Transforming Primary QTS

Primary Professional Studies

Edited by Alice Hansen

m

LearningMatters

First published in 2011 by Learning Matters Ltd
Reprinted in 2011

British Library Cataloguing in Publication Data
A CIP record for this book is available from the British Library

ISBN: 978 0 85725 299 9

This book is also available in the following ebook formats:
Abode ebook ISBN: 978 0 85725 301 9
EPUB ebook ISBN: 978 0 85725 300 2
Kindle ISBN: 978 0 85725 302 6

Cover and text design by Toucan Design
Project management by Deer Park Productions, Tavistock, Devon
Typeset by PDQ Typesetting Ltd, Newcastle under Lyme
Printed and bound in Great Britain by Bell & Bain Ltd, Glasgow

Learning Matters Ltd
20 Cathedral Yard
Exeter EX1 1HB
Tel: 01392 215560
info@learningmatters.co.uk
www.learningmatters.co.uk

MIX
Paper from
responsible sources
FSC® C007785

Transforming Primary QTS

Primary Professional Studies

Contents

Introduction

Right now primary education finds itself in a changing landscape brought about through new curriculum reform. This book, which forms part of the *Transforming QTS* series, supports you as a trainee teacher to address the challenges and exploit the opportunities throughout your training, and into your first years of teaching.

Transforming QTS: The complex role of the trainee teacher

Curriculum reform cannot happen overnight. It is a process that takes a long time and is dependent on the extent to which the profession embraces the imposed changes. As you train to become a teacher you will be exposed to a number of schools, educational settings, tutors, teachers and other students, and all will have different responses. You will observe numerous ways of approaching children, teaching and education. At times you may find this very challenging, but you will always learn more about how you feel about education from the context you find yourself in.

It is the current coalition government's aspiration for schools to have a high level of autonomy, to innovate, have high expectations of children, and deepen academic knowledge through learning from each other (Gove, 2010). In order to be a successful trainee teacher in this climate, you will need to acknowledge and embrace your own highly complex role. Your teacher training is not about ticking off a list of competencies or demonstrating you can deliver a prescribed curriculum. Instead, you will be required to **take risks**, **ask questions**, and make **informed decisions** based on **collaboration** with others in a timely and professional way. Your training will ask you to reflect on your **values**: how do they impact on the way you think of yourself as a teacher and the way you develop relationships with the children you teach and your colleagues? Understanding **child development** and that all children develop in different ways and at different rates because of **prior learning**, **learning styles**, and **individual needs** are explored throughout the book also. It is not enough to focus only on children's learning. Your *own* learning and proactively approaching your own **personal professional development** through **reflective practice** and **research-informed teaching** is a core aspect of the extent to which you will succeed on your course and as a teacher.

These emboldened terms are some of the themes you will find within the book as you read it. Of course these are not new. These aspects have evolved out of existing good practice. Indeed, in one of his earliest speeches as the Secretary of State for Education, Michael Gove stated, 'I want to celebrate the gains which have been made – and one of the most important is the development and deepening of culture in which we recognise that it is professionals, not bureaucratic strategies and initiatives, which drive school improvement' (Gove, 2010). By fulfilling the aspects identified above, you will achieve success in the high status profession you have chosen to enter.

Using this book

Structure of the book

Throughout this book the authors have drawn upon their extensive experience of teaching and mentoring trainee teachers. This book aims to reflect and address aspects that concern you as a trainee teacher at any stage of your course. It is presented in four sections.

Section 1: The Curriculum
This section explores the development of the national curriculum used in primary schools, and shows how schools and trainee teachers can design learning opportunities using a range of approaches.

Section 2: The developing child
Over the last 50 years, the centrality of children in the primary phase has been acknowledged and embraced. Therefore this section considers aspects related to child-centred teaching and learning, issues of inclusion, and transition and progression.

Section 3: The developing teacher
The Standards for QTS Q1–Q9 require you to demonstrate appropriate professional attributes. These reflect teaching as a profession and this section challenges you to consider what it is to be a professional, including amongst other things how to safeguard children and your role as a trainee teacher and teacher in the wider school community. It will also encourage you to think about how you create your own teacher identity. Personal professional development is a key component of your initial teacher training. It began the moment you prepared for an interview on your course, and will continue throughout your career. This aspect of developing as a teacher is discussed in this section also.

Section 4: Teaching skills
The 'nuts and bolts' of teaching are also important, and these are reflected in the Standards for QTS in Q22–Q33. This section will support your assessment of children, planning for teaching, and management of behaviour for learning.

Features

This book contains a number of features to support your learning.

At the start of each chapter you will find a list of **Learning Outcomes**. These provide the intended focus of each chapter. You can skim these to see the structure and content of each chapter.

Each chapter will help you to demonstrate some of the **Professional Standards for Qualified Teacher Status**, and a list of the relevant standards appears at the beginning of each chapter.

You may wish to search for individual standards that you have identified as areas for development, or make a note of your reading and associated activities in your teacher training notes.

Each chapter contains a number of **Activities** that help you to become actively engaged in the content of the chapter. Sometimes the activity will ask you to reflect on your reading or placement experiences, or there may be a task that you will need to undertake. You may find it helpful to undertake the activities with a friend, or discuss the outcomes with your tutors or school mentors.

Case Studies are provided to illustrate how the ideas presented in each chapter can be achieved in a real context.

Research underpins quality teaching. Each chapter contains **Research Focus** features that highlight key literature in the area being discussed. The features provide an overview of the research.

Each chapter concludes with a **Learning Outcomes Review** which asks you to reflect upon the key components of the chapter.

Note: This introduction has explained that education is currently placed within a changing landscape and Chapter 1 particularly explores this further. We are clear about the direction of travel that many areas of primary education are taking, and those areas are addressed in this book – making it the most up-to-date and helpful book available to trainee teachers today. However, as this edition went to print, the Department for Education was continuing to make fast and widespread changes to education. Therefore, please be aware that while every effort was made to reflect the current state of education at the time of writing, there may have been subsequent changes that are not reflected in this edition. Remember that it is a key part of your professional development as a teacher to make sure that you keep up to date with legislation and change at government level, so monitoring the key education websites and specialist press should be a regular part of your practice.

Reference

Gove, M (2010) Speech to the National College Annual Conference, Birmingham, 16 June 2010. Available at www.education.gov.uk/news/speeches/nationalcollegeannualconference Accessed 2/10/12

1. Transforming teaching and learning
Alice Hansen

Learning Outcomes

By the end of this chapter, you will have:

- reviewed the development of teaching and learning in English primary schools since the 1940s;
- reflected on how this development impacts on our current teaching and learning practices in primary schools;
- considered your own professional knowledge and competence, by reflecting on how you are contributing to the 'transformation' of teaching and learning.

Standards

Q8 Have a creative and constructively critical approach towards innovation, being prepared to adapt their practice where benefits and improvements are identified.

Q14 Have a secure knowledge and understanding of their subjects/curriculum areas and related pedagogy to enable them to teach effectively across the age and ability range for which they are trained.

Q15 Know and understand the relevant statutory and non-statutory curricula and frameworks, including those provided through the National Strategies, for their subjects/curriculum areas, and other relevant initiatives applicable to the age and ability range for which they are trained.

Introduction

Teaching is entering a new evolutionary phase, where the Government is committed to a vision of a 'transformed school curriculum' (DfE, 2010a), where 'ministers are committed to giving schools more freedom from unnecessary prescription and bureaucracy' and where teachers are encouraged to 'consider new approaches' (DfE, 2010b).

In order for you to make sense of these statements, this chapter is laid out in three parts.

1. *Where have we been?* provides a historical journey through the development of the national curriculum and other pertinent education milestones since the 1940s.

2. *Where are we now?* outlines the current statutory and non-statutory guidance you must be familiar with.

3. *Where are we going?* asks you to consider curriculum reform and what transforming teaching and learning for the future looks like.

Understanding the historical and current contexts is essential for you to critically and professionally move forward in your teacher training.

Where have we been?

This section reports a very small part of the history of education in England. It is mainly concerned with Government-related documentation from the 1940s to 2010 and is intended to provide for you a skeletal outline of the intention of the government of the day. Although you should be aware that political parties and changes of government impacted significantly at various times during this period, detail about the government in power at the time is not given here. For more information about this, see the Further Reading section.

In the 1920s and 1930s, Sir Henry Hadow wrote six reports about education, which are widely recognised as informing the development of the English education system as we recognise it today (Plowden, 1967; Gillard, 2006). One of these reports *The Primary School* (Board of Education, 1931), stated that 'the traditional practice of dividing the matter of primary instruction into separate subjects, taught in distinct lessons, should be reconsidered [as long as] provision [is] made for an adequate amount of drill in reading, writing and arithmetic' (Board of Education, 1931, p.113). It went on to make the recommendation that 'the curriculum of the primary school is to be thought of in terms of activity and experience, rather than knowledge to be acquired and facts to be stored' (Board of Education, 1931, p.140).

Activity

As you read through this section, consider the extent to which the issues raised in the various decades resonate with what you hear about education today. Are there any issues that you thought were relatively new, but you now see have been a topic of debate or focus for development since before you, or even your parents, were born? How have they developed? Why are they still important aspects to consider in education?

The 1940s–1950s

The Second World War was in full swing in 1942 when William Beveridge chaired the committee that penned the report, *Social Insurance and Allied Services* (Beveridge, 1942). The report identified five 'giant evils' in society: disease (requiring improved health care), ignorance (requiring improved education for all), squalor (requiring adequate housing for all), idleness (requiring all to be in full employment) and want (to be addressed by welfare for children, the elderly and unemployed). As a result of this report, several reforms were developed, including the expansion of National Insurance, the creation of the National Health Service, and the introduction of the 1944 Education Act.

For the first time, the 1944 Education Act provided free education for all children aged five to fifteen. It introduced transport, free milk, medical and dental treatment and free school meals to all children who wanted them. It required all schools to begin each day with an act of worship and it recommended that local authorities educate children with special educational needs in 'ordinary' schools wherever possible. Local Education Authorities (LEAs) were set up, and these were required to appoint a Chief Education Officer who consulted with the Minister of Education.

Given the significant welfare change that was happening during this time, it may be surprising to you that in the early 1940s many forms of corporal punishment were legal, and the 1944 Education Act did nothing to change this. Therefore children were often physically and mentally injured or tortured (McKenzie, 2001).

For primary schools, the next significant document was published at the end of the 1950s: *Primary Education* (Board of Education, 1959). It clearly set out for the first time primary education as a very particular stage in the national system. It published inspection findings from Her Majesty's Inspectors (HMI), and was based on 'discussions with teachers about their work and about the principles on which they act and the standards they achieve' (Board of Education, 1959, p.vi).

It focused on children, and considered them as individuals with interests. There was a clear strand running through about children's learning alongside ways of teaching. Containing information about the expected development at various ages through the primary age range, it explored issues of providing for a wide range of ability, able children and those with special educational needs (referred to at the time as 'handicapped'). There was a section titled 'The fields of learning' (encompassing religion; physical education; language; mathematics; art, craft and needlework; handwriting; music; history; geography and natural history) in which the curriculum was explored. This document set the context for the Plowden Report, published in 1967.

1960S–1970S

The 1960s and 1970s saw a number of big changes within primary schools (Galton et al., 1980, p.156).

Although the 1944 Education Act introduced the opportunity for all children aged five to fifteen to a free education, it was the 1962 Education Act that legislated that parents would become legally obliged to ensure that their children were educated (at school or elsewhere). Alongside this, LEAs were made responsible for ensuring that children attended school.

In the 1960s increasing numbers of immigrants were coming into the country and in 1965 local authorities were advised to avoid heavy concentrations of immigrants in any one school. Circular 7/65 stated that a group containing up to one fifth of immigrant children can fit in a school with reasonable ease, but if the proportion goes beyond a third, serious complications occur.

In the following year, Section 11 of the Local Government Act of 1966 provided for a payment to Local Authorities, a grant that was designed to

> *address disadvantage – brought about by differences of language or culture – that is experienced by members of any ethnic minorities in accessing education, training, employment and a wide range of other opportunities, services and facilities that are available to other people... [in order to] enable members of ethnic minorities [from the New Commonwealth] to overcome such disadvantage, and thereby to play a full part in the social, economic and political life of the country*

(Home Office, 1960)

It was only in the 1993 Local Government (Amendment) Act that the scope was widened to all minority ethnic people.

Research Focus: The Plowden Report

In 1963 the Education Minister, Sir Edward Boyle, commissioned a report that would 'consider primary education in all its aspects and the transition to secondary education' (Plowden, 1967 p.1) and in 1967 the Plowden Report: *Children and their Primary Schools* was published. It focused on a child-centred approach to education, stating that 'at the heart of the educational process lies the child' (p.7). Amongst many other things, it considered:

- Child growth and development (including gender differences, cognitive, physical, emotional, behavioural and intelligence development);
- Increased communication with parents;
- A national focus to positively discriminate towards schools in the most deprived areas to receive extra help, termed 'educational priority areas';
- The need to re-examine the books schools use and the curriculum they teach, overcoming language barriers and educating immigrant children and their parents;
- The need for an 'integration of the social services' so that trained social workers can collaborate with schools;
- That continuity across education stages was required, including that teacher trainees should be trained in more than one stage, and that documentation should accompany children to the next school;
- Some changes in the way subjects are taught (e.g. mathematics and a second language) were 'taking place unusually rapidly';
- Aspects of the curriculum, stressing that 'children's learning does not fit into subject categories' and that the younger the child, the less differentiation should be made between the subjects. These were: religious education, English, modern languages, history, geography, mathematics, science, art and craft, music, physical education, sex education;

→

- That decisions on punishment should be left up to the teacher, within the school's policy; the infliction of physical pain should be forbidden;
- A recommendation on using a combination of individual group and class work was made but it also welcomed the trend towards individual learning;
- The education of 'handicapped children in ordinary schools', suggesting that
  - society has created new stresses and strains
  - the term 'slow learner' should be substituted for 'educationally sub-normal'
  - trainee teachers should be equipped to help handicapped children as far as they can;
- The importance of the education of gifted children should be acknowledged, and that there was a need for further research;
- The suggestion that head teachers should have more say over their schools.

The Plowden Report was welcomed by most educationalists but there were a minority who loudly opposed the 'progressive' education being promoted in primary schools (see, for example, Bennett, 1976). In order to address the growing debate, on the 18 October, 1976 the Prime Minister James Callaghan made a speech that publicly launched what became known as The Great Debate.

The goals of our education, from nursery school through to adult education, are clear enough. They are to equip children to the best of their ability for a lively, constructive, place in society, and also to fit them to do a job of work. Not one or the other but both. The balance was wrong in the past. We have a responsibility now to see that we do not get it wrong again in the other direction. [...]I have outlined concerns and asked questions about them today. The debate that I was seeking has got off to a flying start even before I was able to say anything. Now I ask all those who are concerned to respond positively and not defensively. It will be an advantage to the teaching profession to have a wide public understanding and support for what they are doing.

(Callaghan, 1976)

The 1970s saw an increase in the legislation that was passed that had a direct influence on primary schools. For example, The Education (Handicapped children) Act of 1970 transferred the responsibility for education of severely handicapped children from health authorities to LEAs, The Education (milk) Act of 1971 limited the provision of free milk in schools, The 1975 Sex Discrimination Act affected school admissions, appointments and curricula and The 1976 Race Relations Act also impacted on the way schools operated. The school leaving age was raised to 16 in 1973.

Alongside the current sociological climate schools were in, other influences were beginning to drive government policy. For example, in 1974 the Assessment Performance Unit (APU) was established in order to promote assessment and monitoring methods in order to track children's achievement.

Additionally, a number of seminal reports with a focus on subjects and pedagogy were written in this decade. These included the Durham Report (1970) *The 4th R: Church of England report on church schools and religious education*, Bullock Report (1975) *A Language for Life* related to the teaching of English, Warnock Report (1978) *Special Educational Needs* that considered provision for children and young people with special needs, and the survey by HMI (1978) *Primary Education in England* that reported some aspects of the work of 7, 9 and 11 year old children in over 1,100 classes.

To inform the 'great debate', in the late 1970s LEAs were required to review and report on their curriculum policies. These events were the beginning of the 'process of reaching a national consensus on a desirable framework for the curriculum and consider the development of such a framework a priority for the education service' (HMI, 1980, Foreword).

1980s

A View of the Curriculum (HMI, 1980) called for a lengthy process of consultation in order to establish a curriculum. It reflected the principles of the Plowden Report and placed the Warnock Report explicitly and firmly at the heart of the process. This was followed by further support and advice for LEAs on curriculum development. One such source was a series entitled *Curriculum Matters* by HMI, which was published between 1984 and 1989, covering 17 subjects and other areas of importance in education from 5–16 years of age.

1985 saw the publication of the white paper *Better Schools*. Among other things, it continued the focus on the national agreement about the purposes and content of the curriculum, it took steps to reduce under-achievement and to address truancy.

Later in the decade, a consultation document (DES, 1987) was published. This outlined the proposed ten subjects of the National Curriculum, comprising of three core (English, mathematics and science) and seven foundation (geography, history, technology, a foreign language (for secondary school pupils), art, music, and physical education) subjects, alongside the percentage of time to be allocated to each subject or group of subjects. It identified a need to assess children's attainment at 7, 11, 14 and 16 and it stated that most assessment would be carried out by teachers, with national tests supplementing their work. The latter was followed up in 1988 when The National Curriculum Task Group on Assessment and Testing (TGAT) identified how tests and school league tables would be structured. The report stated that one advantage to operating a national testing regime would be to apply a common set of benchmarks across the age ranges, and acknowledged the key role moderation would play to ensure consistency of judgements (Green, 2002).

Further reports were written into core areas of education provision, such as the Cockcroft Report (1982) *Mathematics Counts*, the Swan Report (1985) *Education for All*, and the Elton Report (1989) *Discipline in Schools*. Another key document to be reported was the ORACLE survey (Galton et al., 1980), which published findings including how, where the curriculum is broadened (beyond literacy and numeracy), children do better (Ross, 1999).

Furthermore, during this period a number of Education Acts were passed, including the two 1986 Education Acts. In the latter, LEAs were required to publish their curriculum policies, governors were required to publish annual reports, and schools were required to hold parents' evenings. Schools were no longer allowed to undertake corporal punishment. Additionally, they were inhibited from indoctrinating children into any political viewpoint. In 1988, the Education 'Reform' Act, which was the most significant act since 1944 (Ross, 1999), was passed. Among other things, it legislated for the introduction of Key Stages, the National Curriculum and its accompanying testing regime with league tables. This meant that for the first time since the abolition of the *Elementary Code* in the 1920s teachers were required by law to teach a prescribed curriculum. More power over education was handed over to central government and the functions of LEAs were limited (Alexander, 2009).

The development of the National Curriculum was overseen by the National Curriculum Council and the School Examination and Assessment Council. The Programmes of Study were handed over to individual subject working groups and perhaps this is why the final documentation was 'substantial and set out in considerable detail the subject content that schools should be required to cover' (House of Commons, 2009, p.13).

The National Curriculum was introduced into schools in 1989 and implementation occurred over the next few years.

Early 1990s

After the introduction of the 1988 National Curriculum and the associated unrest related to unreasonable workload, the Government commissioned Ron Dearing to review the national curriculum. The Dearing Review (1993) suggested that the curriculum be slimmed down, time given to testing should be reduced, and around 20% of teaching time set aside for the use of schools to design their own curriculum. This led to a revised national curriculum in 1995 which saw a significant reduction in content and the introduction of eight level descriptors across the key stages.

The seminal report *Curriculum organisation and classroom practice in primary schools* (Alexander et al., 1992) (often referred to as the 'three wise men report') was written in 1992 to review the delivery of education in primary schools. Reporting on it ten years later, Hofkins (2002) explained how many teachers rejected it at the time, but its influence on today's classrooms is clear. Although it was used in a 'back to basics' election campaign after the progressive years of the 1970s and 1980s, the report itself was calling for a balance in the way teachers taught, using whole-class teaching, group and individual work to teach subjects and topics. It also suggested teachers use questioning and explaining skills more effectively, and focused on teachers having higher expectations of all children.

Where are we now?

Late 1990s–present

The last two decades have seen the most government intervention in relation to the guidance provided about how to teach the curriculum (Wyse et al., 2008).

National Curriculum review

1997 saw the first full review of the National Curriculum and as a result a revision of the National Curriculum occurred again in 1999. It was significantly slimmed down.

Values, aims and purposes

This National Curriculum was the first to provide underpinning values, aims and purposes. The values acknowledge that *education influences and reflects the values of society and the kind of society we want to be* (DfEE, 1999, p.10). Relating to the well-being of all children, there are four main purposes:

- to establish an entitlement (for all children);
- the establish standards (to set targets for improvement, measure progress and monitor and compare performance);
- to promote continuity and coherence (through a flexible, national framework);
- to promote public understanding (and confidence in the work of schools).

There are two aims:

Aim 1: The school curriculum should aim to provide opportunities for all pupils to learn and to achieve.

Aim 2: The school curriculum should aim to promote pupils' spiritual, moral, social and cultural development and prepare all pupils for the opportunities, responsibilities and experiences of life.

The structure of the National Curriculum

Programmes of study for each subject set out what children should be taught. The related attainment targets identify the expected standards of performance. '*It is for schools to choose how they organise their school curriculum to include the programmes of study*' (DfEE, 1999, p.17).

The three core subjects remain the same as the 1988 curriculum. The non-core foundation subjects are: design and technology, information and communication technology, history, geography, art and design, music and physical education. There are also non-statutory guidelines for personal, social and health education, citizenship, and modern foreign languages (MFL). Since then, *Languages for all: languages for life* (DfES, 2000) included the directive for all KS2 children to learn a modern foreign language. Additionally, religious education is a statutory subject, supported by non-statutory guidance.

General teaching requirements

Finally, the National Curriculum outlines a number of general teaching requirements. The first is inclusion. Please see Chapter 4 for a detailed discussion about this. Other requirements include the use of language (writing, speaking, listening and reading) and ICT across the curriculum, and health and safety.

> ### Activity
> Recall the last time you read pages 10–23 of the National Curriculum handbook. Reread it. Why do you think that there are calls for a reform of the National Curriculum?

Literacy and mathematics

In 1997 the white paper *Excellence in schools* announced that at least one hour a day would be spent on English and on mathematics, and that schools were to have targets given to them in order to raise standards. Following this, in 1998 the schools standards minister, Stephen Byers, declared that literacy targets would raise standards so that 80% of children would attain Level 4 or above in English, and 75% of children a Level 4 or above in mathematics by 2002 (although these targets were not met until later).

The late 1990s saw a distinct shift in governmental leadership of schools. Its focus turned from *what* to teach, to *how* to teach and the introduction of the first National Literacy Strategy was soon followed by the National Numeracy Strategy. Both produced frameworks for teaching literacy and mathematics and, while they were designed to be non-statutory, the vast majority of schools adopted their teaching methods.

2006 saw the renewed primary framework for literacy and mathematics come out as an online resource (http://nationalstrategies.standards.dcsf.gov.uk/primary/primaryframework) and in the same year the *Review of the teaching of early reading*, the Rose Report (2006), was published to address the debate about the place of phonics in the teaching of reading. In 2008, the Williams Report *Independent Review of Mathematics Teaching in Early Years Settings and Primary Schools* was published.

The number of publications produced to support primary teachers in recent years has been immense. A search of National Strategies publications for primary literacy and mathematics resources alone (many more for other aspects of the curriculum were also produced) (http://nationalstrategies.standards.dcsf.gov.uk/primary/primaryframework/resourcelibrary) provides 193 resources for literacy, and 576 for mathematics, with the latter including ICT resources.

Activity

Reflect on the planning and teaching that you have undertaken to date. To what extent did you use published materials to support your planning? Who were they published by? What proportion were government-based, and what proportion were private enterprise?

Although the National Strategies and the DCSF (House of Commons, 2009) emphasised that the National Strategies guidance was non-statutory, there was a widespread perception among teachers that National Strategies guidance was mandatory, and that they could be penalised by their local authority or school improvement partner, or through Ofsted inspection, for not following that guidance (Alexander, 2009).

Formal prescription did ensue when, in 2007, the government required phonics to be taught in the early stages of learning to read. This was built on in 2010 when it was announced in the white paper that all children would be taught systematic synthetic phonics and children would be tested in Year 1 to 'confirm whether individual pupils had grasped the basics of phonic decoding [and] identify those pupils who need extra help, so the school can provide support' (DfE, 2010c).

Case Study: Guidance for national testing

Following advice from his mentor, Abdul was searching the QCDA website for some *assessing pupil progress (APP)* resources. He came across a search function that allowed him to search by topic at www.qcda.gov.uk/resources.aspx. He was surprised at the number of resources available for national curriculum tests (over 3,000) compared to APP (just over 30).

He spoke to his mentor the next day about what he had observed. She suggested that while this was indeed a significant proportion, it was important to remember, firstly, that the number included resources for secondary schools as well. Of course there were also the statutory test papers and answer sheets from over the years. She explained to Abdul how the 'standards agenda' had created a focus on assessment and that the QCDA had responded to teachers' needs in wanting to ensure that their children were reaching the highest possible attainment, so guidance for the tests was essential reading for any teachers administering the tests. There was also a need for schools to report school results on documentation from the website. It was also possible to find answer sheets, guides for monitoring visits and maladministration committee procedures. Abdul's mentor explained that one of the types of documents she found most useful in her teacher training were the Standards reports. These annual analyses of children's performance in the standardised tests for Key Stages 1 and 2 concluded with the implications for teaching and learning reading, writing, mathematics and science.

Abdul reflected on the place that standardised tests had on how his placement school's approach to teaching and learning.

In a fairly damning indictment of the way National Strategies' non-statutory guidance was interpreted by schools, formal minutes of the House of Commons (2009) stated: 'We are concerned at the growth of centrally-produced curriculum-related guidance, and we believe that the National Strategies should be discontinued'. This was actioned, and as a result the National Strategies ceased to be in April 2011. Additionally, the QCDA was one of the first government quangos to be axed in the sweeping cuts of 2010.

Every Child Matters

Another key development during this period was the Every Child Matters agenda. In 2003 the government published the Green Paper of the same name and the following year the Children Act 2004 became law, providing the opportunity to put into place a more integrated children's workforce focused on the needs of children, young people and their families.

Central to *Every Child Matters* were five aims that were designed to give all children the support they require in order to:

- be healthy;
- stay safe;
- enjoy and achieve;
- make a positive contribution;
- achieve economic wellbeing.

Case Study: Every Child Matters

Ben, an undergraduate trainee teacher, was undertaking research for a group presentation about *Every Child Matters*. Ben had previously read about the Beveridge Report, particularly the five 'giant evils' in society, that William Beveridge had identified in the 1940s. Ben saw a link. He shared this observation with his group and they decided to include it in their presentation.

THE FIVE OUTCOMES Every Child Matters (DfES, 2003)	THE FIVE 'GIANT EVILS' IN SOCIETY Social Insurance and Allied Services (Beveridge, 1942)
Be healthy	Disease (requiring improved health care)
Stay safe	Ignorance (requiring improved education for all)
Enjoy and achieve	Squalor (requiring adequate housing for all),
Make a positive contribution	Idleness (requiring all to be in full employment)
Achieve economic wellbeing	Want (to be addressed by welfare for children, the elderly and unemployed)

Table 1.1 Handout from Ben's presentation

Ben's tutor praised the group's efforts in drawing on historical documents to make sense of where we are with current educational issues and then asked the whole

→

seminar class how the table reflected significant changes in education over the sixty years. They discussed the changing role of education. For example they considered how the 'giant evils' were about what the government was going to do to support society more widely, and the five outcomes are a promise to children for the future as they become adult members of society. Additionally they felt that the 'giant evils' reflected how government was going to 'look after' people, but the five outcomes seemed to be owned by children so that they could develop the skills themselves to achieve the outcomes (reflecting a shift in stakeholder ownership).

Ben's tutor also kindly reminded the seminar class that because the five outcomes and the 'giant evils' encompass a huge range of complex issues, it was dangerous to interpret them as single entities and link them simplistically the way Ben's group had attempted to. After all, they were overarching themes and aims that were to be addressed over long periods of time.

In the following years the Every Child Matters agenda was further developed and became the central tenet to the *Children's Plan* in 2007. Its launch presented a ten-year strategy to make England *the best place for children and young people to grow up*. This signalled the beginning of a curriculum reform.

Where are we going?

A move towards creativity and personalisation

In addition to a continued focus on literacy and mathematics, the first decade of the new century renewed the focus on creativity and personalisation.

> *The new Primary Strategy will support teachers and schools across the whole curriculum, building on the lessons of the Literacy and Numeracy Strategies, but moving on to offer teachers more control and flexibility. It will focus on building up teachers' own professionalism and capacity to teach better and better, with bespoke support they can draw on to meet their particular needs.*

> Primary National Strategy (2003)

Creativity

The National Advisory Committee on Creative and Cultural Education's (NACCCE, 1999) report *All Our Futures: Creativity, Culture and Education* triggered the government to call on the (then) QCA to lead a three-year research project *Creativity: finding it, promoting it* (QCA, 2004), which investigated how teachers could promote children's creativity across the National Curriculum.

The findings of the project found enhanced levels of children's literacy and numeracy skills, self-esteem, motivation and achievement, individual talents, and life skills.

The 2002 Education Act gave permission for schools to move away from the NC in order to enable 'development work or experiments to be carried out' (2002, Section 90). The government was signalling to schools that they did have more autonomy than many interpreted.

Personalisation

The 2005 white paper *Higher standards, better schools for all* encouraged schools to focus on individual children. In the same year, Ofsted were required to report on the extent to which schools take account of the views of the children. This led to most schools setting up School Councils, if they did not already have one.

Furthermore, *2020 Vision*, the report of the Teaching and Learning in 2020 Review Group (2006), placed personalising learning and teaching and pupil voice central to teaching in the future. It identified that personalising learning is *learner-centred and knowledge-centred, and assessment centred* and outlined the importance of personalisation (Teaching and Learning in 2020 Review Group, 2006 pp.6–7).

Research Focus: Cambridge Primary Review

The *Cambridge Primary Review*, launched in 2006, was an independently funded enquiry into the condition and future of primary education in England. This was the most comprehensive review since Plowden. The process involved the publication of 29 interim reports and two special reports on the primary curriculum. It addressed ten themes: purposes and values; learning and teaching; curriculum and assessment; quality and standards; diversity and inclusion; settings and professionals; parenting, caring and educating; children's lives beyond school; structures and phases; and funding and governance.

The final report, *Children, their world, their education* (Alexander, 2009), contained 75 recommendations (compared to 197 in Plowden and 333 in Bullock) that were signposted in the following summarising headings:

- Respect and support childhood
- Narrow the gap
- Review special needs
- Start with aims
- New structures for early years and primary education
- A new curriculum
- A pedagogy of evidence and principle
- Reform assessment
- Strengthen accountability, redefine standards
- Review primary school staffing
- Leadership for learning
- Reform teacher education
- Schools for the community
- Schools for the future
- Reform school funding
- Reform the policy process
- A new educational discourse

The 'new primary curriculum' that never was

At around the same time as the Cambridge review, Sir Jim Rose was commissioned by the government to lead *The independent review of the primary curriculum*. It focused on curriculum design and content, highlighting that the primary phase of education was unique and that children had different and developing abilities during their time at primary school. It stated that literacy and numeracy remained central, but other aspects included ICT, personal development, transition and progression, and MFL at KS2. It suggested that the curriculum should be organised into six areas of learning:

- Understanding English, communication and languages;
- Mathematical understanding;
- Scientific and technological understanding;
- Historical, geographical and social understanding;
- Understanding physical development, health and wellbeing;
- Understanding the arts.

The Rose Review led directly into the development of the new national curriculum primary handbook (DCSF, 2010) which was published in February 2010. It set out, for the first time, statutory aims which were to enable all young people to become successful learners, confident individuals and responsible citizens. The 1999 National Curriculum stated that its values *do not change over time*, and this proved to be correct in the new version. However, the values were amended to reflect the *values in our society that promote personal development, equality of opportunity, economic wellbeing, a healthy and just democracy, and a sustainable future* (DCSF, 2010, p.4) which were resonant of the Every Child Matters outcomes.

However, three months after its publication, a pending election meant that it did not pass into law and as a result, at the time of this book's publication, another National Curriculum review is being led by the new coalition government.

Transforming teaching: the current debate

It appears that one significant source for current debate in primary teaching is the ongoing tension between teachers having legislative autonomy, but the practical realities of governmental intervention through testing, inspection and non-statutory guidance are causing many teachers to become 'de-skilled' (House of Commons, 2009, p.33). While many (Alexander, 2010; House of Commons, 2009) have called for changes in arrangements for testing and inspection, the government are reforming the curriculum, testing and inspection concurrently, but only time will tell how comfortably these sit alongside each other.

What is clear is that the teaching profession is potentially on the cusp of a significant period of change (see the white paper *The importance of teaching* (DfE, 2010)). From every direction there is a call for a genuinely renewed curriculum. Indeed, there will soon be a new National Curriculum that will provide a further slimmed down statutory requirement. *How* schools decide to engage and motivate their learners will be a decision led by the head teacher, giving back to schools a potentially higher degree of professional freedom. As a trainee teacher, your role will be crucial in seeing this change through.

It is clear from current debate is that that curriculum reform will:

- establish a set of future-facing aims, values and principles;
- continue to address the gap in attainment between various groups of children;
- be shaped through the learner's perspective;
- show a journey from birth (or five) to 19;
- scale down the content of the National Curriculum;
- require local ownership of the National Curriculum;
- challenge the decrease in the overall quality of primary education experienced due to the narrowing of the curriculum and impact of test preparation (Wyse et al., 2008);
- require teachers to become critical and reflective practitioners, basing their professional decisions on sound evidence and data;
- maintain subject knowledge as an essential component of high quality teaching;
- maintain testing as central to a standards agenda.

Activity

Look at the list above. Reflect on how you feel when you read these developments. Make a list of those things that excite you and those you feel more intrepid about. When appropriate, share your list with your tutors/mentors and discuss how you can develop the areas you are excited about as strengths, and how you can develop further the areas that you are more concerned about.

What impact will these curriculum reforms have on you as a trainee teacher, and on the hundreds of children you will teach when you are a teacher working in this transformed curriculum?

Learning Outcomes Review

Thinking about the school in which you are working or have recently worked, respond to the prompts after each intended learning outcome, to identify your knowledge and understanding of the issues covered in the chapter.

- **Review the development of teaching and learning in English primary schools since the 1940s:**
  - Identify as many issues as you can that have continued to be central to educational debate in the last eighty years.

- Which issues do you feel have been satisfactorily resolved in that time?

- **Reflect on how this development impacts our current teaching and learning practices in primary schools:**
  - Reflect on the different schools you have visited as a trainee teacher. Try to write a short paragraph about each school that summarises the a) teaching practices and b) learning practices of the schools. What does this tell you about primary schools?
  - What published documentation do you currently use to inform your planning in school? Which of this is statutory/non-statutory guidance/other published material? Why do you use these?

- **Consider your own professional knowledge and competence, by reflecting on how you are contributing to the 'transformation' of teaching and learning:**
  - What autonomy do you feel you have as a trainee teacher in supporting the development of your school's planning and delivery of the curriculum?
  - What strengths do you bring as a trainee teacher who will be contributing to the 'transformed' teaching profession? What personal/professional aspects of your skills, knowledge and understanding will you need to develop before you qualify or in your NQT year?

Further Reading

Derek Gillard's History of Education website is available at www.educationengland.org.uk/index.html This website contains the text of most of the historical documents discussed in this chapter. It is also a good source of the governments in power.

Excellence and enjoyment: learning and teaching in the primary years. This CPD pack can be downloaded as a zip file from http://nationalstrategies.standards.dcsf.gov.uk/node/85049. It contains units related to planning and assessment for learning, creating a learning culture, and understanding how learning develops.

The Cambridge Primary Review. A very readable booklet bringing together the key messages from the Cambridge Primary Review can be downloaded from http://www.primaryreview.org.uk/downloads/CPR_revised_booklet.pdf

References

Alexander, R. (ed) (2009) *Children, their world, their education: Final report and recommendations of the Cambridge Primary Review*. London: Routledge.

Alexander, R., Rose, J., and Woodhead, C. (1992) Curriculum organisation and classroom practice in primary schools: A discussion paper. London: Department of Education and Science.

Bennett, N. (1976) *Teaching styles and pupil progress*. London: Open Books.

Beveridge, W. (1942) *Social insurance and allied services*. London: HMSO.

Board of Education (1931) *The Primary School*. London: HMSO.

Board of Education (1959) *Primary Education: Suggestions for the consideration of teachers and others concerned with the work of primary schools*. London: HMSO.

Bullock, A. (1975) *A Language for Life*. London: HMSO.

Callaghan, J. (1976) *The Ruskin Speech*. Available from http://education.guardian.co.uk/thegreatdebate/story/0,9860,574645,00.html accessed 7/12/10.

Cockcroft, W.H. (1982) *Mathematics counts*. London: HMSO.

DES (1987) *The National Curriculum 5–16: A consultation document*. London: HMSO.

DCSF (2010) *The National Curriculum: Primary Handbook*. London: QCDA.

DfE (2010ba) The Importance of Teaching: Schools White Paper. Available from www.education.gov.uk/schools/teachingandlearning/schoolswhitepaper/b0068570/the-importance-of-teaching/ accessed 9/12/10.

DfE (2010b) Important information on the primary curriculum and Key Stage 3 level descriptions. Available from www.education.gov.uk/curriculum accessed 15/7/10.

DfE (2010c) Synthetic phonics will drive up basic literacy standards. *Govtoday*. Available from www.govtoday.co.uk/Education/Early-Years/synthetic-phonics-will-drive-up-basic-literacy-standards.html accessed 14/12/10.

DfEE (1999) *The National Curriculum: Handbook for primary teachers in England*. London: QCA.

Durham Report (1970) *The 4th R: Church of England report on church schools and religious education*. London: National Society.

Education Act 2002. London: HMSO.

Elton, R. (1989) *Discipline in Schools*. London: HMSO.

Galton, M., Simon, B. and Croll, P. (1980) *Inside the primary classroom*. Australasia: Law book company.

Gillard, D. (2006) 'The Hadow Reports: an introduction', *The encyclopaedia of informal education.* Available from www.infed.org/schooling/hadow_reports.htm accessed 15/7/10.

Green, S. (2002) Criterion referenced assessment as a guide to learning: The importance of progression and reliability. Paper presented at the Association for the Study of Evaluation in Education in Southern Africa International Conference. Johannesburg, 10 July–12 July 2002. Available from www.cambridgeassessment.org.uk/ca/digitalAssets/ 113775_Criterion_Referenced_Assessment_as_a_Guide_to_Learning._The_.pdf accessed 9/12/ 10.

Hofkins, D. (2002) Wise men's gift is lasting legacy. In *TES* 8th February 2002. Available from www.tes.co.uk/article.aspx?storycode=359478 accessed 14/12/10.

Home Office (1960) *Section 11 Grant.* London: HMSO www.nationalarchives.gov.uk/ ERORecords/HO/421/2/reu/grant.htm accessed 15/12/10.

House of Commons (2006) The schools white paper: Higher standards, better schools for all. First report of session 2005–06. Vol. 1. www.publications.parliament.uk/pa/cm200506/ cmselect/cmeduski/633/633.pdf accessed 14/12/10.

House of Commons (2009) *National curriculum. Fourth report of session 2008–2009.* London: The Stationery Office Ltd.

Her Majesty's Inspectorate (or HM Inspectorate) (1980) *A view of the Curriculum.* London: HMSO.

Primary National Strategies (2003) *Excellence and enjoyment: A strategy for primary schools.* London: DfES.

QCA (2004) *Creativity: Finding it, promoting it.* London: QCA.

National Advisory Committee on Creative and Cultural Education (1999) *All Our Futures: Creativity, Culture and Education.* Available from www.cypni.org.uk/downloads/ alloutfutures.pdf accessed 9/12/10.

McKenzie, J. (2001) *Changing education: A sociology of education since 1944.* Harlow: Pearson Education.

Plowden Report (1967) *Children and their Primary Schools.* London: HSMO.

Primary National Strategy (2003) *Excellence and enjoyment: a strategy for primary schools.* Available from http://nationalstrategies.standards.dcsf.gov.uk/node/85063 accessed 14/12/10.

Rose Report (2008) *The independent review of the primary curriculum: final report.*

Ross, A. (1999) *Curriculum: construction and critique.* London: Routledge.

Swan, M. (1985) *Education for All.* London: HMSO.

Teaching and Learning in 2020 Review Group (2006) *2020 Vision*. Available from http://publications.education.gov.uk/eOrderingDownload/6856-DfES-Teaching%20and%20 Learning.pdf accessed 14/12/10.

Warnock, H.M. (1978) *Special Educational Needs*. London: HMSO.

Wyse, D., McCreery, E., and Torrance, H. (2008) The trajectory and impact of national reform: curriculum and assessment in English primary schools. Primary Review Research Briefings 3/2. Available from www.primaryreview.org.uk/Downloads/Int_Reps/7.Governance-finance-reform/RS_3-2_briefing_Curriculum_assessment_reform_080229.pdf accessed 9/12/10.

2. Curriculum approaches
Adrian Copping

Learning Outcomes

By the end of this chapter you will have explored:

- how beliefs about learning drive curriculum planning and teaching approaches;
- how children's learning and development is at the forefront of curriculum development;
- how a cross-curricular approach deepens learning through the joining of concepts and ideas;
- debates about integrated and single-subject learning opportunities.

Standards

Q1 Have high expectations of children and young people including a commitment to ensuring they can achieve their full educational potential and to establishing fair, respectful, trusting, supportive and constructive relationships with them.

Q8 Have a creative and constructively critical approach towards innovation, being prepared to adapt their practice where benefits and improvements are identified.

Q10 Have a knowledge and understanding of a range of teaching, learning and behaviour management strategies and know how to use and adapt them, including how to personalise learning and provide opportunities for all learners to achieve their potential.

Q14 Have a secure knowledge and understanding of their subjects/curriculum areas and related pedagogy to enable them to teach effectively across age and ability range for which they are trained.

Q15 Know and understand the relevant statutory and non-statutory curricula and frameworks, including those provided through the National Strategies, for their subjects/curriculum areas, and other relevant initiatives applicable to the age and ability range for which they are trained.

Q19 Know how to make effective personalised provision for those they teach, including those for whom English is an additional language or who have special educational needs or disabilities, and how to take practical account of diversity and promote equality and inclusion in their teaching.

Q22 Plan for progression across the age and ability range for which they are trained, designing effective learning sequences within lessons and across series of lessons and demonstrating secure subject/curriculum knowledge.

Q23 Design opportunities for learners to develop their literacy, numeracy and ICT skills.

Introduction

Chapter 1 outlined the statutory requirements and non-statutory components of the National Curriculum. For each subject in Key Stages 1 and 2, the National Curriculum programmes of study set out what children should be taught and it is for schools to choose how they organise their school curriculum to include the programmes of study (QCDA, 2010). Therefore, although teachers are statutorily obliged (that is, by law you are required) to teach the *content* of the National Curriculum (DfEE, 1999), schools and teachers are not bound in any way as to *how* they should teach. In light of that, this chapter explores how schools and teachers might design their curriculum to include effective learning experiences for their children.

Theoretical approaches to curriculum design and designing learning

A curriculum, be it a national one or a derivative made particular to a specific context, is created based on a series of beliefs about learning, and the perceived purpose of the curriculum. This section discusses the impact that your own beliefs have on how you plan for learning. The case study below exemplifies how the National Curriculum for England reflects a theoretical framework of learning.

The National Curriculum for England (DfEE, 1999) is based on the belief that in order for learning to occur, ideas and concepts should be re-examined and re-visited over time. This has been termed a 'spiral curriculum' where '*students return again to the basic concepts, building on them, making them more complex and understanding them more fully*' (Howard, 2007, p.1). Therefore, new learning builds on previous learning where the understanding of a concept is extended and enhanced through a process of *scaffolding*. This approach, outlined by Jerome Bruner, is rooted in the idea that learning is meaningful, has a purpose and that initial concepts have some validity and interest for the learner.

There are many other beliefs about how children learn and some of these are considered in Chapter 4, but it is important to remember as you read this chapter that a school's curriculum or scheme of work arises out of a belief in how children learn. The development of that curriculum, the activities contained therein, the progression of activities and teaching approaches indicated arise out of a particular belief about what learning is, how it happens and how children do it.

Additionally, it is shaped by how teachers perceive the wider curriculum itself. In light of this, the next section explores three ways of conceptualising a curriculum.

Conceptualising the curriculum

Activity

Read through the models below and consider to what extent they reflect how you see the curriculum. If necessary, have a go at developing your own model that uses a metaphor to reflect your own perceptions.

The curriculum as a blueprint for learning

This belief suggests that the curriculum is a blueprint on which knowledge is built. Instructions for the building suggest that the pre-ordained outcome must be reached and particular ways of working must be followed in order to get there. It is safe, secure and comfortable, provided the blueprint is accurate. It implies that there are no opportunities to explore alternative ways of constructing knowledge and is clearly focused on outcomes. This way of conceptualising the curriculum suggests a belief about knowledge which is propositional or declarative (knowing about facts, e.g. knowing the important events in Tudor England, how the water cycle works, or that Paris is the capital city of France) and that learning is procedural. Biggs (2003, p.41) explains that declarative knowledge *is what is in libraries and text books, and is what teachers "declare" in lectures. Students' understanding of it can be tested by getting them to declare it back.*

Whilst it could be argued that there is knowledge that should be known, it is limited in its use and application. Donald Schön, who developed the notion of reflective practice, explains how propositional knowledge or declarative knowledge is of limited value (Schön, cited in Brockbank and McGill, 2003). The implications of this belief are that learning could become rigid, concepts remain abstract and potentially irrelevant to the learner and that any learning that could take place through the process of an activity or created context is negated by the focus being on the arrival at the correct endpoint as provided by the instructions.

The curriculum as a set of outcomes to be able to quantify

This belief implies that a scheme of work (listing the statutory objectives, providing indicative activities that allow the learner to meet those and identifying suggested assessment designed to test the meeting of that outcome) can be tested, and the objective can be ticked off as having been taught and learnt.

This conceptualisation suggests something about how knowledge is gained. In this case, it is about knowledge being *procedural*. Biggs (2003) states that this procedural knowledge *is a matter of getting the sequences and actions right having the right... competencies* (2003, p.42). Just like the blueprint model, this is a very linear approach to the curriculum where the focus is on the outcome and passing the test which may indeed negate meaningful, constructed learning because in a sense this approach to curriculum is about the end result.

The curriculum as a map

This belief continues to use declarative knowledge as an end point. However, it may address the concerns of the models discussed above. The curriculum as a map model suggests that the curriculum is set within a particular environment and that participants within the environment are able to use a map to journey and explore within it. As long as a participant has the skills to be able to interpret the map, it is possible to reach a given destination using a number of possible routes. The route chosen will in turn offer new experiences and opportunities on the way to reaching the destination.

Boyle (2002, p.11) explains how a map metaphor can be used.

> *A map provides a systematic, integrated description of a particular geographical domain. This description, it should be noted, is both abstract and conventionalised. This knowledge base can be used to construct a route from any location on the map, through a series of 'valid steps', to any other location on the map. This is far more powerful than any set of procedural descriptions.*

This belief builds on the notion that a curriculum should be designed to match the needs of the learners for whom it is intended because external guidance cannot be put into practice unless the context is considered. Boyle's map metaphor suggests a flexible and creative approach to learning knowledge and this places the learner (as the user of the map) and the teacher (as the expedition guide) in a position of being decision makers. Therefore, this takes into consideration the 'softer' skills a learner should possess, such as collaboration.

This approach reflects a belief that knowledge is useful and functioning. Biggs (2003) calls this *'functioning knowledge' (2003, p.42)*. However, in order for a functioning knowledge to exist, Biggs suggests that the learner must have high levels of both declarative and procedural knowledge. These types provide the learner with the *what* and *how*. Additionally, Biggs (2003, p.42) suggests that the learner needs a further type of knowledge which he terms *'conditional'* that provides the learner with the *why* and *when*. As Biggs summarises *'if the target is functioning knowledge, the declarative knowledge needs to be developed to relational levels in order to provide both the knowledge of the specific context, and the conditional knowledge that enable skills to be performed adequately* (2003, p.43).

Activity

Reflect on a recent school placement experience. Identify how the school's curriculum was designed. Which of the three beliefs about the curriculum, outlined above, were most prevalent in that design? Note down how the belief was exemplified in the learning and teaching. Also note what you consider to be the impact on children's learning.

Research Focus

In her work on trainee teachers' subject knowledge development in English, Twiselton (2006) identified three categories of trainee teacher: task managers, curriculum deliverers and concept/skill builders. She suggests that trainee teachers pass through these stages on a continuum.

The stages are important in thinking about curriculum design and the nature of knowledge. The belief about curriculum as a set of outcomes is very much about teaching through delivering the curriculum. Twiselton's findings suggest that *Curriculum Deliverers appeared unable to link concepts and skills. Instead they appeared to treat knowledge as isolated and atomised pieces. In this view learning can be represented as a series of 'products' seen as ends in themselves (2006, p.91)*. The implications for this approach to curriculum design are that the curriculum may lack cohesion and children may not be as able to make links between subject areas through the joining of concepts.

Twiselton's (2006) notion suggests that trainee teachers move through categories on a continuum, rather than stay within discrete categories. Her research identified that ultimately trainee teachers should be aiming to develop into a 'concept/skill builder': a trainee teacher whose subject knowledge is not closed and who is able to link concepts and skills to situations outside of the classroom.

Earlier this section explored how Biggs suggests a joining up of knowledge types, and Twiselton (2006, p.93) supports this by stating that *'the bringing together of knowledge is the key to effective teaching'*. It is also evident that this is one key to effective learning.

The implications for this research and the 'curriculum as a map' model above are significant. It allows children to explore, problem solve and investigate. It also suggests that the learning that takes place during the process of meaningful activity is as, if not more, important than meeting a prescribed objective. However if this approach is the only one applied, a question must be asked about where does the solid foundation of declarative knowledge become built.

The case study below provides an example of how a trainee teacher on his final block placement planned and taught a lesson using Alfred Noyes' classic poem 'The Highwayman' as a stimulus.

Activity

As you read the case study, consider:

- Tom's beliefs about learning and teaching;
- how those beliefs may have directly impacted upon the children's learning and motivation to learn;
- where on Twiselton's continuum you would place Tom's subject knowledge.

Also consider your own response to the case study: would you be able to work in a similar way? As you read the case study, consider your own beliefs about learning and teaching and how they might impact upon how you would approach a similar unit of work.

Case Study: 'The Highwayman'

Tom, a trainee teacher working in a Year 6 class, planned an English unit for his placement class. The purpose of the unit was for the children to produce a news report about the two deaths that occur in the poem using processes such as enquiry, problem solving, reasoning and communication.

Prior to the children arriving, Tom had set the classroom up like a police murder scene using police cones and hazard tape to cordon off an area, taping outlines of two dead bodies on the floor and using anglepoise lamps to create subdued lighting. The chairs were arranged like a police investigation room, in pairs and in rows with police desk badges ready for the children to write their names on. A rolling slide presentation of images of highwaymen was playing on the interactive whiteboard and an action soundtrack supported this.

The effect was startling. The children came in for registration and were immediately asking questions about the classroom, investigating the artefacts, watching the slide show, discussing the images and there was an excited buzz of chatter and smiles and anticipation as to what would happen next.

Tom burst into the room in costume and introduced himself as the ghost of the highwayman lying dead on the floor and read/told the story from Noyes' narrative poem.

Tom then changed role to Detective Chief Inspector and charged the children with enquiring into the characters in the poem, what further information was needed to be found out, what might their motivation be for committing the murder and what questions might they like to ask the suspects. Tom used the dramatic technique of hot-seating and played the roles of the three main suspects. The children (in role as detectives) asked probing questions of the characters as to their motivation and 'where were you on the night of...' type questions whilst another child scribed useful information onto the board under a picture of each character. There was then an opportunity to share initial hypotheses and reflect on the views of others through small group discussion.

The children moved into role as journalists with the purpose of creating a news piece (a video presentation) in small groups. The teacher gave roles to each child (news anchor, camera operator, court reporter, crime scene reporter) and each group collated their ideas to form a news piece. A recording of a news programme was watched and the style analysed. A script was planned and prepared

→

collaboratively in groups and then shared with the whole class. A 'good news report checklist' was used for evaluation purposes and each group had strengths and areas to improve to work on before final recording.

After recording, the class watched the news reports and assessed their performance in terms of news report criteria as well as understanding of the poem and story and a discussion about the key aspects of learning they had engaged in followed.

At the end of the unit some of the children made these comments:
- *I enjoyed being detectives, today we got be real police interviewing people;*
- *We were involved in everything;*
- *I learnt that English can be a bit like drama and acting;*
- *... that I'm more confident than I thought;*
- *... you got to do English physically as well as mentally.*

Interestingly, most of the comments came from the process of learning and were not particularly related with the end product of the video piece.

You are likely to have noticed that Tom was a very confident and creative trainee teacher. Crucially, he believed that children learn best from co-constructing their knowledge through experience and as a result he planned and taught in a way that reflected this. We see a social contructivist belief (Lambirth, 2005), where, in small groups, children bring their ideas and expertise together, share it and in so doing jointly construct new knowledge and skills with their peers.

Research Focus

Vygotsky (1978) and Bruner (1983) both emphasise the role of talk in learning. They claim that discourse can enhance thinking and support learning. Vygotsky even suggests that thinking and learning can come into existence through the act of talking, taking the idea that the verbal expression of a thought brings it into being. Both believed that learning was socially constructed. Firstly that new learning is built upon previous learning and experience and secondly that this construction process can occur through social discourse, a process that Bruner termed *scaffolding*.

Models of designing learning opportunities

This section focuses on the ways that you might design learning opportunities for the children you teach on placement. Regardless of the ways you conceptualise the curriculum, it is possible to approach planning the curriculum in several different ways.

Fogarty's models of curriculum design

Robin Fogarty has been writing about curriculum integration since the early 1990s. She has developed ten models for how school curricula may be conceived. This section considers four of these, but if you want to read more, see the further reading section at the end of this chapter. Fogarty suggests that curriculum areas, knowledge, skills and understanding can be integrated in meaningful ways and that different models can be used by different teachers and in different times of the school year.

Shared

The shared approach is concerned with looking at two particular subjects and emphasising the common skills and concepts in them. Fogarty (1991, p.62) explains how the model *views the curriculum through binoculars, bringing two distinct disciplines together into a single focused image.* For example let's take English and history. Each circle in Figure 2.1 represents selected subject specific elements from the National Curriculum, and the area of overlap contains elements that appear in both. Therefore these can be shared when curriculum planning.

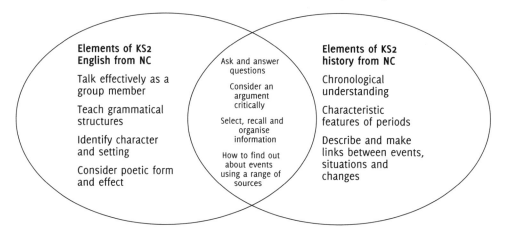

Elements of KS2 English from NC

Talk effectively as a group member

Teach grammatical structures

Identify character and setting

Consider poetic form and effect

Ask and answer questions

Consider an argument critically

Select, recall and organise information

How to find out about events using a range of sources

Elements of KS2 history from NC

Chronological understanding

Characteristic features of periods

Describe and make links between events, situations and changes

Figure 2.1 Example of shared integration: English and history

This approach has many advantages. It ensures that there is a strong link between two subjects and that any links made are meaningful and purposeful. It means that ideas and concepts can be applied easily and is relatively easy to organise. It does however mean that the rest of the curriculum might remain fragmented.

Threaded

The threaded approach is concerned with emphasising particular skills that can run through a subject and draws attention to the value of the process of learning, in particular thinking, social and study skills that can be threaded through a particular subject. Fogarty (1991, p.63) likens this model to viewing the curriculum *through a magnifying glass: the 'big ideas' are enlarged throughout all content with a metacurricular approach.* Let's take ICT as an example.

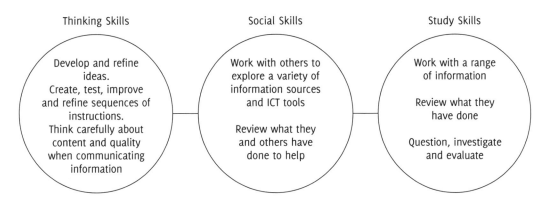

Figure 2.2 Example of threaded integration: Key Stage 2 ICT

This list is by no means exhaustive but it does demonstrate how skills in different areas can be considered through a subject, meaning that as a subject is taught or a curriculum area covered, key process skills can be threaded through to make learning more meaningful and coherent. With this approach there is the explicit teaching of thinking skills and the explicit consideration of multiple intelligences. It means that the transfer of skills is easier and provides opportunity for children to gain insights into their own skills, strengths and weaknesses. Brown and Campione (1998, cited in Watkins, Carnell and Lodge, 2007, p.72) suggest that these insights, known as *meta-cognition* are where 'effective learners operate best'. This approach does however mean that subjects remain separate and meaningful links may not be fully exploited and therefore arguably the full learning potential may not be fully realised.

Integrated

With the integrated approach there is a common theme and subjects are not explicitly emphasised. Fogarty (1991, p. 63) likens this to looking through a kaleidoscope where *interdisciplinary topics are rearranged around overlapping concepts and emerging patterns and designs.* The theme may be a curricular topic such as 'Britain and the world in Tudor times' but the emphasis is on the joining up of skills, concepts and attitudes rather than a focus on the subjects themselves. Let's use the theme of 'Britain and the wider world in Tudor times' as an example. The objectives stated within Fig. 2.3 are taken from the National Curriculum for History, Key Stage 2.

With this approach the interdependence of knowledge, skills and attitudes is clearly mapped out. This is the main advantage of this approach as learning is clearly identified as more than just knowledge being gained but to do with transferable skills and underpinning concepts as well as recognising that developing attitudes is a major part in learning. This approach emphasises whole child development and the role that these different elements play in learning.

Place events, people and
changes into correct periods

How to find out about events
from a range of sources

Describe and
make links
between main
events and
changes

Use dates
and historical
vocabulary to
describe
periods
studied

Understand
factors that
contribute to
a certain
interpretation
of a historical
event

The past is
represented
and interpreted in
different ways

Social, cultural,
ethnic diversity
of societies
studied

Know about ideas,
beliefs and attitudes
and experiences of
men, women and
children in the
past

*Figure 2.3 Example of 'integration' approach using a KS2 British History unit
'Britain and the wider world in Tudor times'*

Webbed

Within the webbed approach a central theme or topic is identified, subjects treated separately but the consideration is what skills and concepts can each of those subjects contribute to the central theme. Fogarty (1991, p.63) suggests that this is like viewing the curriculum through a telescope, *capturing an entire constellation of disciplines at once.* As an example let's take a Key Stage 1 focused topic, 'the seaside' (Fig. 2.4).

The purpose of this approach is to consider the skills that can be taught through the theme. The advantages of this are that the central theme or hub pulls everything together and integrates the content. It also provides a holistic approach to learning and allows children to see links between concepts whilst also providing an opportunity for concepts, skills and content to overlap and be reinforced. However, its success is dependent on an appropriate theme and avoiding tenuous links. The content must also be relevant and meaningful.

Figure 2.4 Example of webbed approach using a topic heading and KS1 curriculum objectives

Activity

Consider a plan for a unit of work you have undertaken. Which of Fogarty's models of integration do you see and how did your planning in these ways impact on on the children's learning? Now that you have read about Fogarty's models of curriculum design, how might you amend the unit of work?

Integration versus single subject curriculum design

Case Study: The International Primary Curriculum

One published integrated curriculum growing in popularity is the International Primary Curriculum (IPC). The IPC is ostensibly a thematic approach to the curriculum. For schools that subscribe, it provides a menu of thematic units. These can be selected by schools so they best fit the interests of the children in the school. Each unit includes learning outcomes, a stimulus or entry point activity, tasks or activities, an explanation of the purpose of the theme and ideas for extending learning beyond what the unit suggests.

Fundamentally important to the thematic approach the IPC presents are the principles behind it. The IPC aims to ensure children:

- *Learn the essential knowledge, skills and understanding of a broad range of curriculum subjects.*

- *Engage with their learning so that they remain committed to learning throughout their school careers and their lives.*

- *Develop the personal qualities they need to be good citizens and to respond to the changing contexts of their future lives.*

- *Develop a sense of their own nationality and culture at the same time as developing a profound respect for the nationalities and cultures of others.*

www.internationalprimarycurriculum.com

This, like all other curriculum approaches, is built upon a strong set of beliefs about how children learn best and also about what knowledge is. For the IPC, knowledge is not just about the acquisition of sets of facts but about the desire to learn, to become life-long learners with a thirst for knowledge. Their approach is also more global, on two levels. The first level being about a more international perspective, children recognising and understanding the culture in which they live which will help them understand and develop a respect for the cultures of others. There is also a recognition that learning is about developing personal qualities such as flexibility, tolerance, interpersonal and intrapersonal skills essential in preparing them for jobs that may not yet exist. The IPC is also designed to take into account the idea that intelligence is multi-faceted.

There are other approaches and models to curriculum design. Although this chapter has focused on Fogarty's curriculum approaches that support ways of integrating subjects and consider the process of learning, Fogarty also identified as a curriculum approach a traditional, single subject design for organising the curriculum, which he called the *fragmented* model (Fogarty, 1991, p.61).

There is some debate to be had around many of the ideas suggested in this chapter. This debate primarily concerns two arguments: an integrated approach with the joining up of concepts from subjects and a single subject approach. The first argument is that an integrated approach to curriculum encourages the joining up of subjects, concepts, skills, knowledge and understanding and so, the proponents of this approach suggest, makes learning more coherent.

An integrated approach

A *fully* integrated approach to the curriculum by its very nature suggests that all subjects, including the daily mathematics lesson and the literacy hour will be absolutely amalgamated. It is interesting to note that the IPC does not include mathematics within its units and it also provides complex mapping guides for schools for them to identify where they need to address potential gaps in their bespoke unit choices in relation to statutory National Curriculum content. The question therefore must arise about what drove most schools to make the decision to have each morning dominated by these two subjects.

Alexander (2009) suggests that the government's drive to have schools demonstrate high standards in these subjects is likely to be the reason. This concerns government targets for schools at the end of Key Stage 2 to achieve certain percentages of levels four and five in Standard Assessment Tests (SATs).The publication of schools' results to parents, OFSTED and the world means that schools want to get the best results possible as these results can often be the first impression that a school gives. This in turn often gives rise to extensive preparation and a lot of SATs anxiety. Alexander (2009) goes on to say that this approach to curriculum and assessment compromises children's entitlement. The National Curriculum (2002, p.11) aims to *provide rich and varied contexts for pupils to acquire and develop a broad range of knowledge and skills*. There seems to be some conflict between this entitlement to a broad and balanced education and the emphasis on publically reported outcomes for English and mathematics. Alexander (2009) goes on to say that:

> The most conspicuous casualties are the arts, the humanities and the kinds of learning in all subjects which require time for talking, problem-solving and the extended exploration of ideas. A policy-led belief that curriculum breadth is incompatible with the pursuit of standards in 'the basics' has fuelled this loss of entitlement (2009, p.22).

This illustrates the two elements in the debate: curriculum breadth and pursuit of standards. Alexander reminds us that these do not have to be two opposing sides but that curriculum breadth can facilitate higher standards, but higher standards of what? This debate can only really have meaning once the question of the purpose of primary education is considered. If primary education is about enabling *pupils to think creatively and critically, to solve problems, to make a difference for the better...to become creative, innovative, enterprising and capable of leadership to equip them for their future lives as workers and citizens* (Alexander, 2002, p.11) then it seems that an integrated approach that supports the development of these in a joined up way may be more effective in achieving this first aim of the National Curriculum.

A single subject approach

One concern with an integrated approach to the curriculum is that individual subjects may lose some of their integrity. Indeed, OFSTED's summary of evidence related to improving primary teachers' subject knowledge across the curriculum begins with *The Independent Review of the Primary Curriculum accents the importance of subjects in primary education and the need for high quality teaching to ensure that pupils make all the progress that they are capable of* (2008, p.1). Additionally, it is not possible to ignore statistics about more students taking A-level mathematics in 2010 than ever before (STEM Advisory Forum, 2010) and how this is being linked to the implementation of the National Numeracy Strategy (NNS) which occurred when those students were in Year 2. This suggests that the NNS was a success in improving attitudes towards the subject. Furthermore, 80% of children in Year 6 achieved a level 4 or above in 2010. This is difficult to ignore when 54% achieved level 4 or above in 1997 (DfE, 2010).

Therefore, a single subject approach to curriculum design can also be highly effective. However, a clear progression of skills should be identified, planned for, and linked together in a structured way so that learners can gain initial skills and then learn how to use them effectively, particularly where an end product is identified. However this does not mean that links cannot be made to other curriculum subjects. Designing the curriculum in this way allows the teacher to use the skills, knowledge and understanding gained through one subject to transfer them to another.

Opposite is an example of a term's worth of work in Art. As you look at it, consider the build up of skills taught working towards the final product. You may notice opportunities for critical thinking, creative thinking, problem solving and also opportunities for developing meaningful cross curricular links.

Activity

Using the Art Medium Term Plan in Fig. 2.5, add any cross-curricular links you think are appropriate. Despite this being a plan for a single subject can you integrate any concepts and skills using any of Fogarty's models for integration? Use this to see how these different approaches to design are not incompatible.

During the activity you may have been able to pull in lots of ideas and thoughts and used the ideas in the plan as a central hub for other ideas around, perhaps a topic of Africa, continents or more specifically, 'Kenya'.

Now let's step back and consider what beliefs about learning drove this plan. First a belief in scaffolding: children need to have a purpose and then be taught the skills necessary to achieve that purpose. Each skill is then followed by an opportunity to try out, practise and explore. Just as in Tom's case study, we see a social contructivist belief (Lambirth, 2005) where, in small groups, children bring their ideas and expertise together, share it and in so doing jointly construct new knowledge and skills with their peers. Through this activity it is also possible to

Medium Term Plan Checklist: Art and Design: Year 5

Learning objectives – linked to NC: skills, vocabulary, concepts and knowledge.	Learning experiences	Resources
To understand that landscape painting involves viewing from a single point and using perspective and scale according to distance. (4a, 5a,1b)	Children look at a range of landscape paintings: Constable, Monet, Cezanne, African landscapes in photographs and paintings, discuss similarities and differences. Look at colours: intense colours in foreground and paler colours further away. Look at scale and diminishing size.	Examples of landscapes by various artists and photographers
To have an appreciation of the use of colours to blend in paint and pastel. (2a,b,c)	Experiment mixing paler colours and intense colours and making patterns. Experiment with blending colours for African landscapes and creating vivid coloured skies and land with 'overpainting' areas, use pastels and watercolours in conjunction and blend together.	Paints, pastels, paper Mixing trays Pencils, paper
To use colours, lines and 3D materials to create an impression of texture. (4b, 5b,c)	Experiment sketching a landscape with diminishing features in the distance, looking at landscapes by a range of artists.	As above and examples of African landscapes
Outcomes	Put painting and sketching together to produce an African landscape focusing on African prints and photographs.	
● To make detailed observations of African landscape paintings.	In small groups, use papier mache to make landscapes of Kenya based on pictures and photographs. Cover balloons with papier mache to produce hot air balloons to fly over African landscapes.	Papier mache, balloons, wire, card
● To imitate African landscapes taking into account colours used, blending and moods created.	Paint the papier mache when dry.	Paint, fabrics, thread, other media such as dried pasta and printing blocks.
● To make 3D African landscapes, using papier mache, vivid colours and hot air balloons.	Use mixed media to create banners depicting people, flags, animals and symbols of Kenya, use different textures, threads, embroidery in small groups.	Canes to hang work

Figure 2.5 Medium term plan for Art (single subject approach)
PoS taken from revised National Curriculum 2002

see how an integrated approach to curriculum design and a single subject approach do not have to be mutually exclusive. A skills-based art and design plan can certainly provide stimulus for an integrated approach to curriculum, similarly an integrated, perhaps webbed curriculum approach can facilitate a deep and exciting single subject plan. As stated before, subject knowledge is very important to success as a teacher, but it is what you do with that knowledge that is more important.

The case study below provides an example of how a group of trainee teachers in a year three class on a creative themed week placement. They planned and taught a series of lessons around the theme of enterprise.

Activity

As you read the case study, consider:
- the trainee teachers' beliefs about learning and teaching;
- how those beliefs may have directly impacted upon the children's learning and motivation to learn;
- what learning took place and how this was scaffolded for the children.

Also consider your own response to the case study: would you be able to work in a similar way?

Thematic approaches

Case Study: Enterprise week

A small group of PGCE trainees were planning a week on the theme of 'enterprise'. Their placement was undertaken as part of a module in their training and involved planning with members of staff in the school. The group began with a main end-product: creating a CD and/or podcast to help raise money for an appeal important to the children in the school. The idea was to post it on the school website and sell the CD at the school fair.

The week began with a role play and subsequent hot-seating and discussion about what it may have been like to be in the situation for which the appeal was raising money. It allowed children to respond physically, verbally and emotionally and begin to understand the world in someone else's shoes. This provided an excellent stimulus for the week as the children could mind map their thoughts and ideas and share them with others. The trainees brought in a range of subjects to their theme, providing subject knowledge in geography and science, marketing, persuasive writing and design. They were in role as rappers as well as business executives over the course of the week. The children had a large variety of learning opportunities not always measured in National Curriculum outcomes. The children learned how to make fruit smoothies, the technology behind making a music CD, the business of marketing and recording music using a mixing desk. They also had the opportunity to learn to express their thoughts, feelings and emotions and experience to a degree life in the shoes of people much less fortunate than themselves. Whilst some of the outcomes of this learning were demonstrated in more traditional acts of writing, drawing and mathematics, the main learning was taken from the processes the children went through and the shared experiences they had during the week of activities.

$\rightarrow$

One teacher commented that the children were more enthusiastic and engaged to work hard and the children's knowledge and understanding of issues outside their locality was definitely heightened. Interestingly the activities the children enjoyed most and articulated most learning from were those which they got practically involved in and made or created something. There was also a definite purpose to this week of work, raising money for people less fortunate than themselves and this purpose captured the enthusiasm and imagination of the children. This purpose was enabled by the theme of enterprise and all the learning opportunities derived from the activities shared that common goal. Fig 2.6 is a theme map such as the trainee teacher group used.

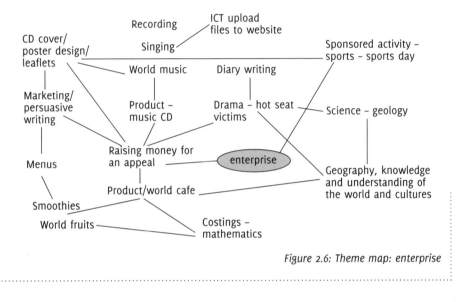

Figure 2.6: Theme map: enterprise

You are likely to have picked up on the children's comments about learning best and enjoying most the activities where they could get practically involved. When planning this themed week of work, the trainee teachers were keen to promote practical and purposeful activity, believing that the children would learn most if they could engage in a full experience that involved not just their minds but their bodies too. The children gained a lot from experiences not traditionally associated with school work such as making smoothies and making a CD. The trainee teachers believed that purposeful activity that was relevant and useful promoted learning and that the children would gain from it. They were able to define learning in broad terms.

This varied range of experiences and broad definition of learning encouraged more of the children to be successful and not 'turn off' those who found more traditional school work activities a challenge. Their planning demonstrates that they believed in the value of a range of different intelligences and that a child's intelligence is not defined by their ability in literacy and mathematics.

Research Focus

Howard Gardner (2006) terms this 'multiple intelligences'. This way of looking at intelligence recognises that intelligence should not just be measured in terms of being literate and numerate but in many other areas too. Alongside more 'traditional' intelligence, Gardner places spatial intelligence, interpersonal and intrapersonal intelligence, kinaesthetic intelligence and musical intelligence as part of a child's unique blend of intelligence and should not be ignored or allowed to stagnate at the expense of literacy and mathematics. This approach is clearly a way to provide children with the National Curriculum's aim of a broad, balanced and relevant curriculum through the profile raising of foundation subjects and mirroring the blending of intelligences with the blending of subjects through a themed approach. Perhaps this approach can offer an alternative to the government's standards agenda and assist in looking at education and approach to curriculum design and assessment in a more holistic way.

Activity

Examine the thematic web in Fig 2.6. Plot onto it opportunities for developing Gardner's intelligences: Visual/spatial, bodily-kinaesthetic, musical, interpersonal, intrapersonal, linguistic, logical/mathematical. More information on each of these is available at www.tecweb.org/styles/gardner.html. Consider whether you think the above approach is an effective approach to planning.

Now go to this website: www.infed.org/thinkers/gardner.htm. This article presents more information on Howard Gardner and on his multiple intelligences theory and identifies some additional intelligences for consideration. Towards the end there are some key questions or problems with his theory, surrounding his criteria for deciding on a particular intelligence, his conceptualisation of intelligence and a lack of empirical evidence. Read these carefully and add the information gained to your thinking about whether considering these intelligences is a good approach to planning.

Learning Outcomes Review

From your reading and from thinking about the school in which you are currently placed, or in which you most recently undertook a placement, respond to the questions which follow each of the intended learning outcomes, as a means of identifying your knowledge and understanding of the issues covered in the chapter.

- **How beliefs about learning drive curriculum planning and teaching approaches:**
  Give some reasons why some of the class teachers you have worked with have
  - organised their classroom in a certain way;
  - used particular teaching approaches;
  - used particular resources.
  Look at the planning that the class teacher uses for their teaching. Identify the main learning theory(ies) that underpin this planning. Find the evidence in the plan.

- **That children's learning and development is at the forefront of curriculum development:**
  - What can you do in your planning for teaching to ensure that children's learning is at the forefront of all that you do?
  - Think about a class you have recently taught, how did they learn best? How did you know? What will you do in the future?

- **How a cross-curricular approach deepens learning through the joining of concepts and ideas:**
  What different approaches could you use in your planning to join skills, concepts and ideas across subjects? Using the National Curriculum devise some examples.

- **Debates about integrated and single-subject learning opportunities:**
  Reflect on and evaluate your own planning on placement. Did you use integrated and/or single subject? Why? What was the impact on the children's learning and on your own subject knowledge understanding?

Further Reading

The texts below relate directly to the research foci outlined throughout this chapter. They will provide you with more knowledge and understanding of some of the key principles that have been outlined.

Brown, A. and Campione, J. (1998) Designing a community of young learners: theoretical and practical lessons. In Lambert, N. and McCombs, B. (eds) *How Students Learn: Reforming schools through learner-centred education.* Washington DC: American Psychological Association.

Cordon, R. (2000) Chapter 1 in *Literacy and Learning through talk: Strategies for the primary classroom*, pp.7–10. Buckingham: OUP in Lambirth, A. (2005) *Reflective Reader: Primary English.* Exeter: Learning Matters. pp.72–75.

Fogarty, R. and Stoehr, J. (2008) *Integrating Curricula With Multiple Intelligences: Teams, Themes, and Threads.* (2nd ed). Thousand Oaks, California: Corwin Press.

Gardner, H. (2006) *Multiple Intelligences: New Horizons*. New York: Basic Books.

References

Alexander, R. (2009) *An Introduction to the Cambridge Primary Review*. Available at: www.primaryreview.org.uk/Downloads/Finalreport/CPR-booklet_low-res.pdf accessed 22/7/10.

Alexander, R. (2004) Still no pedagogy? Principle, pragmatism and compliance in primary education. *Cambridge Journal of Education* 34 (1) pp.7–33.

Arthur, J. and Cremin, T. (2010) (2nd ed) *Learning to Teach in the Primary School.* London. Routledge.

Biggs, J. (2003) (2nd ed) *Teaching for Quality Learning at University.* Maidenhead: Open University Press.

Boyle, T. (2002) Towards a theoretical base for educational multimedia design. *Journal of Interactive Media in Education*. Vol. 2. From: http://www-jime.open.ac.uk/2002/2 accessed 14/5/08.

Brockbank, A. and McGill, I. (2003) *Facilitating Reflective Learning in Higher Education.* Buckingham: SRHE.

Brophy, J. and Good, T. (1986) Teacher behaviour and student achievement. In Wittrock, M.C. (ed) *Handbook of Research in Teaching.* London: Macmillan.

Brown, A. and Campione, J. (1998) Designing a community of young learners: theoretical and practical lessons. In Lambert, N. and McCombs (eds) *How students learn: Reforming schools through learner-centred education.* Washington DC: American Psychological Association. p.540.

Bruner, J.S. (1983) *Child's talk: Learning to use language.* Oxford: Oxford University Press.

DfE (2010) *Analysis of Year 6 Attainment in Maths by Level.* London: National Strategies.

DfEE (1999) *The National Curriculum: Handbook for primary teachers in England Key Stages 1 and 2.* London: HMSO.

DfEE (2002) (2nd ed) *The National Curriculum: Handbook for Primary Teachers in England Key Stages 1 and 2.* London: QCA.

Fogarty, R. (1991) Ten ways to Integrate Curriculum. *Educational Leadership*, 49 (2): pp.61–65.

Gardner, H. (2006) *Multiple Intelligences: New Horizons*. New York: Basic Books.

Howard, J. (2007) *Curriculum Development.* Available at: http://org.elon.edu/catl/documents/curriculum%20development.pdf accessed 20/7/10.

Lambirth, A. (2005) *Reflective Reader: Primary English.* Exeter: Learning Matters.

QCDA (2010) *The Structure of the National Curriculum.* http://curriculum.qcda.gov.uk/key-stages-1-and-2/Values-aims-and-purposes/about-the-primary-curriculum/index.aspx accessed 20/10/10.

STEM Advisory Forum (2010) *Maths A-level Numbers Increase.* London: National Strategies.

Twiselton, S. (2006) The problem with English: the exploration and development of student teachers' English subject knowledge in primary classrooms. *Literacy: Teacher Education and Development.* 40 (2) pp.88–96.

Vygotsky, L. (1978) *Thought and Language.* Cambridge, MA: MIT Press.

Watkins, C., Carnell, E. and Lodge, C. (2007) *Effective Learning in Classrooms.* London: Paul Chapman.

5. Child-centred teaching and learning
Denis Hayes

Learning Outcomes

By the end of this chapter you will:

- be aware of the multi-dimensional nature of learning;
- understand different theories of child development and their implications for teaching;
- recognise the significance of memory and memorising for learning;
- identify different learning styles and their implications for teaching;
- understand the place of learning through experience;
- be able to distinguish between individualised and personalised learning.

Standards

Q10: Have a knowledge and understanding of a range of teaching, learning and behaviour management strategies and know how to use and adapt them, including how to personalise learning and provide opportunities for all learners to achieve their potential.

Q18: Understand how children and young people develop and that the progress and well-being of learners are affected by a range of developmental, social, religious, ethnic, cultural and linguistic influences.

Q29: Evaluate the impact of their teaching on the progress of all learners, and modify their planning and classroom practice where necessary.

Q30: Establish a purposeful and safe learning environment conducive to learning and identify opportunities for learners to learn in out-of-school contexts.

Theories of learning

For further information about theories of learning, see also Chapters 4 and 7 of this book.

Definitions of learning

The nature of learning and how it takes place has dominated the education debate in recent years. The term is normally used to describe any situation in which the brain assimilates knowledge but the processes that combine to produce a learning outcome (i.e. the thing being learned) are difficult to define and explain. One of the challenges for primary teachers is to know when it is correct to claim that a child has 'fully' learned something and, in due course, to formally register the achievement.

Learning can be defined in various ways, including:

- the process that helps the learner to make sense of information and create something new from it;
- the means of sharpening current understanding;
- utilising knowledge and insights gained from earlier experiences to respond effectively to new ones;
- the ability to step back from the security of familiar knowledge to explore less familiar areas;
- the ability to think and reason.

With respect to the last point, Robson (2006) suggests that learning is a necessary *consequence* of thinking, 'which includes use of the imagination, a playful disposition, persistence and the ability to learn with and from others' (p.3). It is therefore important for you to be aware that children are not merely recipients of learning but active partners and initiators of it.

Learning can also be broadly classified into *functional* (immediate use) or *transferable* (usable in other contexts). Take, for instance, a situation where children are learning to use a software program. Some children will doubtless become adept at using the program (functional) and may even be called upon by the teacher to act as tutor to other children. However, only a proportion of the same group of well-informed children will make connections with the implications for using other, similar programs, and transfer their knowledge to the new situation. Again, children who learn a set of spellings for a test may get them all correct (functional learning) yet misspell some of the words in free writing. The aim is, of course, to ensure that children not only master the word list but also utilise their learning in a variety of active, writing situations where spelling is only one of the required skills. Both of the above examples illustrate that apparent 'mastery' of the immediate knowledge is far from being the end of the process.

One explanation about learning is that different forms of it are associated with the right and left parts of the brain. The left part deals principally with language acquisition, sequences and number; it works to analyse information and responds best to structured and sequenced learning. The right part interprets images, looks for patterns, creates metaphors (figures of speech) and strives to synthesise (pull together) and consolidate information. Interplay between the left side and right side of the brain is necessary for the development of deep understanding, creative expression and problem solving. To speak of a person solely as 'left-sided' or 'right-sided' is simplistic, though one dimension is normally prominent.

Research Focus: Bloom's Taxonomy

To explain the functions of learning, Bloom and his colleagues developed what came to be known as *Bloom's Taxonomy* in the 1950s (Bloom, 1956). Taxonomy simply means 'classification', so the taxonomy was an attempt to classify forms of learning. The team suggested a hierarchy of six major classes of learning,

$\rightarrow$

supposedly moving from simple learning (knowledge) to very complex forms of learning (evaluation), as follows:

1. knowledge;

2. comprehension;

3. application;

4. analysis;

5. synthesis;

6. evaluation.

The taxonomy is of interest when you are planning and teaching or evaluating children's work because it offers a yardstick against which to monitor the level of demands that are being placed on them and what level of difficulty they can handle. However, as in all models of learning, it is important to appreciate that Bloom's Taxonomy is meant to be a guide and not a rigid formula. The same applies to Piaget's model (see next section under 'Child development') and any other model applied to education.

Activity

Use Bloom's Taxonomy to evaluate the sorts of demands you are placing on a group of children during a lesson or series of lessons. Consider whether there are ways in which more capable children can engage with the higher-order demands, notably levels 4, 5 and 6.

The learning process

Whichever learning theory is in vogue, it is a fact that children of similar age take varying amounts of time to absorb information and grasp concepts (ideas). Children do not learn in a smooth, uninterrupted fashion with bits of knowledge added in a neat, efficient way like engine parts on an assembly belt. Their experience of learning is more akin to the movement of the tide up and down the beach – sometimes gaining ground, sometimes falling back and occasionally surging forward. Learning has also been likened to a spiral staircase, as a pupil returns to the same point to reinforce and deepen his or her existing understanding but 'higher up' the stairway. The spiral staircase analogy is helpful to illustrate the fact that the learner not only needs to 'look down' to see where he or she has come from but also 'look up' to gain an idea of what comes next (see Chapter 2 for further discussion of spiral learning and the spiral curriculum). Skilful teachers encourage children to make such links by asking them to recall previous learning and introduce them to the hoped-for 'next step' in the learning process.

Child development

Interest in the field of child development grew significantly in the early twentieth century, with particular attention being paid to children and young people who exhibited abnormal behaviour. Only later were these ideas applied to all children.

Theories about child development

There were a number of key theories proposed to explain development, including those by Sigmund Freud, who stressed the importance of *childhood events and experiences*. Erik Erikson was a Danish/German/American developmental psychologist and psychoanalyst, famous for his theory on social development of human beings and coining the phrase 'identity crisis'. He suggested that life could be organised into eight stages that extend from birth to death, the first four stages of which have some applicability to the primary phase.

1. *Infancy*: from birth to 18 months – children learn to trust.

2. *Early childhood*: from 18 months to 3 years – children build self-esteem and autonomy.

3. *Play age*: from 3 to 5 years – children try to copy the adults around them and take the initiative in creating play situations.

4. *School age*: from 6 to 12 years – a social stage of development during which we master many new skills and increase our knowledge.

By contrast with Freud, Erikson claimed that each stage of development is dependent on *overcoming conflict* – because success or failure in dealing with the conflict impacts on the child's future development. For instance, if children aged 3 to 5 years are not given opportunities to play and deal with the social and emotional issues attached to this activity, they may struggle later in life when required to show initiative and relate to others.

Theorists such as the Russian psychologist Ivan Pavlov and the American, Burrhus Frederic (BF) Skinner dealt only with *observable behaviour* rather than the thinking and reasoning that underpinned it. In their view, development was a spontaneous reaction to rewards, punishments, stimuli and other reinforcing behaviours (such as praise).

John Bowlby was an English psychiatrist who developed *attachment theory*, one of the century's most influential theories of personality development and social relationships. Bowlby believed that early relationships with caregivers, especially parents, play a major role in child development and continues to influence social relationships throughout life.

The work of the Swiss/French biologist and psychologist Jean Piaget has significantly influenced the way that learning is organised in school. Piaget's approach is central to the school of cognitive theory known as *cognitive constructivism*. He suggested that children think differently from adults and proposed a *stage theory of cognitive development*. Piaget was among the first people to promote the idea that children play an active role in gaining knowledge of the world. He considered the most critical factor in children's cognitive development to be interaction with their peers. Most famously, Piaget stressed the role of maturation (growing up) in children's increasing capacity to understand their world. He also proposed that children's thinking does not develop smoothly but rather that there are certain points at which it moves into completely new areas and capabilities, as described in the following model:

- sensori-motor stage: birth to 18 months/2 years;
- pre-operational stage: 2 years to 7 years;
- concrete operational: 7 years to 11 years;
- formal operational stage: 11 years and beyond.

By the 1950s Piaget's ideas had become world-known, especially in the field of early childhood education where they were seen as legitimising the idea of learning through play that was free from direct adult influence, thereby reflecting the nursery school tradition (Penn, 2005).

Initially, teachers interpreted the model to mean that children are not capable of understanding certain things before they reach specific ages and it was therefore used as the basis for organising the school curriculum on an age-based structure. However, experience with children shows that Piaget's model is too rigidly structured. For example, some children manage concrete operations earlier than the Piagetian model suggests and even some adults don't function at the level of formal operations or are not called upon to use them, so lose the ability to do so. You should be therefore be careful not to make too many assumptions based on the child's age; it is only one indicator of likely capability.

Piaget is associated with *cognitive* constructivism. Cognition is defined as the mental process of knowing, including aspects such as awareness, perception, reasoning and making judgements. More simply, it is the process of perceiving, thinking, reasoning and analysing. Cognitive functions deal with logic, rather than with areas of the emotions. However, theorists such as Lev Vygotsky (Russian) and Jerome Bruner (born 1915 in the USA) are known as *social constructivists* because they placed considerable emphasis on the part played by language and the influence of others in facilitating learning. Vygotsky argued that mature mental activity involves 'self-regulation' through social interaction, which affects thought, language and reasoning processes. Consequently, instruction and schooling play a central role in helping children to discover how to pay attention, concentrate and learn effectively. Vygotsky claimed that a more experienced partner (buddy), such as another child or a teaching assistant, can provide help to the less knowledgeable partner in the form of an 'intellectual scaffold', which facilitates more rapid progress than would be possible alone.

Jerome Bruner's theories are based upon the premise that the process of constructing knowledge of the world happens within a social context and argues that 'there is no unique sequence for all learners and the optimum progress in any particular case will depend upon a variety of factors, including past learning, stage of development, nature of the material and individual differences' (Bruner, 1966, p.49). Bruner emphasised his opposition to the theory of 'readiness' espoused by Piaget, arguing that any subject can be taught effectively in some intellectually honest form to any child at any stage of development. He also insisted that interest in the material to be learned provides the best motivation, rather than external goals such as grades, being top of the class or merits. From the wide range of explanations above, you can see that there are many factors influencing individual development; no single theory explains everything that happens in education.

Significance of the emotions

In recent years there has been a growth of interest in the way that learning is affected by the emotions and the concept of *emotional intelligence*. The study of emotional intelligence evolved from theorists such as Howard Gardner (1983) – who worked with Bruner for a time – and Williams and Sternberg (1988). However, Salovey and Mayer are credited with coining the expression 'emotional intelligence' (Salovey and Mayer, 1990). Daniel Goleman popularised emotional intelligence in the business realm by describing its importance as an ingredient for successful business careers and as a crucial component for effective group performance (Goleman, 2005). However, whereas Goleman equated high emotional intelligence with maturity and character, Salovey and Mayer firmly resisted making such a link.

Claude Steiner coined the term *emotional literacy* during the 1970s, defined broadly as being aware of your own emotions and understanding the emotions being experienced by others. He went on to develop his ideas about emotional literacy as 'emotional intelligence with a heart'. It is worth noting that emotional literacy is a term that is often used interchangeably with *emotional intelligence* (Steiner, 2000). Hein (2008) claims that emotional literacy is the ability to express feelings with words that convey specific feelings in three-word sentences; for example, *I feel confused*; he argues that the purpose for developing our emotional literacy is to precisely identify and communicate our feelings. In England and Wales, emotional literacy is commonly linked with the Social and Emotional Aspects of Learning (SEAL) initiative in the belief that by assisting children to articulate their feelings and negotiate with peers and adults – a process formerly known as 'assertiveness' – their confidence will grow and they are more likely to take a positive approach to learning.

Note that another expression, *emotional education*, is also entering the education lexicon, loosely defined as understanding others and understanding ourselves in a deeper and more insightful manner. Emotional education draws on the research from emotional intelligence and emotional literacy and is said to improve our life chances, health and wellbeing, in addition to reducing conflict in social interactions.

Activity
Observe the differences in the way that children apply themselves to a task when they work:
- independently;
- with a partner;
- as a member of a group.

Note in particular the influence of social and emotional aspects of learning (SEAL) on:

- their concentration level;
- application to the task;
- quality of learning outcomes;
- relationships with others.

What do these results tell you about the educational benefits of social, emotional aspects of learning?

Memory and remembering

It is common to hear teachers telling children that they must remember a fact, way of working/ behaving or a procedure. However, memorising is a complex phenomenon, the most familiar aspect being an *active working memory* that children can use immediately after they see, hear or otherwise experience something. The active working memory provides a mental 'jotting pad' to store information for everyday activities such as remembering times, following instructions and keeping track of lists of things to do. A working memory allows children to hold information in their heads and manipulate ideas mentally; for example, adding up numbers without a calculator or doing the summation ('sums') on paper.

Research Focus

Gathercole and Alloway (2008) found that the majority of children with poor working memories are slow to learn in the areas of reading, mathematics and science. Children with memory strengths are easy to identify because they can accommodate large amounts of information and retain it effortlessly from a variety of sources. By contrast, children who struggle with memory weaknesses need a considerable amount of repetition, careful explanation and opportunities to explore ideas through problem-solving and investigations.

Weak memory

You will be alerted to a pupil's weak memory when written work is characterised by poor sequencing, missing words and inadequate grammar, despite the fact that they may be able to explain their ideas in speech. If children have problems in absorbing verbal information or are poor listeners they need to have directions explained and visually reinforced (with a diagram, for instance). If children have poor visual recall they may forget what they have read or been shown and need to have their learning supported through careful explanation and 'hands-on' experiences. See VAK types of learning, later in this chapter.

Memory and learning

One of the teacher's most important roles is to ascertain what children have learned after exposure to a planned educational experience, drawing on observations, talking with children, asking questions and marking their completed tasks. In doing so, it quickly becomes apparent that memory affects learning, such that something may be:

1. learned for now but likely to be forgotten very soon;

2. learned, never to be forgotten;

3. learned within defined limits;

4. learned but requiring updating and reinforcement to be secure;

5. learned and understood so thoroughly that the learning can be used successfully in different situations.

Memory and knowledge

The *retention of knowledge* through memorising is a key factor in learning; for example, it is possible for children to master words from a modern foreign language early in the school year but forget them after a short time unless they are regularly practised. In this instance, the learning has been temporary and functional and the fourth of the above statements is relevant. Again, a child may learn how to multiply two numbers by using a certain technique but flounder when given the same problem in a different form – for example, to know that five times eight is forty but struggle to understand that eight items at five pence each costs 40 pence. In such cases, the third statement above is relevant.

Effective learning

Learning that consists of memory *without understanding* has limited value. For example, children might be systematically taught to read words correctly, recite multiplication tables or chant a religious creed, but unless they grasp their meaning and significance, the depth of learning remains shallow. Furthermore, learning that is purely functional, such as knowing how to subtract two numbers, has limited usefulness unless it can be employed in a genuine life situation (such as shopping). Watkins (2003) argues that characteristics of effective learning implies that the learner is:

• active and strategic;

• skilled in cooperation, dialogue and creating knowledge with others;

• able to develop goals and plans;

• able to monitor his or her own learning and is versatile across contexts (different life situations).

Consequently, children need to reflect on their own learning as an essential ingredient in their development, assisted by talking to peers or adults, a point emphasised by both Vygotsky and Bruner (see earlier).

The ideal is for children to have such a grasp of knowledge, skills and understanding that they can use their existing abilities to forge ahead confidently and apply their existing knowledge in unfamiliar situations, as noted in the fifth option listed on p. 51. This deep and expansive type of learning, involving *long-term memory*, extends beyond the boundaries imposed by a task or technique and allows knowledge and understanding to be applied more widely. You cannot rightly claim that children have learned something until these conditions apply.

Classroom practice

Helping children learn

Although learning is taking place continuously, it is in a formal educational setting (such as a school) that it is structured and closely monitored through the curriculum, programmes of study, levels of attainment and so forth. Whatever the specific nature of these imposed structures, educationists agree that the process benefits from well-informed and capable teaching. In other words, though children are capable of learning without experiencing a formal period of education – you only have to observe children playing to realise that a great deal of learning takes place spontaneously during play and personal interactions – pupil progress can be enhanced by a teacher's understanding of how children learn, what they learn and how best to organise learning. MacGilchrist (2003) makes five important points about the nature of learning that have implications for classroom practice.

1. Learners construct and integrate new knowledge in a way that makes sense to them.
2. Learning about learning ('meta-learning') and making sense of experience is a hallmark of effective learners.
3. The relationship between learning and performance is complex and is influenced by motivation and self-image.
4. Learning can be enhanced through developing a variety of social skills and a willingness to persevere and stay on task.
5. The social contexts of the school and classroom are significant in promoting or inhibiting learning.

(Amended list)

Reinforcing learning

You cannot learn for the children but you can do a lot to assist them by providing the right resources, providing them with adequate information, enthusing them to find out more, encouraging them to ask questions and using every possible means to reinforce their learning.

Ultimately, all significant learning must be embedded and etched in the mind of the learner (long-term memory) through repetition and reinforcement by means of discussion, problem solving and activities appropriate to the intellectual capacity and maturity of the child. For instance, memorising a poem 'off by heart' to present to an audience requires practice, rehearsal, coaching and the gradual development of natural speech as the words become more familiar and their significance comprehended. It is quite possible, however, that this mastery may be temporary and largely forgotten after a period of time has elapsed. Contrast this temporary sort of memorising with the ability to interpret words on a page for the purpose of reading, in which the regular use of the words in a variety of contexts (books, work sheets, text on a whiteboard, screen, etc.) will more or less ensure that they can be read at any time in the foreseeable future. Your task is to help children to maintain their understanding and capacity to handle ideas beyond the point at which they are needed for task completion.

Learning styles and preferences

One way in which you can assist the learning process is by taking account of the 'learning styles' or 'learning modes' of children. A widely-used model is referred to as VAK, the three letters standing for: **V**isual learning, **A**uditory learning and **K**inaesthetic learning. *Visual* learners are those who learn best by seeing (e.g. pictures, graphs and diagrams). *Auditory* learners learn best by hearing (e.g. listening to a poem). *Kinaesthetic* learners learn best through practical work. Some educationists separate Kinaesthetic from *Tactile* (as a fourth category): kinaesthetic referring to 'constructing' (e.g. building kits; using computer programs) and tactile emphasising 'touch' (e.g. work with clay). Yet other educators include a fifth category of *Written* learning style. None of the definitions is watertight and there is a degree of overlap between them but the basic principle is for teachers to take account of individual learning preferences as they prepare lessons and actively engage in teaching.

Another way of determining preferred learning styles is by allocating children into four basic categories: (1) innovative and imaginative learners (2) analytical learners (3) pragmatic learners (4) dynamic learners. Thus, *innovative and imaginative* children seem to learn particularly effectively when they have opportunity to use the full range of their senses and ask questions about why things happen. Children with more *analytical* minds tend to process information by studying a range of possibilities closely, thinking deeply and reflecting on the issues involved, developing their own ideas and comparing them with what they observe happening. *Pragmatic* learners first speculate and make suggestions before finding out if their ideas work in practice, then adjust their ideas accordingly. *Dynamic* learners learn best when they have a chance to experiment with ways in which they can use their present level of information and probe other possibilities without fear of being rebuked for doing so.

In practice, the most effective learning takes place when children are given the opportunity to use a combination of tactile senses, visual stimuli, careful listening, enquiry-based activities, conversation and paper and pencil exercises, supported by teacher explanation and reinforced through individual or group activities.

Differentiation

You will need to take account of these different learning preferences when you plan lessons, such that there is sufficient freedom to satisfy the innovative pupil; sufficient intellectual challenge to satisfy the analytical pupil; sufficient opportunity for practice to satisfy the pragmatic pupil; and sufficient investigative element to satisfy the inquisitive pupil. You also have to take account of the needs of children with special educational needs (SEN) and those for whom English is not the primary tongue. Cultivate the habit of speaking at a steady pace and articulating words carefully. Using 'street language' may be fine in an informal social setting but is inappropriate in class and can bewilder second language speakers. See Chapter 4 for further discussion on meeting individuals' needs.

Every class group contains children with different learning preferences and you cannot possibly hope to recognise, process and deliver them all. As a new teacher, the best you can manage is to organise learning situations using groups, varying the stimuli and providing differentiated tasks. For example, the stimuli might include pictures, discussions, making, doing, saying and hearing (Garnett, 2005). The more that children can see the relevance and usefulness of their learning, the more likely it is that they will engage enthusiastically with the lesson content, gain understanding and retain knowledge. Children also need to be given the opportunity to transfer what they have learned to new situations; this is often the acid test for whether or not deep learning has been achieved.

Jeffrey and Woods (2003) declare that real learning and children's personal knowledge are encouraged through hands-on, active engagements, through role-play and through generating positive feelings about learning. Learning then becomes exciting, fun, inspiring, rewarding and motivating. Teachers gain this information when they get alongside children, converse with them, ask questions, allow them to respond, offer advice and explanation and discuss the next steps in the learning process.

Differentiation is a term used to describe a means by which lessons and the associated questions, tasks and evaluation of achievement take close account of children's abilities and aptitudes. In practice, differentiated work often means that children engage with different tasks of varying degrees of difficulty. A teaching assistant will often support children who find learning a challenge. If children are all given the same work, teachers take account of their abilities when assessing work and offering feedback.

Important note: As meeting the high standards described above is a challenge for even the most experienced teacher, don't expect overnight success!

Child-centred education

Child-centred education is a term frequently associated with the American philosopher and educationist, John Dewey, to describe a teaching approach in which children actively construct knowledge by exploring the outside world through free-play, though in fact Dewey did not especially advocate such an approach. Teachers that motivate children to discover new skills and knowledge for themselves are sometimes referred to as 'child-centred teachers'. Such teachers do not favour transmitting facts to (largely) passive children through a 'lecture' style of teaching but prefer to facilitate the discovery of knowledge that is interesting to the children through (for instance) establishing areas around the room with different activities for children to access or assigning children to work together in groups on a chosen project. Relatively little whole-class teaching takes place and limited systematic direct instruction (step-by-step) is employed in helping children to master basic skills. Rather, children discover for themselves through play, investigation and using adults as sources of information and guidance.

A key aim of child-centred learning is to empower children in the belief that a full education is not just about verifiable facts (information) but also about helping children to develop positive attitudes, sensitive judgement and thoughtful evaluation of evidence. Smith (2006) argues that pupil empowerment is a crucial factor in learning and that all children, regardless of ability, should be involved in decision-making in two ways. First, and principally, by contributing to decisions about the effectiveness of their own provision. Second, by participating in decision-making at a wider level and thus influencing school policy.

Supporters of a 'child-centred' approach claim that it helps children to develop greater social competency and creativity than in a more formal setting. However, sceptics point out that children need to be taught basic skills before they can employ them creatively and consider child-centred methods to be unreliable. It is still common to hear sceptics refer to the damage caused by the emphasis on 'child-centred learning' in the Plowden Report, published as long ago as 1967 – though such allegations do not bear close scrutiny. In 2009, the *Rose Review* revived the fortunes of a child-centred philosophy by advocating cross-curricular links in learning (see Hayes, 2010). In addition, ICT was added to mathematics and literacy as the 'core' of the curriculum and spoken communication and personal development are to be developed intensively.

Experiential learning

Outside school, most learning is gained or enhanced by first-hand experience, for which no amount of direct teaching will substitute; for example, exploring a pond; absorbing the sights, scents and sounds in a wooded valley; or a visit to a local craft centre. Similarly, children benefit from listening to visiting poets and authors reading their own work; practical drama; playing with construction materials; handling unfamiliar objects; and shopping in the local market.

Schools that promote experiential learning encourage self-motivation, harmonious social relationships, spontaneous enthusiasm, sharing with others about the work in hand and 'learning about how they learn best' – sometimes referred to as 'meta-learning' or 'meta-cognition' (see Chapter 2 for further discussion). Children's learning is also improved through *investigations* such as science experiments; special effects through random mixing of paints;

researching a topic; and creative computer simulations. These investigative approaches to learning assist children's conceptual understanding, skills acquisition and factual knowledge, and differ markedly from sterile approaches with set procedures and outcomes.

Research Focus: Meta-learning

The concept of meta-learning was introduced by Maudsley (1979) as the process by which learners become aware of and increasingly in control of habits of perception, inquiry, learning and growth that gradually become natural to them. Put simply, meta-learning is becoming more sensitive about and aware of the ways in which we learn.

Discovery learning

Discovery learning is an open-ended form of problem solving in which the teacher provides an introductory activity or stimulus on a relevant theme or topic to gain the children's interest, stir their natural curiosity and raise the level of enthusiasm and motivation. Children are then permitted considerable latitude to decide how they will proceed and shape the enquiry. When they have found out as much as they can in the allocated time, the children determine how they will present their findings – orally, formally written or presented diagrammatically. Younger children with limited ability to write, offer feedback about their discoveries through the spoken word or in the form of a drawing.

Discovery learning is closely associated to work by the French psychologist, Jean Piaget and 'constructivist' theory (see earlier in this chapter), in which learners draw on their existing knowledge and past experiences to discover facts and relationships and insights. Robson (2006) refers to Penn (2005) and notes that by the 1950s Piaget's ideas had become known worldwide, especially in the field of early childhood education 'where they were seen as legitimising the idea of learning through "natural" or "free" play [i.e. free from direct adult influence], very much part of the nursery school tradition' (p.13).

Proponents believe that discovery learning encourages active pupil engagement; promotes autonomy motivation, responsibility and independence; develops creativity and problem solving skills; and offers an individualised learning experience. Critics cite disadvantages, such as the danger of cognitive overload (i.e. too much to think about at one time); the possibility of misconceptions (i.e. developing wrong ideas); and teachers failing to detect and correct mistakes and misconceptions (*Learning-Theories.com*).

In primary schools, discovery learning is normally carried out in pairs or small groups and a report of findings is then made to the rest of the class. Resources are provided by the teacher in advance or created by the children as they proceed with their investigations. The use of information technology (notably through computers) is particularly helpful where the discovery is factual, rather than practical knowledge from hands-on application using materials (kinaesthetic learning). Discovery learning has become more difficult to employ in recent years with the onset of timetabling and increases in curriculum content, with its accompanying time pressures. It is most effective when it is guided by a knowledgeable adult and used in conjunction with the more familiar direct instruction method.

Activity

Observe groups of children engaged in discovery learning and note: (a) which child or children dominate proceedings; (b) which children are passive; (c) how much genuine collaboration exists among the children; (d) the nature of the verbal and non-verbal interactions. Think carefully how your observations will affect the way that you organise such learning.

Case Study: Collaborative learning

Becky organised a collaborative learning activity based on four children per group. She provided the resources and explained broadly what she expected them to do, while stressing that they should discuss their decisions and actions with other members of the group. She was surprised about four things. First, some children were anxious to avoid 'mistakes' and so kept checking with her that they were doing the right thing. Second, some children were strongly dominant and insisted on 'taking charge'. Third, some children copied ideas from other groups instead of using their own. Fourth, the conversations were frequently 'off-task'. Becky soon realised that merely organising children into groups and giving them tasks without first educating them in ways to cooperate, discuss, resolve different viewpoints and reach decisions was unsatisfactory. Over the coming weeks, she spent time helping the children to improve these skills, which resulted in a noticeable improvement in their concentration levels, application to task and final results.

Individualised and personalised learning

The concept of 'personalisation' is based on the belief that it is possible to assess children's progress accurately and tailor-make teaching and learning in such a way that those needs are met. Personalised learning is seen as a highly structured and responsive approach to each child's and young person's learning in order that every pupil is able to progress, achieve and participate in the work (DCSF, 2008; see also Hargreaves, 2006). More recently, *assessment of pupil progress* (APP) has been specifically linked to personalised learning. APP materials include resources that teachers need to help them assess children's progress in mathematics, science and reading and writing from Year 1 (5-year olds) through to the end of Year 6 (11-year olds). Teachers use diagnostic information about children's strengths and weaknesses in planning lessons. National assessment guidelines may be accessed via http://nationalstrategies.standards.dcsf.gov.uk. See Chapter 12 for further discussion about assessment.

Personalised learning should not be confused with the *individualised* learning of the past, characterised by each child engaged on solitary learning paths – often dominated by work sheets – or letting children choose what they want to do.

Research Focus: Personalised learning

In a major study of the ways that schools use personalised learning, Sebba et al. (2007) describe how schools were using their personalised learning approaches to target specific interventions that were then developed more widely. Thus, literacy interventions, programmes and support initially aimed at children with identified special educational needs and provision for gifted and talented children could be targeted at one group of children and gradually extended across the school. The case study schools seemed to have developed activities that reflected greater involvement of the parents through review days and use of ICT for linking home to school.

Some schools have created leadership roles or teaching posts to manage and disseminate best practice in support of the personalised learning agenda, including information to parents and opportunities for them to receive advice about how they may better contribute towards their children's education; see West-Burnham (2008). Schools now hold a lot of assessment information about children in their management systems that are available to staff and parents to provide information about measurable pupil attainment that can be valuable in planning for personalised learning. Hansen and Vaukins (2011) explore this further.

Concerns have been raised about the implementation of personalised learning. First, that it is an unattainable ideal because no teacher, however, skilled and knowledgeable, can offer a bespoke education to each child. Second, learning does not depend solely on teaching methods, so even the most carefully designed programme cannot guarantee outcomes. Third, personalised learning can become unduly rigid in format and thereby constrain creativity and innovation. Finally, a good education does not only consist of high attainment in measurable areas of learning but encompasses (for instance) the ability to relate well to others, act with integrity and make sensible decisions and appropriate choices, none of which can be identified through a specific grade or mark.

Learning Outcomes Review

Thinking about the school in which you are working or have recently worked, respond to the prompts after each intended learning outcome, to identify your knowledge and understanding of the issues covered in the chapter.

- **To be aware of the multi-dimensional nature of learning:**
  - What types of learning are likely to be taking place in the classroom?

- **To understand different theories of child development and their implications for teaching**
  - Make a list of the theorists referred to in the Child Development section and for each of them: (a) Write down a one-sentence summary of his principal belief about learning (b) Suggest a classroom application for the idea.

- **To recognise the significance of memory and memorising for learning**
  - What part does memory play in learning?

- **To identify different learning styles and their implications for teaching**
  - What range of learning styles exist across a class of children?

- **To understand the place of learning through experience**
  - What benefits do children gain through experiential learning?

- **To distinguish between individualised and personalised learning**
  - What are the three distinguishing features of individualised and personalised learning?

Further reading

Hayes, D. (2009) *Learning and Teaching in Primary Schools: Achieving QTS*, Exeter: Learning Matters.

Hayes, D. (2010) *Encyclopaedia of Primary Education*. London: Routledge.

Smidt, S. (2006) *The Developing Child in the 21st Century*. London: Routledge.

References

Bloom, B.S. (ed) (1956) *Taxonomy of Educational Objectives, the Classification of Educational Goals – Handbook I: Cognitive Domain*. New York: McKay.

Bruner, J.S. (1966) *Toward a Theory of Instruction*. Cambridge, MA: Belknap Press of Harvard University Press.

DCSF (2008) *Personalised Learning: A practical guide*. London: HMSO.

Department for Children, Schools and Families (2009) *Independent Review of the Primary Curriculum: Final Report* (The Rose Review). Annesley, Nottingham: DCSF.

Gardner, H. (1983) *Frames of Mind*. New York: Basic Books.

Garnett, S. (2005) *Using Brainpower in the Classroom*. London: Routledge.

Gathercole, S.E. and Alloway, T.P. (2008) *Working Memory and Learning: A practical guide for teachers*. London: Sage.

Goleman, D. (2005) *Working With Emotional Intelligence*. New York: Bantam Books.

Hansen, A. and Vaukins, D. (2011) *Primary Mathematics Across the Curriculum*. Exeter: Learning Matters.

Hargreaves, D. (2006) *Personalising Learning 6: The final gateway – school design and organisation*. London: Specialist Schools Trust.

Hayes, D. (2010) 'Cross-curricular, Rose Review', *Education 3–13*, forthcoming.

Hein, S. (2008) *Emotional Literacy*, accessed through >http://eqi.org/elit.ht<.

Jeffrey, B. and Woods, P. (2003) *The Creative School: A framework for success, quality and effectiveness*. London: Routledge.

Learning-Theories.com: *Discovery learning (Bruner)*, on-line at >http://www.learning-theories.com/discovery-learning-bruner.html<.

Penn, H. (2005) *Understanding Early Childhood*. Maidenhead: Open University Press.

MacGilchrist, B. (2003) 'Primary learners of the future', *Education 3–13*, 31 (3), 58–65.

Maudsley, D.B. (1979) A Theory of Meta-Learning and Principles of Facilitation: An organismic perspective, University of Toronto, (40, 8, 4354–4355–A).

Penn, H. (2005) *Understanding Early Childhood*. Maidenhead: Open University Press.

Robson, S. (2006) *Developing Thinking and Understanding in Young Children*. London: Routledge.

Salovey, P. and Mayer, J.D. (1990) 'Emotional intelligence', *Imagination, Cognition, and Personality*, 9, 185–211.

Sebba, J., Brown, N., Steward, S., Galton, M. and James, M. (2007) *An investigation of personalised learning approaches used by schools*. DfES Research Report RR843. Available from http://www.canterbury.ac.uk/education/tf-mentors/ActivitiesforMentoring/Personalised/documents/DfESReport.pdf last accessed 17/12/10.

Smith, C. (2006) 'From special needs to inclusive education', in Sharp, J., Ward, S. and Hankin, L. (eds) *Education Studies: An issues-based approach*. Exeter: Learning Matters.

Steiner, C.M. (2000) *Emotional Literacy: Intelligence with heart*. Fawnskin, CA: Personhood Press.

Watkins, C. (2003) *Learning: A Sense-Maker's Guide*. London: Association for Teachers and Lecturers.

West-Burnham, J. (2008) *Leadership for Personalising Learning*. National College for School Leadership, on-line via >http://www.ncsl.org.uk<.

4. Including all learners
Jonathan Glazzard

Learning Outcomes

By the end of this chapter you will be aware of:

- definitions of inclusion and associated issues;
- current over-arching policy agendas and legislation which regulate classroom practice;
- the characteristics of inclusive environments;
- the three principles of inclusion in the statutory inclusion statement and ways in which these can be addressed in the classroom.

Standards

Q1 Have high expectations of children and young people including a commitment to ensuring that they can achieve their full educational potential and to establishing fair, respectful, trusting, supportive and constructive relationships with them.

Q2 Demonstrate the positive values, attitudes and behaviour they expect from children and young people.

Q3a Be aware of the professional duties of teachers and the statutory framework within which they work.

Q19 Know how to make effective personalised provision for those they teach, including those for whom English is an additional language or who have special educational needs or disabilities, and how to take practical account of diversity and promote equality and inclusion in their teaching.

Q20 Know and understand the roles of colleagues with specific responsibilities, including those with responsibility for learners with special educational needs and disabilities and other individual learning needs.

Introduction

This chapter introduces you to the three principles of inclusion as outlined in the National Curriculum. The historical development of inclusion as a policy agenda is briefly addressed as well as the underpinning statutory framework which guides practice is discussed. The chapter emphasises the importance of trainee teachers and teachers formulating a set of inclusive values upon which to base their practice.

Defining inclusion

According to Sikes et al. (2007, p.366) attempting to define inclusion 'is a thorny and controversial task which has occupied many commentators over the years'.

Activity

What is your own definition of inclusion?

What factors have helped you to develop that definition?

How important are values and attitudes in shaping inclusive practice and how important is knowledge?

Is knowledge more important than your personal values?

Personal interpretations of inclusion

It has been argued that 'inclusion is a bewildering concept which can have a variety of interpretations and applications' (Avramidis et al., 2002, p.158). Thus, your own interpretation of inclusion and inclusive practice will fundamentally affect the way you perform in the classroom. According to Sikes et al.:

> Whilst policy, structure and culture might shape the broader social and institutional contexts in which teachers and teaching assistants operate, it is their personal interpretations and understandings, their day-to-day enactments, how they perform inclusion, their agency which determines how the policy is formulated and re-formulated in practice.

(Sikes et al., 2007, p.366)

On placements you will gain experience of working with several teachers in different schools and it is likely that you will witness a range of inclusion practices. Professional autonomy allows teachers a degree of freedom in translating policy into practice and teachers interpret policy frameworks in different ways. Inclusive classrooms are central to providing all children with high quality learning experiences and the school's interpretation of inclusion should be articulated within the inclusion policy and it is important that you read this carefully.

Including all learners

You might think about inclusion only in relation to the education of children with special educational needs and disabilities in mainstream environments. However, inclusion is a broad concept which embraces **all** learners. When you think about inclusion, reflect on how you are going to set suitable learning challenges, respond to children's diverse learning needs and overcome potential barriers to learning and assessment for all learners. There is no easy way that constitutes a minimum statutory entitlement for every child.

As a trainee teacher you will need to think about inclusion on different levels, such as:

- the needs of all learners when planning and teaching;
- how you might develop inclusive classroom environments;
- the ways in which you form effective, mutually respectful partnerships with parents, carers and other adults.

Personal values and inclusion

Before you can start to put inclusion into practice it is beneficial for you to reflect on your own values. These will inevitably shape and define your practice. A useful starting point is to reflect on whether you hold any prejudices towards specific groups. Negative stereotypes can lead to discrimination and therefore have no place in the modern world of education. In Chapter 7 you will read about how you are a role model and you need to demonstrate that you welcome and respect all individuals and groups of learners.

Mainstream and special education

Earlier definitions of inclusion focused on the inclusion of all learners into mainstream schools. However, Warnock has argued that:

> Inclusion is not a matter of where you are geographically, but of where you feel you belong. There are many children, and especially adolescents, identified as having special educational needs, who can never feel as though they belong in a large mainstream school.

> (Warnock, 2005, p.38)

Warnock (2005) stresses that 'the idea of inclusion should be ... redefined so that it allows children to pursue the common goals of education in the environment within which they can best be taught' (p.54). In this sense it might be useful for you to conceptualise inclusion in terms of inclusion into the enterprise of education rather than inclusion into mainstream environments. Special schools can and do create inclusive learning environments if the learners thrive, make progress, feel valued and feel that they belong. Despite this there has been a wealth of literature which has emphasised that special schools are exclusionary, oppressive and marginalise learners with special educational needs (see Barton, 1998a; Skirtic, 1991; Tomlinson, 1982). These writers have stressed the point that the education of all children in mainstream schools is part of an international human rights agenda which emphasises that any form of segregation is discriminatory.

Activity
Reflect on the above arguments relating to mainstream and segregated education.
- Do you agree with Warnock's perspectives on inclusion?
- What are your views on special schools?
- Do you think all learners can be educated in mainstream schools?

Inclusion as acceptance and respect for all

According to Farrell (2001) the term 'inclusion' refers to the extent to which a school or community values diversity and welcomes all people as full members of that community. Increasingly inclusion is defined as a broad concept which aims to eliminate social exclusion (Ainscow, 2007). Thus, inclusion embraces issues related social class, disability, gender, ethnicity, religion and sexuality. Corbett (2001) has stressed that inclusion should be thought of as an active rather than a passive process. It represents a continual commitment from all staff to challenge and eliminate all forms of discrimination. Inclusion demands a radical transformation of policies and practices within schools so that barriers to learning, participation and achievement are identified and removed. It represents a whole school commitment to social justice, equity, mutual respect and social diversity which consequently shapes the ethos and philosophical position of all those who work in the school. Inclusive schools celebrate diversity and challenge discriminatory attitudes which ultimately create barriers to learning, participation and achievement.

According to Giroux:

> *Educators should reject forms of schooling that marginalize students who are poor, black and least advantaged. This points to the necessity for developing school practices that recognise how issues related to gender, class, race and sexual orientation can be used as a resource for learning rather than being contained in schools through a systemic pattern of exclusion, punishment and failure.*

(Giroux, 2003, p.10)

Activity
How does the current education system marginalise specific groups of learners? How can this problem be overcome?

Inclusion as a policy agenda: a critique

Inclusive schools enable all learners to thrive. However, recent and current governments have advanced a policy of *normalisation* under the umbrella of inclusion (Armstrong, 2005) which focuses on closing the achievement gap between different groups of learners. Inclusion policy has focused on the use of intervention and support programmes to maximise opportunities for all learners to achieve narrow performance indicators.

Inclusion as a process of normalisation

Research Focus

Christine Lloyd's critique of government policy in relation to inclusive education shows that current practices and policies focus on the normalisation of individuals and groups rather than the 'denormalization of institutions, systems and rules which comprise education and schooling' (Lloyd, 2008, p.228). Consequently, vulnerable learners are pressurised into achieving national performance indicators, regardless of whether these are appropriate.

Denormalising schooling involves the development of different curriculum frameworks and assessment systems to meet the needs of all learners. Lloyd emphasises the inaccessibility of the schooling system through a system which measures individual and school success through the achievement of norm-related standards. For Lloyd, the standards agenda and the way in which the education system currently measures success and achievement is exclusive rather than inclusive. The standards agenda therefore erects barriers to participation and achievement rather than breaking them down (Benjamin, 2002; Lloyd, 2008) through constructing vulnerable learners as failures.

According to Lloyd (2008) inclusive education demands not only a radical transformation of classroom practice, but also a radical transformation of policy. She argues that:

> *Achievement conceived in this way can be seen to create the greatest barrier to success. To remove the barrier it is necessary to reconceptualize achievement in such a way that it is attainable and accessible to all.*

> (Lloyd, 2008, p.229)

Activity

What do you think Lloyd means by 'reconceptualising' achievement? Can you think of alternative approaches to measuring achievement so that all learners can experience and enjoy success?

Inclusion agenda versus standards agenda

Many have argued that there is an incompatible relationship between the standards agenda and the inclusion agenda (Warnock, 1996; Barton, 1998b; Armstrong, 1998; Armstrong, 2005; Lloyd, 2008).

··

Research Focus

According to Cole (2005), within the relationship between the standards agenda and the inclusion agenda 'there will be winners and losers and it is suggested that the losers will be the children who are deemed as having special educational needs' (p.334). Goodley (2007) supports this argument, explaining that 'educational environments, curricula content, teacher identities are all normatively associated with environments, standards and achievements that are at odds with the quirkiness of disabled learners' (p.319). He goes on to explain that 'academic excellence is troubled by those who might never be capable of (nor interested in) such achievements' (p.322).

Goodley (2007) argues that the marketisation of education constructs all learners as 'able', productive and skilled as current educational policy links education to entrepreneurship, which is 'hugely problematic for students with disabilities and or special educational needs who require the support of others' (p.321).

Goodley (2007) encourages us to think of more socially just pedagogies which 'resist over coding and the subtle forms of segregation brought about by assessment' (p.324).

··

Activity

How can educational environments be more flexible to cater for a diverse range of learners? In what ways is the inclusion agenda incompatible with the standards agenda?

It could be argued that inclusive education demands a radical re-think at the level of governmental policy. Current policies related to narrowing the achievement gap between learners with and without special educational needs, have resulted in the marginalisation and exclusion of some learners. The current policy of inclusive education uncritically assumes that all learners are able to meet the same socially constructed norms. This policy instrumentally fails the most vulnerable, thus resulting in further marginalisation and exclusion. The current agenda of personalised learning deludes educators into thinking that they are providing a child-centred curriculum. In reality personalised learning focuses on all children achieving a set of norm-related national performance indicators. Socially just or inclusive pedagogies celebrate difference and define achievement in various ways. Within a socially just inclusive education system learners would be empowered to develop strengths in areas which they are both interested in and feel confident in. Genuine personalised child-centred education is the route to an inclusive education system which recognises that one curriculum and one assessment system cannot meet the needs of all learners.

The development of inclusive education

The documents in the research focus below mark milestones in the evolution of inclusion as a policy agenda. It is important that you are aware of these and understand the impact their publication made on approaches to education for all after their publication.

Research Focus

- The Warnock Report (DES, 1978) introduced the terminology of *special educational needs* and recommended the *integration* of children with special educational needs into mainstream schools.

- The Salamanca Statement called on all governments in the United Nations to 'adopt as a matter of law or policy the principle of *inclusive* education, enrolling all children in regular schools, unless there are compelling reasons for doing otherwise' (UNESCO, 1994).

- Both the Green Paper (DFEE, 1997) and *Removing Barriers to Achievement* (DFES, 2004) emphasised the need for schools to plan for inclusion and to raise outcomes for children with special educational needs.

- The Code of Practice (DFES, 2001) set out a graduated response to support children with special educational needs and emphasised the importance of consultation with children and parents/carers.

- The National Curriculum (DFEE, 1999) included a statutory inclusion framework.

- The Special Educational Needs and Disability Act (SENDA, 2001) emphasised that discrimination on the grounds of disability is illegal.

- *Every Child Matters* (HMSO, 2003) emphasised the need for multi-agency collaboration to raise outcomes for all learners, parent partnership, child participation and intervention to support vulnerable learners and their parents. This strategy aims to tackle the negative impact of social deprivation on learners' attainment.

- The Disability Discrimination Act (2005) emphasised the need for schools and other educational institutions to make reasonable adjustments to cater for the needs of all learners with disabilities.

Inclusive environments

Despite the issues associated with personal interpretations of inclusion there are several key characteristics of inclusive learning environments which you need to embed into your practice. Inclusive environments:

- value difference and celebrate diversity;
- recognise what each child can do and build on this by providing suitable learning challenges;

- respond to children's diverse learning needs;
- identify and remove barriers to learning and achievement;
- are warm, friendly and positive so that all adults and children feel as though they belong;
- demonstrate an ethos of mutual respect;
- value the views of all (child, parents, carers and all adults working within the school);
- create a climate of hope, success and possibility.

The statutory framework for inclusion

The National Curriculum (DFEE, 1999) clearly states that schools have a statutory responsibility to provide all children with a broad and balanced curriculum and that all children have an entitlement to effective learning opportunities. The statutory framework for inclusion in the National Curriculum sets out three principles that schools must address in order to develop inclusive practices. All schools must:

- *set suitable learning challenges for all children;*
- *respond to children's diverse learning needs;*
- *overcome potential barriers to learning and assessment for individuals and groups of children.*

(DFEE, 1999)

When you are undertaking placements ensure that you provide opportunities for all children to experience success in learning. To address these principles you will need to:

- plan appropriate learning objectives which match your learners' needs;
- use varied teaching styles to cater for your learners differing learning styles;
- plan access strategies to make learning accessible to all children.

Setting suitable learning challenges

As you move towards achieving QTS, you must demonstrate that you are able to provide suitable learning challenges for every child in your class (Q1; Q19; Q22; Q26b). The following will help you to prepare for your placements and support you to develop your pedagogical understanding in order to meet all children's needs effectively. Chapter 10 identifies methods you can use to develop these essential areas.

Know your learners

Spend time getting to know your learners before you start to teach them. Observe them in a range of curriculum areas. Talk to your mentor about their learning needs, and ask if you can have access to any prior assessment records which detail your learners' attainment. You will be able to plan for progression in learning once you have a clear understanding of your learners' starting points and prior attainment (see standard Q13).

Subject knowledge
Only with adequate subject knowledge (Q14) will you understand strands of progression in various aspects of learning in specific subjects. You will then be able to identify children's next steps in learning.

Using assessment to build on prior learning
You need to ensure that you assess your learners frequently (Q26, Q27, Q28). Much of the assessment you carry out will be informal and formative and help you to identify what children can do and whether they have any misconceptions. Read more about assessment in Chapter 14.

Identifying appropriate learning outcomes
In some instances you might be able to build in access strategies to enable all learners to achieve the same learning outcomes (Q19). In others it may not appropriate to have all your learners working on the same learning outcomes, so differentiate the outcomes to match the needs of your learners.

Using appropriate grouping arrangements
Although your ability to influence grouping arrangements as a trainee teacher on placement will vary, the ideal situation is to operate flexible grouping arrangements so that children can switch groups according to their needs (Q25d). For example, a child may have specific difficulties with reading and writing but may excel in speaking and listening activities. Another child may struggle in mathematics with number and calculations but may excel in shape, space and measures. It is also important to remember that children respond differently to different areas of the curriculum. Mixed-ability grouping can often provide children with a suitable context for peer-peer scaffolding.

Personalised learning
When planning for children's needs, think carefully about setting personal learning targets for individuals if appropriate (Q19). Involve support staff in the assessment process and encourage them to suggest possible next steps for the learners they are supporting. Remember that you need to demonstrate that you are able to work collaboratively as part of a team (Q32). See Chapter 12 for planning for other adults.

Taking responsibility for all learners
You must take your responsibilities seriously in relation to planning for the education of *all* learners (Q1; Q19). The important point to bear in mind is that learners with additional needs should only be withdrawn when necessary. Additionally, ensure that the education of learners with additional needs is not left solely to support staff or specialist classroom assistants.

High expectations of all learners

It is your responsibility to ensure that every child makes progress (Q1; Q13; Q22). Planning for progression will help children move forward in their learning. You will be required to demonstrate that all of your learners have made good rates of progress in relation to their abilities and starting points. Maintain high expectations of all learners and track their progress regularly. You will also be able to forecast progress rates more accurately once you have a clear picture of their prior attainment and rates of progress (Q13).

The principle of high expectations for all learners means ensuring that learners who have been identified as gifted and challenged receive appropriate learning challenges. Ensure that these learners make rapid rates of progress and be confident that you have the necessary subject knowledge required to challenge learners who are working above age-related expectations. 'Target setting' (Q26b) for/with your learners is fundamental to securing the very best outcomes for all your children.

Using appropriate curriculum frameworks to aid differentiation

Schools have a statutory duty to teach all primary-aged children the content of the National Curriculum. This entitlement ensures that all children have access to a broad and balanced curriculum. However, teachers have the flexibility to select programmes of study from earlier or later key stages to ensure that all children are provided with appropriately differentiated learning challenges.

Understanding child development

Chapter 3 outlines the need to ensure you have a very secure understanding of child development. Having a secure understanding of the steps children progress through, and knowledge of what stages children have reached in relation to those steps, is pivotal to planning appropriate learning challenges.

Activity

Imagine that you are teaching literacy to a Year 3 class. You are planning guided writing and the focus is to compose sentences using adjectives, verbs and nouns for precision, clarity and impact. Adam finds literacy difficult and is not yet able to write in sentences. Beth is able to cope with this task and needs to be challenged further.
- Identify a more suitable learning objective for Adam.
- Identify a learning objective which will challenge Beth.

Responding to children's diverse learning needs

Your learners may come from very diverse social and cultural backgrounds. During your teaching placements and teaching career it is likely that you will gain experience of teaching different groups of children. These may include:

- children with special educational needs and disabilities;
- children from different ethnic groups;
- travellers, refugees and asylum seekers;
- boys and girls;
- children from diverse linguistic backgrounds.

As Chapter 4 outlines, children have different interests and learning styles. To ensure that your curriculum engages all children, think about the resources you use to support your teaching and the extent to which these reflect children's diverse backgrounds. Try to draw on children's social and cultural experiences in your teaching. You must challenge any form of bullying or harassment, including racial harassment.

Children's interests can often be used as a starting point for learning in the classroom. Boys and girls may have different interests so reflect these interests in:

- the books available for children to read;
- the writing tasks you present;
- the topics and themes you plan.

You will need to respect children's cultural beliefs. Additionally you must ensure that all children have the opportunity to participate in the learning experiences that you have planned. Think carefully about:

- your classroom environment reflecting aspects of social, linguistic and cultural diversity;
- images around your classroom reflecting positive images of disability;
- the choice of famous people that you choose to study in history;
- how you present other countries in geography to avoid stereotypical views.

Think about how you might embed aspects of social and cultural diversity through art, dance, music or drama. Try to be creative in your approach. Think carefully about your word choices and avoid generalisations. Children do not all live in houses, they do not all live with a mum and a dad and they do not all celebrate Christmas or shop in the local supermarket. Although this is obvious, teachers may inadvertently transmit white middle class values onto learners. You should demonstrate your sensitivity to the diverse backgrounds of the learners in your class.

The Race Relations (Amendment) Act (2000) clearly states that schools must:

- promote good race relations;
- eliminate racial harassment;
- promote equality of opportunity.

This legislation places a duty on schools to take a proactive stance towards race equality. It is not sufficient just to address racist incidents as and when they occur (Knowles, 2006). Children need to be taught about race equality. Try to demonstrate your commitment to diversity by embedding every aspect of it into your planning, teaching, classroom environment and ethos.

Activity

When on placement, discuss with your class teacher how their planning responds to the diverse needs of the children in their class and more broadly in their local community.

Case Study: Gender differences

Jane was on placement in a mixed R/Y1 class. She created a writing area to support children's independent writing. Over a period of several weeks Jane began to notice that many of the boys in her class were reluctant to enter the writing area in self-chosen activities. The boys often chose to play in the outdoor area or in the construction area. If they did go in the writing area they did not persist with activities for any length of time.

Jane decided to carry out a small-scale action research project. The aim of the research was to improve boys' motivation in writing. She initially observed a small group of boys during independent play. Jane noticed that the boys frequently played at being superhero characters that they had watched on television. Jane informally asked them about the characters they were playing and she discovered more about the characters they liked. Jane decided to capitalise on the boys' interests in developing the writing area to reflect these.

She focused on a 'Superman' theme and put resources (pictures, comics and stationery) into the area to reflect this character. After the writing area had been enhanced Jane immediately noticed that the boys wanted to use it, and continued to do so.

Activity

- How might Jane use the children's diverse learning styles to develop other areas of the classroom?
- Can you think of any dangers with this approach?

Overcoming potential barriers to learning and assessment

You play a major role in addressing under-achievement in school. You are responsible for identifying vulnerable groups: these are children who are likely to under-achieve. You will need to monitor achievement carefully and plan for individuals and groups of learners to help them make further progress. You will need to be prepared to justify the progress of all of your learners.

Groups of learners at risk of under-achievement include:

- travellers;
- children identified as being gifted and talented;
- children who are learning English as an additional language;
- looked after children;
- children with special educational needs and disabilities.

To overcome barriers to learning you may need to:

- break tasks down;
- vary your teaching styles e.g. by providing children with visual, auditory and kinaesthetic learning opportunities;
- build in access strategies to enable children to access a piece of learning.

Access strategies will vary depending on the specific barrier to learning but typically might include:

- use of additional support e.g. support staff and peer support;
- use of ICT;
- specific equipment;
- visual timetables.

Activity

The above list is not exhaustive. What strategies have you seen being utilised to support children with specific impairments, e.g. dyslexia, autism, speech and language, sensory difficulties and social, emotional and behaviour difficulties. Draw on your experiences from your school-based training to help you.

Working with travellers

Lloyd and McCluskey (2008) identify some of the key issues facing the education of children who are travellers. These include:

- *low educational participation/ attendance;*
- *high incidence of exclusion (DFES, 2003);*
- *low attainment;*
- *racist harassment, physical bullying, name calling;*
- *interrupted learning;*

- *inadequate support;*
- *failure of schools to pass on records;*
- *inappropriate identification of special educational needs.*

(Lloyd and McCluskey, 2008, p.335)

Travellers are entitled to a flexible system of education and the use of ICT/internet based home learning is having a positive impact on attainment. The Race Relations Amendment Act, 2000 places a duty on schools to promote racial equality and challenge discrimination. Schools and teachers should embrace and accept the cultural differences between travelling and non-travelling children and offer differentiated and flexible provision accordingly. Inclusion necessitates additional and different provision, not provision which is the same. Schools should develop effective partnerships with the local Traveller Education Service to help develop inclusive ways of working. Above all teachers should reflect on their own values and prejudices. Ignorance and negative teacher attitudes potentially result in the marginalisation of learners from this community. Teachers should celebrate the culture of travellers and use this as an opportunity to educate other children about the history of travellers and their cultural beliefs.

Gifted and talented children

Giftedness is usually seen as the potential *a child may posses in any particular subject or area of human activity; it is characterised by the child's ability to learn in that area faster than its peer group. Talent is seen as the* realisation *of that giftedness; in effect, the performance of that giftedness.*

(Knowles, 2006, p.150)

Essentially children in this category could be those who have advanced vocabularies or are able to reason. These children may master concepts, knowledge and skills at a quicker rate than their peers. These learners may disengage if the learning is not sufficiently challenging and they may be socially aloof. The term *talented* is often used to describe children's abilities in sport, music or the visual/performing arts, whilst giftedness is often used to refer to ability in academic domains.

Children who are gifted and/or talented need access to:

- a differentiated and challenging curriculum;
- extension activities which advance learning;
- opportunities to think, problem solve, reason and evaluate (Bloom's Taxonomy of thinking skills may help you to extend children's thinking skills further – see Chapter 3);
- opportunities to consider a range of perspectives/viewpoints;
- opportunities for learning through personal enquiry/research;
- a teacher with excellent subject knowledge who is capable of extending their learning within specific strands;

- regular assessments to identify their individual learning needs.

It is important that you abandon stereotypical views when identifying children who are gifted and talented. These learners may well come from working class backgrounds or socially deprived backgrounds.

Research Focus

Porter's work (Porter, 1999) illustrates how children who are formally identified as gifted and talented are often punctual; attend school regularly; have parents who are interested in education and behave. It is possible for a range of factors to mask a child's giftedness.

Children with English as an additional language, refugees and asylum seekers

During your course it is likely that you will work with children with English as an additional language (EAL). Children will need support to access the language across the curriculum and not just in English lessons. Environmental print should display children's first languages so classroom labels, posters and displays need to include words using children's first languages as well as English. This will demonstrate that their first language is valued. First languages can be used during class greetings so that all children have opportunities to hear the language.

Encourage children to use both languages. Gardner (2006) recommends the use of dual language texts and the use of 'code switching' so that children can use both languages when writing if they struggle to write an English word. Teachers should celebrate the children's cultural backgrounds and use this as an opportunity to enrich their teaching.

You might wish to consider using the following strategies to support language development in these children:

- use of visual teaching strategies;
- use of tactile resources such as objects to represent words;
- use of puppets;
- use of bilingual support workers.

Instructions need to be precise and supported by visual stimuli as appropriate. Think carefully about how to develop partnerships with parents and carers and the use of family literacy programmes may be useful in helping to break down barriers. Letters and notes to parents and carers may also need to be translated.

Children with special educational needs and disabilities

Read the case study overleaf.

- How did Sally help Sam to overcome any barriers to learning?
- In what ways did Sally minimise categorisation?
- What actions could have been undertaken by the Head Teacher in relation to Chris?
- How important are teacher attitudes in facilitating (or erecting barriers to) inclusion?

Case Study: Sam

Sam was a four year old child with Asperger syndrome or high functioning autism. In his previous school he had been labelled as a 'disruptive' child. Sam's parents decided that the case study school would be a better option for Sam, due to the fact that there was an autistic resource base on site and the mainstream teachers were experienced at including children like Sam in their classrooms. Sam's parents were keen that he was educated in mainstream provision, despite the fact that there was special provision for autistic children on the premises. Sam came to the school with twenty hours of support. He was immediately placed in the reception class (Sally's class) because of his age.

During Sam's first two days at the school he was accompanied by a member of staff from the Communication and Interaction Team from the Local Authority. His teacher commented that the member of staff:

... seemed to have 'textbook' strategies for dealing with autistic children. She insisted that he had a daily schedule, even though I thought that we should try him without one in the first instance. I was anxious not to make him feel different. She said that he had to be escorted to the toilet. She wanted him to go out to play before the others so that he was not distressed by being in a busy cloakroom. She said that he would need one-to-one support on the playground. She wasn't very happy because I said 'no' to all of her recommendations. These strategies would have isolated Sam and were not practical in a mainstream classroom and a mainstream school. There was simply no way that we could escort him everywhere and the bottom line was that his parents had chosen to send him to a mainstream school for a reason. They did not want us to operate a mini special school. She also wanted Sam to have one-to-one teaching which I am totally opposed to. I was glad when she left us alone. After a couple of days he settled brilliantly. He didn't need a schedule. He didn't need one-to-one supervision and he didn't need to be taught in a one-to-one situation. He coped with getting ready to play with the other children. He coped with our normal classroom routines. Sometimes I remember that he used to throw himself on the floor. This was often when he needed his own space. We used to withdraw him to give him the space he needed but not as a punishment. It allowed him to calm down (Sally).

→

Sally was determined to avoid implementing strategies that would emphasise and draw attention to Sam's differences. Rather than using an individual schedule with Sam, Sally used a whole class visual timetable on a 'planning board' so that all the children could clearly see which areas of the classroom they were supposed to be working in. This also enabled all adults to identify where children were. Sally prepared Sam for changes in routine through pre-warning him. In addition she used social stories as an approach to talk him through new experiences in advance. Sally talked about his obsessions with books and computers:

> I used them as a bargaining tool. If I wanted him to do a task I would tell him that he couldn't go in the book area or use the computers until he had done what I had asked him. It worked a treat! (Sally).

Sally recalled how Sam's mother was more relaxed about him being in mainstream provision than his father:

> His father wanted us to watch him like a hawk. I told him that this was not necessary but he still wanted us to protect him more than the others (Sally).

After a very successful year in Sally's class, Sam moved to another teacher (Chris). She explained that Chris operated a much more formal classroom and had very little patience for children who were not always able to behave in appropriate ways:

> He had very low tolerance levels. He would shout at Sam all the time and Sam used to cry constantly. He used to send him out of class with his TA when he couldn't cope with him. Sam became a very distressed little boy. Chris just doesn't recognise that children are not all the same and cannot be programmed to behave in the same ways. Children are not robots. I saw all my hard work going down the drain and it made me so angry. One day Sam was wailing and screaming because Chris had shouted at him. I was furious and so was Julie, the SENCO. Julie was deeply disturbed and she told Chris that it said more about him and his classroom ethos than it did about Sam. I asked the Head to move Sam to a teacher who would continue what I had started. The Head luckily agreed and within a matter of weeks, Sam's behaviour improved (Sally).

This case study provides an example of successful inclusion. Barbara Cole's research with *mother-teachers* (Cole, 2005) demonstrated that above all, the notion of being 'wanted' was an important factor in developing an inclusive ethos. For these parents, their overriding concern was that the teachers wanted their children. In the case study Sally clearly wanted to teach Sam but Chris was reluctant. Sam's case study illustrates that children with autism are capable of internalising negative teacher attitudes and this can affect their behaviour. In inclusive environments children need to feel that they are welcome in mainstream settings and have a right to be there. There is clearly a need for some practitioners to reflect on their own values in relation to the education of learners with special educational needs and until all teachers accept their shared responsibility for the education of all children, genuine inclusion will remain problematic.

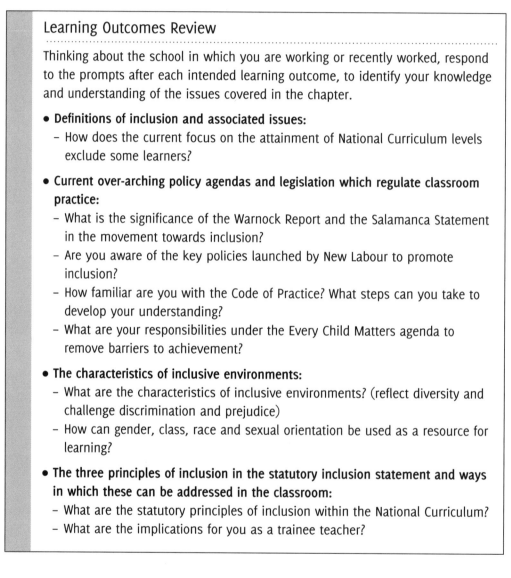

Learning Outcomes Review

Thinking about the school in which you are working or recently worked, respond to the prompts after each intended learning outcome, to identify your knowledge and understanding of the issues covered in the chapter.

- **Definitions of inclusion and associated issues:**
  - How does the current focus on the attainment of National Curriculum levels exclude some learners?

- **Current over-arching policy agendas and legislation which regulate classroom practice:**
  - What is the significance of the Warnock Report and the Salamanca Statement in the movement towards inclusion?
  - Are you aware of the key policies launched by New Labour to promote inclusion?
  - How familiar are you with the Code of Practice? What steps can you take to develop your understanding?
  - What are your responsibilities under the Every Child Matters agenda to remove barriers to achievement?

- **The characteristics of inclusive environments:**
  - What are the characteristics of inclusive environments? (reflect diversity and challenge discrimination and prejudice)
  - How can gender, class, race and sexual orientation be used as a resource for learning?

- **The three principles of inclusion in the statutory inclusion statement and ways in which these can be addressed in the classroom:**
  - What are the statutory principles of inclusion within the National Curriculum?
  - What are the implications for you as a trainee teacher?

Further Reading

Billington, T. (2000) *Separating, Losing and Excluding Children: Narratives of Difference.* London: Routledge Falmer.

Skidmore, D. (2004) *Inclusion: the dynamic of school development.* Maidenhead: Open University Press.

References

Ainscow, M. (2007) Taking an inclusive turn, *Journal of Research in Special Educational Needs,* 7, (1), 3–7.

Armstrong, D. (1998) Changing faces, changing places: Policy routes to inclusion, in P. Clough and L. Barton (eds), *Managing Inclusive Education: From Policy to Experience.* London: Paul Chapman Publishing.

Armstrong, D. (2005) Reinventing 'inclusion': New Labour and the cultural politics of special education. *Oxford Review of Education,* 31, (1), 135–151.

Avramadis, E., Bayliss, P. and Burden, R. (2002) Inclusion in action: an in-depth case study of an effective inclusive secondary school in the south-west of England. *International journal of Inclusive Education,* 6, (2), 143–163.

Barton, L. (ed) (1998a) *The Politics of Special Educational Needs.* London: Falmer Press.

Barton, L. (1998b) Markets, Managerialism and Inclusive Education, in P. Clough and L. Barton (eds) (1998) *Managing Inclusive Education: From Policy to Experience.* London: Paul Chapman Publishing.

Benjamin, S. (2002) *The micropolitics of inclusive education.* Buckingham: Open University Press.

Cole, B. (2005) Good Faith and Effort? Perspectives on Educational Inclusion. *Disability and Society,* 20, (3), 331–344.

Corbett, J. (2001) Teaching Approaches Which Support Inclusive Education: A Connective Pedagogy. *British Journal of Special Education,* 28, (2), 55–59.

Department for Education and Science (DES) (1978) *Special educational needs: report of the committee of enquiry into the education of handicapped children and young people (The Warnock Report).* London: HMSO.

Department for Education and Employment (DFEE) (1997) *Excellence in Schools.* London: Department for Education and Employment.

Department for Education and Employment (DFEE) (1999) *The National Curriculum for England.* London: DFEE.

Department for Education and Skills (DFES) (2001) *Special Educational Needs Code of Practice.* Nottinghamshire: DFES.

Department for Education and Skills (DFES) (2003) *Aiming High: Raising the attainment of Gypsy Traveller children.* London: DFES.

Department for Education and Skills (DFES) (2004) *Removing Barriers to Achievement: The Government Strategy for SEN.* London: DFES.

Department for Education and Skills (2006) *Primary Framework for literacy and mathematics.* Nottingham: DFES.

Department for Education and Skills (2007) *The Early Years Foundation Stage: Setting the standards for learning, development and care for children from birth to five.* Nottingham: DFES.

Farrell, P. (2001) Special Education in the Last Twenty Years: Have things really got better? *British Journal of Special Education,* 28, (1), 3–9.

Gardner, J (2006) Children who have English as an additional language, in Knowles, G. 'Gifted and Talented' in Knowles, G. (2006) (ed) *Supporting Inclusive Practice.* London: David Fulton.

Giroux, H.A. (2003) Public pedagogy and the politics of resistance: notes on a critical theory of educational struggle. *Educational Philosophy and Theory,* 35, (1), 5–16.

Goodley, D. (2007) Towards socially just pedagogies: Deleuzoguattarian critical disability studies. *International Journal of Inclusive Education,* 11, (3), 317–334.

HMSO (2003) *Every Child Matters.* Norwich: The Stationery Office.

Knowles, G. (2006) Gifted and Talented, in Knowles, G. (2006) (ed) *Supporting Inclusive Practice.* London: David Fulton.

Lloyd, C. (2008) Removing barriers to achievement: a strategy for inclusion or exclusion? *International Journal of Inclusive Education,* 12, (2), 221–236.

Lloyd, G. and McCluskey, G. (2008) Education and Gypsies/Travellers: 'contradictions and significant silences'. *International Journal of Inclusive Education,* 12, (4), 331–345.

Porter, L. (1999) *Gifted Young Children: A Guide for Teachers and Parents,* Buckingham: Open University Press, in Knowles, G. 'Gifted and Talented', in Knowles, G. (2006) (ed) *Supporting Inclusive Practice.* London: David Fulton.

Sikes, P., Lawson, H. and Parker, M. (2007) Voices on: teachers and teaching assistants talk about inclusion, *International Journal of Inclusive Education,* 11, (3), 355–370.

Skirtic, T. (1991) *Behind Special Education: A critical analysis of professional culture and school organisation.* Denver: Love Publishing.

Tomlinson, S. (1982) *The Sociology of Special Education.* London: Routledge and Kegan Paul.

UNESCO (1994) *The UNESCO Salamanca Statement and framework for action on special needs education.* Paris: UNESCO.

Warnock, M. (1996) The work of the Warnock Committee, in P. Mittler and V. Sinason (eds) *Changing Policy and Practice for People with Learning Difficulties.* London: Castle.

Warnock, M. (2005) *Special Educational Needs: A New Look.* Impact No.11, Philosophy of Education Society of Great Britain.

5. Transitions and progression
Mary Briggs

Learning Outcomes

This chapter will introduce you to the topics of transitions and progression and what they means for children, parents/carers, teachers and other adults working with children, schools and other settings. By the end of this chapter you will have:
- an understanding of the concepts of transitions and progression;
- an understanding of the relationship between transitions, continuity and progression;
- become aware of the need to plan for transitions in your teaching;
- an awareness of transitions as a continuous process rather than a one off event and everyone involved needs time to adapt to new situation;
- an understanding that smooth transitions can ensure continuity and progression in children's learning.

Standards

Q4 Communicate effectively with children, young people, colleagues, parents and carers.

Q6 Have a commitment to collaboration and co-operative working

Q7(a) Reflect on and improve their practice, and take responsibility for identifying and meeting their developing professional needs.

Q10 Have a knowledge and understanding of a range of teaching, learning and behaviour management strategies and know how to use and adapt them, including how to personalise learning and provide opportunities for all learners to achieve their potential.

Q18 Understand how children and young people develop and that the progress and well-being of learners are affected by a range of developmental, social, religious, ethnic, cultural and linguistic influences.

Q21(b) Know how to identify and support children and young people whose progress, development or well-being is affected by changes or difficulties in their personal circumstances, and when to refer them to colleagues for specialist support.

Q25(d) Demonstrate the ability to manage the learning of individuals, groups and whole classes, modifying their teaching to suit the stage of the lesson.

Q29 Evaluate the impact of their teaching on the progress of all learners, and modify their planning and classroom practice where necessary.

Q32. Work as a team member and identify opportunities for working with colleagues, sharing the development of effective practice with them.
Standards also related to transitions and progression are: Q1, 2, 3a,b, 5, 14, 21a.

Introduction

Activity
Before starting to read this chapter think about the kinds of transitions that children experience. If possible discuss this with others on your training programme and/or school-based tutors/mentors or teachers.

Here are some of the ideas you may have thought about. It is not an exhaustive list but one just to get you started thinking about transitions:

- into play group/pre-school/care outside the home;
- into school;
- between each Key Stage;
- smaller transitions in relation to identity (e.g. arrival of brothers and sisters);
- between tasks;
- within the settings/schools for example for specific subjects within the curriculum or specific classes.

Defining transitions

Transitions are changes in the situation for children and those associated with them and can include the transition between home and a play group or pre-school, or care outside the home particularly in the early years. We often just associate transitions with children's entry into formal school but there are other transitions for children. For example, there can be changes for children at home in relation to their position in the family when a new brother or sister arrives which means children consider their role in the family, for example no longer the baby and now a big sister or brother.

This section will begin to unpack some of the issues in relation to transitions in education between home and school, within school between key stages which may be in different buildings, within the class with transitions between tasks and groups and between schools.

Research Focus

In her review of the literature related to transitions for children and young people Annmarie Turnball (2006) came up with the following list:

Starting nursery	Illness of family members	Changing friends
Starting primary school	Death of family members	Coming out as lesbian or gay
Starting secondary school	Separation from parents	Diagnosis of illness
Changing school	New siblings	Diagnosis of a disability
Moving house	Moving through year groups	Living with illness/disability
Puberty	Entering care	New step parents
First exams	First sexual experience	Living in a new country

(Turnball, 2006, p.2)

She describes how these transitions are 'potentially challenging episodes of change' which may be gradual or sudden and last for a short or longer period of time.

Transition between home and an educational setting

The first major transition that children and their families often experience is between home and an educational setting. This can be a source of stress and anxiety for all those involved partly as a result of not knowing what to expect. You may remember your first visit to a new school or more recently to university and the feelings you had about the event, which could help you begin to understand some of the anxieties around the situation. Any teacher working within this age range will want to establish relationship with children and their families before the children start in the new setting. This can often involve home visits with photographs being taken of the child at home with permissions which are then used to identify drawers or pegs for the new child when they start attending the new setting.

Children or schools ready?

The NFER have carried out considerable research into the issue of transitions and particularly in relation to the school starting age in different countries. Caroline Sharp has been a key researcher of this early years issue. Over the years in the UK we have had varying policies for children starting school at different ages. At one point schools took children in three times a year which meant that summer born children always had less time in school before any assessments. This group have been seen as disadvantaged by their age. The following quotation from the conclusions of a presentation encourages us to consider the purpose of transitions and for whose benefit are all the activities associated with this area.

The challenge is to ensure that the system minimises inequalities due to relative age. We need to make schools ready for children, rather than focusing on making children ready for school.

(Sharp, 2009)

The case study of activities below is taken from a study in the USA by Kagan et al. (2010). This specific study is of 'Countdown to Kindergarten' in Boston Massachusetts.

Case Study

The project is a non-profit collaborative effort of the City of Boston, Boston Public Schools (BPS), and more than two dozen public and community agencies. The program engages families, educators, and community members in a citywide effort to celebrate and support the transition into kindergarten, recognizing it as a significant educational and developmental milestone for children and their families. The program has developed a series of educational activities that create a continuum of services supporting families from birth through kindergarten entry. The aims of the project are to raise awareness within the community but particularly targeting parents/carers, of the importance and availability of kindergarten provision. This project wants parents and carers to know about:

- the kindergarten curriculum to ensure that families take advantage of the academic and social benefits kindergarten provides.

- the processes of choosing schools, registering, and entering kindergarten and that they are clear and welcoming to all families.

This project aims to lay the groundwork for primary caretakers to be active partners in their children's education in BPS elementary schools and beyond. They also coordinate and expand social and learning activities that help children transition from home or preschool into kindergarten. The kinds of activities that are offered are set out in a calendar of local events for children and families and include:

- an 'I'm Ready' DVD, Countdown to Kindergarten information sheets, registration guides, and readiness activities;

- an 'I'm going to Kindergarten' T-shirt that allows children to access child-friendly community resources (e.g., museums) for free;

- School Preview Time: opportunities to visit schools and learn about how to choose and then register for school;

- School Welcome Sessions: opportunities for families to explore their newly assigned school and receive a 'Counting Down to Kindergarten' readiness guide;

- Neighbourhood Kindergarten Days: celebrations held at neighbourhood Boston Public Library branches for children and families entering kindergarten;

$\rightarrow$

- Annual Kindergarten Celebration at the Boston Children's Museum: Boston's citywide celebration where children have the opportunity to meet teachers, sample typical kindergarten activities, climb on board a real school bus, and receive free health screenings;
- a Countdown exhibit at the Boston Children's Museum;
- free Playgroups groups for families with children 1- to 3-years-old.

Activity

After you have read the case study about early transitions in one US city, find out about the information and activities that are available for families in your area. Is there a children's centre were information and activities might take place?

Early Years Foundation Stage to Key Stage 1

This particular transition has become an international focus of attention for research with educationists concerned about providing the very best start for children as they enter school. This section looks at different approaches from a variety of countries.

Australia

Research carried out in Australia which was reviewed by Petriwskyj (2005) suggests that one of the major issues with the transitions at this point are around the conception of children's readiness for more formal learning and there are still tensions for teaches related to the academic expectations of the move from the Foundation Stage Curriculum to the National Curriculum and the overall approach taken. Peters (2000) found that teachers and parents viewed continuity between preschool and school as essential to successful transition into school but that many saw increasing structure in preschool curriculum and pedagogy as providing this continuity.

Denmark

In Denmark Broström (2000) describes the need to make the child feel '*suitable*, that is to have a feeling of well being and belonging'. The argument for this is that research on starting school shows that children who feel suitable, relaxed, well adjusted in kindergarten are much more likely to experience success in school than children who do not feel well adjusted at the beginning (Margetts, 2006). In many ways this might appear to be common sense but as a trainee teacher you will need to be aware of the feelings of the children and parents as well as being versed in the routines and practices.

Whose perspective?

There can be a tendency to consider this very important transition purely from the adults' perspective, concentrating on what parents/carers and teachers need to know and this has been a focus of much of the research. This is rather than focusing on what children may need and want to know. From Margett's (2006) work in Australia asking children what they thought children needed or wanted to know about starting school the following themes emerged, peer relationships; school rules; general procedures; classrooms; academic skills; and feelings.

It is not just the classroom and potential changes in practice that the children must learn to adapt to but negotiating the playground environment can be a very daunting one for the youngest children in school. Although they often have a separate space outside from the rest of the school this is still a place to learn new things. These include learning about being friends, dealing with unfriendly behaviour and aggressive behaviour, fighting or quarrelling, sharing, turn taking, being comforted, being lonely and telling a secret (Smith, 2003). Part of the role of being a teacher related to the QTS standards is 'Q30. Establish a purposeful and safe learning environment conducive to learning and identify opportunities for learners to learn in out-of-school contexts', which includes considering the playground and play times as part of this environment.

In *Excellence and Enjoyment: A Strategy for Primary Schools* (DfES, 2003) the Government set out its intention to ensure continuity between the areas of learning in the Foundation Stage and the Key Stage 1 programmes of study. It also made a commitment to gaining a better understanding of whether there were still difficulties around transition and whether teachers need more support. Two recent major studies published by the DfES and Ofsted have examined the transition from Reception to Year 1. Saunders et al. (2005) found that schools had adopted a variety of strategies aimed at smoothing transition. These tended to focus on three areas: induction of children into Year 1; continuity of practice between Reception and Year 1; and communication between staff, parents and children. The study found that: '...the best transitions for children take place where conditions are similar, communication is encouraged, and the process of change takes place gradually over time' (Sanders et al., 2005).

The other study was carried out by Ofsted (2004) and this found there was an imbalance in the curriculum with a much stronger emphasis on numeracy and literacy than other areas of the curriculum. Since this study was published the curriculum balance has been reconsidered for the whole of the primary age range with a greater focus on creativity across the curriculum. Although from a professional perspective learning is very important in the dialogue between parents/carers and school the key issue is the emotional well being of the children from the parental perspective as indicated in the following quote from the report.

> *... a means of keeping in touch, not only with reading but other issues affecting their children. One father commented about his daughter: 'I want to know is she is settling in well and is beginning to start to read and write a bit as well as recognising numbers. But above all, I want to know if she is happy.'*

> (Ofsted, 2004, p.16)

Activity

Discuss with your school-based tutor or mentor the school's approach to the transitions and the issues discussed between the staff at both end of the transition. What do you notice about the tensions that they experience? How do they support children and parents during this period? Do they have a specific programme of events for the children and their parents? Does this happen at specific times of the year or is this a continuous process?

Research Focus

One important aspect of transitions is how children feel about the changes to come and this was a focus of research at the National Foundation for Educational Research (NFER) by Caroline Sharp and Gabrielle White in their 2005 paper 'How children make sense of the transition to Year 1.'

When asked about what they anticipated Year 1 would be like these are typical answers which illustrate how they are thinking about the changes to come:

Girl: *We will do all writing and stuff ... They don't have any toys, only some, not lots...*

Boy: *When you go in Year 1 you get older so you will have to do harder work.*

Where children had visited the year one classes previously they appeared to have a clearer idea of what to expect.

Girl: *I already know because I have been there because we had "change over classes".*

Sharp and White followed the children to ask them about what they noticed after the transition

In Reception we used to dress up and we could play on the carpet with the dressing-up stuff. We can play in Year 1, but not lots of times any more.

You only go outside at playtime and lunchtime. They don't have any toys outside though.

Every time we do [work] sheets there is always a more difficult sheet to go on to next, and you can't go and play when you finish your work because there is always another sheet.

These comments illustrate a key and current approach in educational research that is including 'pupil's voice' in their work. This changes the focus of the research

$\longrightarrow$

from looking at events or activities undertaken here as part of the transition to exploring the children's views of the process and their thoughts about the changes to come. 'Pupil voice' comes from a growing recognition that children and young people are not simply citizens of the future, but are capable persons willing and able to be involved in their communities and schools and perhaps above all as a teacher we can learn from children's views about improving the learning process.

Sharp and White's research demonstrated there was a clear distinction between the Early Years Foundation Stage and Key Stage 1 practice.

Play-based ⟶ Work-based

Active ⟶ Static

Led by adult/child ⟶ Directed by adults

Thematic ⟶ Subject-based

Emphasises a range of skills ⟶ Emphasises listening and writing

Their conclusions were:

- most children coped well with the move to Year 1;
- school transition strategies were important;
- growing up brought new challenges and harder work;
- curriculum and pedagogy had a clear impact on children's enjoyment of learning.

As the issues identified in the research above have been a focus of continuous professional development and review in many schools, it would be worth you exploring how much practices have changed since this research was undertaken.

The short case study below is drawn from information available on Teachers' TV and focuses on the transition between the children's centre just down the road and the primary school. Clapham Manor Primary School in London looked closely at the issues in relation to transitions and some of their work can be seen on Teachers' TV: www.teachers.tv/videos/transitions-building-on-learning. When reading this case study consider what you have learnt about the school's approach to transitions and how this might compare to your experiences so far.

Case Study: One school's approach

The staff reviewed the results of children's learning for end of Key Stage 1 and saw that they were not as high as end of Key Stage 2. They draw the conclusion that they need to improve on their transition periods at Clapham Manor Primary School and Children's Centre in London. They identify relationships with parents as

→

playing a key part during the transitional periods, especially in the children's move from the nursery to reception. They developed a transitions policy for the school which sees transition as a continuous process rather than a one off event. This resulted in more activities across the phases of the school and an acknowledgement that for some children an individual transition plan was needed to further support the process and ensure progression of children's learning. One unique aspect of the school is their use of learning partners with each class in the school linked with a class of older children and visits take place between the classes helping to establish friendships and mentoring. Staff and learning partners from the school visit the nursery to make themselves familiar to the children and this goes on throughout the year with longer visits each time. The children also keep a celebration book to highlight their achievements up to Year 1. All these activities have helped them to establish smooth transitions between the nursery and school. One result of the review of transitions has resulted in staff development and changes in practice in Year 1 to support the movement of children into key stage one.

Activity

If possible, when you are on placement, observe in a reception class and a year one class during the morning sessions as this is when you may see differences in approach. Although you may find more similarities depending upon the school philosophy and the teaching staff involved, what do you notice about the similarities and differences in practice? You may also be able to talk to your school-based tutor/ mentor about the changes that may have occurred since this research was completed and what the teachers, parents/carers and children think about the changes made.

Smooth transitions

Smooth transitions are essential for children to experience continuity and minimal disruption to their learning and security. The recommendations from Sanders et al. (2005) for the transition between the Foundation stage and Year 1 are:

- more play-based learning in Year 1;
- maintenance of friendship groups;
- good communication between staff and parents.

The key features of good transitions are around consistency.

- Consistency is important to and identifiable in young children (e.g. schemas).
- Effective educational provision needs consistency:
  - adults;

– routines and information;
– experiences and materials.

• Consistency enables children to be active and independent learners.

Transitions for individuals in the class

At a micro level there are a number of transitions for children within the classroom throughout the day and as the teacher you need to consider these when planning your lessons, activities and the use of resources.

Transitions between different phases of a lesson and location in the class

This can be a difficult activity for trainee teachers as some children can find it difficult to make transitions between activities or use this as the opportunity to behaviour inappropriately. Part of planning for the transitions often involves movement between activities and there is a need for quiet before instructions can be given to facilitate the movement. Trainee teachers talking on the Behaviour4learning website (www.behaviour4learning.ac.uk) discussed the use of something like a rain stick to shake and make a relatively quiet noise to gain the class's attention, or children repeating a clapping pattern started by the teacher. You can read further strategies for managing behaviour in Chapter 13. These techniques help with transitions during teaching times and at the end of lessons.

Activity
Either through observation, or by reflecting on a previous experience in school, make notes about the following transitions and how teachers handle them.
• Entry to the classroom.
• Exiting the classroom.
• From carpet to table activities.
• Break and lunch times.
• Moving to assembly.
• Moving from the class to the hall or outside for PE/games.
Do teachers employ different techniques for different occasions or do they have one method that they stick to? Do they use the transitions as a teaching activity, e.g asking children to identify if they have lace up shoes or answer a spelling or a mental calculation in order to be able to leave the class?

Transitions between groups within the class

Sometimes you find that children are in different groups for different areas of the curriculum particularly if grouping is based on attainment so you may find that groups have names to distinguish them apart. There can be routines established in the class that assist the transitions between different groupings which can involve the collection of books and the handing out of a different set sometimes by 'book monitors'. With groups like guided reading groups this could include children collecting their copies of the book the group is working on.

Relationship between transitions, progression and guided group work

Children can be grouped in a number of different ways to ensure progress in their learning. *Progression* is seen in this book as the moving through the phases of education. It is often explicitly linked with continuity of experiences and learning. It can also be seen as progression in learning though this is more closely related to assessment and will be addressed in Chapter 12. It is also essential that you understand how *continuity* (how academic and pastoral arrangements are made in a way which ensures progression), is taken into account when planning provision for them. Guided group work can be one way of organising children for teaching purposes. Guided work is continued focused teaching designed to support children's learning. It can be used to move learning forward, to extend and challenge all learners or to focus on a particular concept, skill or strategy that needs developing; or to develop the children's language and communication skills in order to express their ideas and build up their confidence. Guided group work can provide opportunities for:

- focused teaching, structured to address the shared needs of the group, identified by ongoing and periodic assessments;
- to teach core routines for tasks/games;
- interactive teaching and scaffolding;
- planned talk – opportunity for sustained discussion;
- opportunities to assess learning – to diagnose and address barriers to progress.

These are all part of the teacher's role in ensure continuity and progression for all learners. One reason for discussing this under transitions is that children need to understand why they are being grouped in particular ways in the classroom and how they might use the learning that takes place in these guided groups in the usual teaching groups that might occur in the class. Teachers play a crucial role in helping children to make the transition between different groups in the class.

Activity
List the particular features of guided group work, and how this is different to self-facilitated work. Consider how guided group work would assist you to ensure pupils progress in their learning.

Transitions for setting across the year or years within the school

We don't always associate transitions from class to class with primary education but tend to think about this as a secondary school issue. However many schools set within year groups or across years for English and mathematics and as a consequence children must move between classes mostly in the mornings when these subjects are taught. This may be something you encounter when in schools on placement. If this is the case, think carefully about how they manage the transitions. For example:

- How much time is allowed for the transfer of children from class to class?

- How does the class teacher know about children in his or her class's progression in learning if they are taught either or both subjects or mathematics and English by another teacher?

- How can they build on the learning in those subjects when teaching the rest of the curriculum?

Transitions for groups between classes

This can be particularly important for children who attend intervention sessions within the school day or other special educational needs support groups. Transitions can also apply to children who take music lessons where they are out of a specific lesson and may miss explanations. When children return to the class, making the transition into the class lesson they will need guidance and support to take part in the learning. As the teacher you will need to ensure that their learning progresses in the same way as the rest of the class. Think about how individual differences are taken account of in planning the timing of such sessions. What will you do about any work that is missed? It may be useful to talk to some of the children involved and ask about their feelings with regard to the transitions they need to make and what makes it easier or harder for them returning to the class. You can then use this information to help you plan your own actions for individuals/groups where this occurs.

Transitions between classes at the end of the school year

Most primary-aged children change classes at the end of the academic year though you may find yourself in a school where there are mixed aged classes. The short case study below based in a primary school in the Midlands details the kinds of activities that go on before, during and after transitions between classes in a primary school each academic year.

Case Study: Planning and preparing for transition and progression

Much of what happens appears to be behind the scenes. Teachers meet to look at the numbers of children within a particular year group and this can often make the difference between having a single year class or a mixed year class. For mixed year

$\rightarrow$

classes the discussion involves how the mix is to be decided. If it is just one or two classes that are mixed the decision can often be on age alone as this can be the easiest way to explain why some children may appear to have 'moved up' whilst others 'stayed down'. If there is more than one class in a year group the discussion can be about the grouping of children to allow all children to learn and maybe to separate those who don't always work well together. This discussion can also be influenced by the strengths and interests of the teachers who will teach the classes. Once the makeup of the classes is decided then parents and children are usually informed (a few weeks before the end of the term). Visits usually take place on the same day that the Year 6 visit their secondary schools so all teachers can receive the next year's group. This can also be a time that NQTs are invited to meet their classes before taking up their appointments in the new academic year. Teachers can then receive internal records for the class they are going to teach to ensure continuity and progression in the children's learning.

Transition and progression to secondary school

Moving to secondary school is a challenging time for children. Children have a variety of concerns but those raised most often include concerns about bullying, queries about school uniforms, queries about discipline or queries about new subjects (Powell et al., 2006). A key to effective transition and progression from primary to secondary is the flow of information and the following research highlights a number of specific issues in relation to ensuring that the information get to the right people involved in the process.

Research Focus: From primary school to secondary school

Powell et al.'s (2006) research focused on practice in Wales but many of the issues are the same for England. All the secondary schools organised parents' evenings to introduce the school to parents of Year 6 children, although the frequency and timing varied.

Powell et al. identified a number of activities that supported good liaison and therefore transition for children between primary and secondary schools:

- termly meetings between primary school head teachers and staff;
- meetings between primary school curriculum area leaders and the relevant staff in the secondary school;
- links between secondary learning support staff and the primary schools;
- pastoral links;
- more extra-curricular activities, for example sports and music.
  (Powell et al. 2006, p.38)

$\rightarrow$

A key issue is the progression and continuity of learning between KS2 and KS3 and in this study of practice cooperating to develop schemes of work for the primary schools or to bridge the KS2/KS3 transition was seen as effective in maintaining the learning across the change of school.

It is worth considering the different perspectives of those involved in the transition process at this stage of a child's life. The information that parents/carers want can be different from that needed by their children. Secondary schools often provided parents the following kinds of information:

- a general introduction to the school, its staff and the National Curriculum;
- the school's results at GCSE and A level (where appropriate);
- registration procedures, including where to go at the start of the first day;
- information about the number of lessons each day;
- details of what equipment the children would require;
- lunchtime arrangements;
- what was needed in terms of school uniform and where it could be purchased.

Transitions to ensure progression in learning

In order to ensure that there is continuity and progression in children's learning between schools' information about prior learning across the curriculum and in and outside school needs to be passed between the schools. This would help you understand the requirements for Q6 related to collaboration. Typically the kinds of information on pupil attainment supplied by primary to secondary schools are:

- national KS2 test and task levels;
- national KS2 test marks;
- teacher assessments for a range of subjects not just the core curriculum;
- reading ages and other information for children with SEN;
- teacher comments which may include particular strengths or areas of concern.

In addition to data about academic subjects and attainment, schools find other information helpful in settling children into a new school and making decisions about form tutors or pastoral groupings as well as any early subject setting. The type of information passed on to secondary schools can include:

- information about children's strengths and weaknesses;
- attendance;
- extra-curricular activities;
- friends;

- language used at home;
- religious affiliation if appropriate;
- health;
- behaviour;
- potential for sport;
- musical or performing talents.

Activity

When you are in a primary or junior school find out which Year 6 teacher is responsible for transfer liaison with the secondary schools. Find out what kinds of information is transferred between schools. How are the children supported in their transition to secondary school?

For specific groups of children transitions can be more problematic and this was highlighted by Robinson and Martin (2008) when reviewing the experience of Traveller and Roma communities where at age 11 school and parental expectations and desires may come into conflict. The importance of specific outreach work was indicated as being the best way to work with these particular communities. Chapter 4 explores issues related to supporting all learners further.

Research Focus

The Strengthening Transfers and Transitions project (DSCF, 2008). Seven local authorities selected families of schools to engage in action research to explore what strengthens transfers and transitions. The action research projects clearly identified seven key principles that underpin effective transfers and transitions for progress.

- Assessment for learning (AfL) principles underpin progress across transfers and transitions.
- Transfers and transitions are key drivers in raising standards.
- Children need confidence, understanding and skills to advance their own progress across transfer or transition.
- Partnership working is essential for effective transfers and transitions for progress.
- Effective partnerships are built on a common vision, shared responsibility and trust.
- Partnership working requires mutual understanding through shared experiences and a common language.

$\rightarrow$

- Sustained collaboration requires systems and structures that support formal and ongoing links between partners.

The following elements emerged in a number of the schools' projects as having particular leverage.

- Head teacher/SLT involvement. The crucial element here is a 'leader' with the status to give importance to transfers and transitions, but additionally able to align it with wider school improvement priorities.

- Ongoing collaboration before and after transfer in the context of both key stages. This has not been one key stage 'doing' transfer to the other, but an equal partnership that has professionally developed all stakeholders.

- Cross-phase network meetings whose agenda and discussions have focused on professional dialogue about teaching and learning within the contexts of transfers and transitions, and not about the cohort or individual children that are involved.

- The development of children's skills through either a part- or full-time competency-based curriculum designed to build on prior learning and to facilitate successful movement to the following year/key stage.

- Building capacity and sustainability for ongoing improvement by involving children and parents in the monitoring, reviewing and planning process and strategically sharing effective practice through a planned process, both within an LA and a school.

Learning Outcomes Review

Thinking about the school in which you are currently placed, or in which you most recently undertook a placement, respond to the questions which follow each of the intended learning outcomes, as a means of identifying your knowledge and understanding of the issues covered in the chapter.

- **An understanding of the concepts of transitions and progression, and the relationship between transitions, continuity and progression:**
  - What do the terms transition, continuity and progress mean?
  - What transitions have the children in your class experienced?
  - Which of these are in school and which are out of school?
  - What features of the school's organisation and day-to-day operation provide children continuity with experience and ensures progression in children's learning?
  - What structures are in place in the class to ensure that there is progression of children's learning with each transition? How do you do this, and how effective is it?
  - What features or structures support continuity of learning in school?

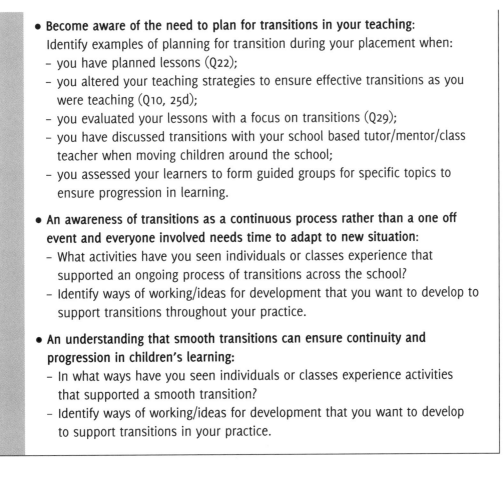

- **Become aware of the need to plan for transitions in your teaching:**
  Identify examples of planning for transition during your placement when:
  - you have planned lessons (Q22);
  - you altered your teaching strategies to ensure effective transitions as you were teaching (Q10, 25d);
  - you evaluated your lessons with a focus on transitions (Q29);
  - you have discussed transitions with your school based tutor/mentor/class teacher when moving children around the school;
  - you assessed your learners to form guided groups for specific topics to ensure progression in learning.

- **An awareness of transitions as a continuous process rather than a one off event and everyone involved needs time to adapt to new situation:**
  - What activities have you seen individuals or classes experience that supported an ongoing process of transitions across the school?
  - Identify ways of working/ideas for development that you want to develop to support transitions throughout your practice.

- **An understanding that smooth transitions can ensure continuity and progression in children's learning:**
  - In what ways have you seen individuals or classes experience activities that supported a smooth transition?
  - Identify ways of working/ideas for development that you want to develop to support transitions in your practice.

Further Reading

Further issues associated with continuity and progression will be addressed in the assessment chapter of this book.

www.behaviour4learning.ac.uk/ This site will give you access to behaviour management techniques you could use with transitions in the class and around school.

DCSF (2008) *Strengthening Transfers and Transitions: Partnerships for progress.* Department for Children, Schools and Families.

DfES (2006) Seamless Transitions – supporting continuity in young children's learning. Norwich: DfES. This is a support pack including DVD for schools and early years settings.

More about children's voice research can be found on www.pupil-voice.org.uk
Also on www.ttrb.ac.uk/viewArticle2.aspx?contentId=13008 as well as current publications on transition issues.

Underwood, L. and Ward, L. (2004) *Staveley and Brimington Learning Community Community Transition Package* http://www.ttrb.ac.uk/attachments/d34fa91d-6861-40a7-a620-b8a521445647.pdf. This is a package of ideas for teachers to use as part of the transition process at different stages.

References

Broström, S. (2000) 'Communication and continuity in the transition from kindergarten to school in Denmark'. Paper related to poster symposium on 'transition' at EECERA 10th European Conference on Quality in Early Childhood Education, University of London, 29 August to 1 September 2000.

DfES (2003) *Excellence and Enjoyment: A Strategy for Primary Schools.* Nottingham: DfES Publications.

DCSF (2008) *Strengthening transfers and Transitions: Partnerships for progress.* Department for Children, Schools and Families.

Kagan, S.L., Karnati, R., Friedlander, J. and Tarrant, K. (2010) *Compendium of Transition Initiatives in the Early Years: A Resource Guide to Alignment and Continuity Efforts in the United States and other Countries.* Columbia: National Center for Children and Families/Teachers College.

Margetts, K. (2006) ' "Teachers should explain what they mean": What new children need to know about starting school'. Summary of paper presented at the EECERA 16th Annual Conference Reykjavik, Iceland, 30 August–2 September 2006.

Ofsted (2004) *Transition from the Reception Year to Year 1: An evaluation by HMI.* HMI 2221. London: Ofsted.

Peters, S. (2000) 'Multiple perspectives on continuity in early learning and the transition to school'. Paper presented at EECERA Conference, London, August–September.

Petriwskyj, A. (2005) 'Transitions to school: Early years teachers' role'. *Journal of Australian Research in Early Childhood Education,* 12 (2) pp39–49.

Powell, R., Smith, R., Jones, G. and Reakes, A. (2006) *Transition from Primary to Secondary School: Current Arrangements and Good Practice in Wales.* Final Report. Slough: NFER.

Robinson, M. and Martin, K. (2008) *Approaches to working with children, young people and families for Traveller, Irish Traveller, Gypsy, Roma and Show People Communities:* A literature review. Leeds: CWDC.

Sanders, D., White, G., Burge, B., Sharp, C., Eames, A., McCune, R. and Grayson, H. (2005) *A study of the transition from the Foundation Stage to Key Stage 1.* Nottingham: DfES Publications.

Sharp, C. and White, G. (2005) 'How children make sense of the transition to Year 1.' Paper presented at the 2005 EECERA Annual Conference, Dublin, 31 August–3 September.

Sharp, C. (2009) 'International research and policy on season of birth'. Westminster Education Forum on the Future of the Primary Curriculum, 22 June.

Smith, N. (2003) 'Transition from nursery to school playground: An intervention programme to promote emotional and social development.' Paper presented at the 13th European Early Childhood Education Research Association Conference, Glasgow, 3–6 Sept. http:extranet.edfac.unimelb.edu.au/LED/tec/

Turnball, A. (2006) *Children's Transitions: A literature review*. Cambridge: Cambridgeshire's Children's Fund.

6. Teaching as a profession
Tony Ewens

Learning Outcomes

By the end of this chapter you should have developed and clarified:

- an understanding of the concept of a profession and what makes teaching a profession;
- knowledge of professional and legal frameworks within which teachers operate;
- an appreciation of ethical principles underpinning teachers' practice;
- an awareness of the professional knowledge, understanding, skills and attitudes which teachers must display;
- your knowledge of the mechanisms by which teachers' accountability to pupils, parents/carers, employers, fellow-professionals and the public is monitored.

Standards

Q3(a) Be aware of the professional duties of teachers and the statutory framework within which they work.
Q3(b) Be aware of the policies and practices of the workplace and share in collective responsibility for their implementation.
It also addresses the relationship between Q3 and other standards.

What makes teaching a profession?

Before beginning teacher training, you probably made yourself familiar with some of the repertoire of skills that teachers deploy, and became aware of the type of education and training associated with becoming a teacher.

Activity

Reflect on why you think teaching is a 'profession'. Do you agree with this description? What characteristics do you think entitle an occupation to be called a profession, rather than a trade, a vocation or simply a job? Who do you think monitors teachers' work, to ensure that their practice is professional? What should happen if teachers fail to display professional conduct?

The following research focus asks you to check your initial thoughts about teaching as a profession in the light of general principles associated with professionalism.

The General Teaching Councils

Politically, education is a devolved responsibility within the four countries of the United Kingdom, and the last twenty years have seen increasing divergence in policy and practice. Each country has had a General Teaching Council (GTC), responsible for maintaining registers of qualified teachers and for regulating the profession. Scotland's GTC, set up in 1965, is the oldest of these, and works with the Scottish Government, universities, school inspectors and teaching unions to determine the standards of knowledge and competence needed by qualified teachers in Scotland. England's GTC was the last to be established. Following the election in 2010, the incoming Secretary of State for Education expressed his intention to abolish it, claiming that it did little to raise teaching standards or professionalism (HC Deb 2 June 2010 C460). This abolition raises a question about the ability of the teaching profession in England to act as 'an organised body involved in testing competence and regulating competence and conduct', a feature of professions identified by Jacques and Hyland. However, the concept of qualifying to enter and continue in the profession remains significant.

The GTCs of Scotland, Wales and Northern Ireland continue, and this is significant if you move around the United Kingdom. If you qualify in England, then wish to work in another UK country, you must register with that country's GTC. If you took a four year degree with QTS or a full-time PGCE this should be straightforward. However, if you took a three year degree with QTS, an employment-based route (EBITT) or a part-time PGCE, check that your award is recognised for registration in the country to which you are moving. If leaving the UK, find out whether your qualifications are accepted in your new location, and whether additional qualifications or experience are needed for recognition as a teacher there.

The Training and Development Agency for Schools (TDA)

The requirements for teacher training in England, and the standards to be achieved to qualify, are handled by the Training and Development Agency for Schools (TDA), the national agency responsible for the training and development of the school workforce. The requirements for courses of Initial Teacher Training (ITT), the standards for Qualified Teacher Status (QTS) and further guidance can be accessed at www.tda.gov.uk.

The ITT requirements and QTS standards illustrate how teaching matches Jacques and Hyland's description of professions. For example, their attribute 'the successful completion of intellectual and practical education and training' (Jacques and Hyland, 2007, p.202) matches the ITT requirements detailing what must be included in ITT courses. The standards cover three categories, attributes to be demonstrated by candidates for QTS, their knowledge and understanding, and the skills they must display. These account for Jacques and Hyland's categories of 'specialised knowledge and skills' and 'conformity to ethical standards in relation to dealings with clients, commitment to the competence and integrity of the profession as a whole' (p.202).

Achieving the standards is only the first stage of your career. You are expected to maintain and enhance your competence. For example, during the first year of teaching you address the core standards for classroom teachers, which include and amplify the QTS standards, emphasising improvement and extension of your abilities. Further standards cover later stages in your career.

Working with others

As well as being responsible to fellow teachers for upholding high standards of professional practice, you must work effectively with colleagues from other professions. An example occurs in most classrooms, when teachers and teaching assistants work together to support children's learning. Standard Q6 requires you to have a commitment to collaboration and cooperative working. Non-teacher colleagues will expect you to lead, by sharing your planning with them and allocating them particular tasks. It takes careful diplomacy to develop your professional relations with these colleagues, especially if they are experienced practitioners. Give thought to ways of valuing their expertise while being confidently assertive in your lead role as teacher.

When working with children with special educational needs (SEN), you will collaborate with other professionals, for example educational psychologists and the school's Special Educational Needs Coordinator (SENCO).

Another example of inter-professional work is in child protection, covered in Chapter 8, when cooperation with professionals in social work, health and police can play a crucial role in safeguarding children. This is set out in Q21 (a): Be aware of the current legal requirements, national policies and guidance on the safeguarding and promotion of the well-being of children and young people.

The responsibility for maintaining and enhancing your professional competence is yours. Others, such as your mentor or tutor, will meet you to review your progress, and later in your career you will experience regular appraisals with senior colleagues. However, you are expected to take the initiative, by monitoring your own performance, knowing your strengths and weaknesses and identifying where you need training or guidance from more experienced colleagues. Placements provide an excellent opportunity to practise this, as the following example illustrates. Notice how the trainee initiates discussion and seeks her mentor's advice:

Case Study: Shainaz's placement progress review meeting

Three weeks into her placement, Shainaz meets her mentor to review her progress. She has identified assessment as an area for improvement and has worked on the skills described in Q27: Provide timely, accurate and constructive feedback on learners' attainment, progress and areas for development. Shainaz has used various assessment strategies and demonstrates consistency in assessing pupils' work accurately. Reflecting on her performance, Shainaz asks, 'How do I know whether a child's achievement represents real progress? I'm not sure whether I set tasks at the right level of difficulty'. Commending her incisive insight, the mentor suggests addressing Q26 (b): Assess the learning needs of those they teach in order to set challenging learning objectives. After discussion, Shainaz decides to seek evidence of pupils' previous attainment, by looking through exercise books, consulting earlier test results and using questioning to identify their levels of understanding. The mentor agrees that this should help her to set appropriately challenging expectations for groups and individuals.

This case study is an example of the notion of reflective practice, notably described by Schön (1983) and Eraut (1994). For these authors, using techniques of analyaing your own practice, then deducing ways of improving it, is fundamental to professionalism.

Research Focus

Although Schön and Eraut wrote some time ago, both volumes remain invaluable for understanding professionalism. Schön studied a variety of ways in which a range of professionals reflected on their practice, and outlined sophisticated variations, for instance the ability to build reflection into ongoing professional tasks. Eraut further extended an understanding of how professionals develop their knowledge and skills, with examples of reflection in action. For example, his explanation of 'routinisation' (Eraut, 1994) may help to explain how and why teachers seem to function as if on 'autopilot', when particular aspects of practice become integrated into their regular routines and are repeated automatically.

Teachers, professionalism and the law

Many of a teacher's professional responsibilities are linked with legal requirements, so you should know something about the legal framework within which you work. Ignorance of the law is not accepted by courts as an excuse.

Some laws affecting teachers are part of general legislation applicable to everyone, especially employees. For example, the Health and Safety at Work Act 1974 requires you to protect the safety of others in the workplace. When applying for jobs you are protected by laws prohibiting discrimination, such as the Race Relations Act 1976, Sex Discrimination Act 1975, Disability Discrimination Act 1995 and Employment Equality Regulations regarding sexual orientation (2003), religion or belief (2003) and age (2006). In return, you must be open and honest in job applications. It is for example an offence to misrepresent your qualifications or to attempt to conceal a conviction.

Other laws relate specifically to teachers. The Secretary of State can bar people from teaching, for example, on certain medical grounds or following serious misconduct. Some criminal convictions, for instance offences against children, and being on the Sex Offenders' Register, are also reasons for being barred from teaching. An 'enhanced' CRB check is required before you are employed, and teachers cannot have previous convictions treated as 'spent', as described in the Rehabilitation of Offenders Act 1974.

You should join one of the teaching unions, which can advise you about your professional responsibilities under the law, and provide support and representation should you encounter any legal difficulty.

Your contract of employment

In maintained schools in England and Wales teachers' contracts are based on *The School Teachers' Pay and Conditions Document*, known as the Blue Book. Local Authorities and schools are obliged to implement these regulations, which prescribe what you are required to do as a teacher and what you will be paid. The obligations and payscales are updated annually. Your point on the payscale is determined by the school's governing body, within the national framework. Other, non-statutory conditions of service, agreed between the teaching unions and the Local Government Employers, cover entitlement to sick leave, maternity and paternity leave, periods of notice and entitlement to belong to a union. They are in *The Conditions of Service for Schoolteachers in England and Wales*, the Burgundy Book, which is revised regularly. Local Authorities accept these conditions as binding.

Maintained schools include Community Schools (formerly County Schools), Voluntary Controlled Schools (mostly Church Schools, where the Local Authority is the employer but the governors may make conditions related to the school's religious character), Voluntary Aided Schools (mostly of a religious character, where the governing body as the employer may make conditions including reference to candidates' religious commitment), and Foundation Schools, where the governing body is the employer.

The conditions of employment in the Blue Book include a requirement to be available for 195 days annually, and to teach on 190, the remainder being 'teacher days' for staff training and development. 1265 hours is treated as 'directed time', when you are required to attend at specific times and places, for example for parents' evenings or staff meetings in addition to teaching. The 1265 hours include the 10% allowance for planning and preparation (PPA time), but not the entire time needed for preparation, marking and associated tasks. You must do these in your own time. After-school activities are not usually counted within the 1265 hours.

Teachers' duties, according to the Blue Book, include:

- planning and teaching;
- assessing, recording and writing reports;
- participating in staff meetings;
- collaborating with colleagues in planning;
- covering for absent colleagues (up to 38 hours per year);
- directing and supervising support staff;
- contributing to the professional development of other staff;
- contributing to your own and others' appraisal;
- participate in further professional development;
- communicate with parents and carers.

(extracted from The Blue Book, 2010, para. 61)

Note that non-maintained schools (including independent and private schools, academies and other categories of school inaugurated following changes in public policy) are not bound by the Blue and Burgundy Books, although many choose to use them. They may have different payscales, require different hours of work and expect additional duties. Check carefully before signing a contract, and ask your union for advice. Ask whether work in a non-maintained school will count towards the induction period (normally, one year's satisfactory full-time work or its part-time equivalent) required before final accreditation as a fully qualified teacher.

Teachers and pupils

Several areas of legislation and regulations deal with relations between teachers and pupils, for example regarding discipline. Each school will have its own policies and procedures, and these must conform to statutory requirements. When on placement you should read the school's policies and procedures covering your interactions with children, and ensure that you operate within them. Schools have public liability insurance, which would cover you against claims arising from an incident while on school business. However, if you have acted outside the school's policies you could be summoned to a disciplinary meeting and, if your actions have been wilfully reckless, you could at worst face legal action for which you are only insured through your union membership. This situation is worth avoiding!

Discipline and sanctions

School Discipline and Pupil Behaviour Policies: Guidance for Schools (DfES, 2007) describes what teachers may and must do to promote and ensure discipline. Paragraph 3.1.6 expresses the purposes of a behaviour policy:

> *School behaviour policies should aim to establish a positive school ethos and promote effective learning by establishing:*
>
> • *clearly stated expectations of what constitutes acceptable behaviour;*
>
> • *effective behaviour-management strategies;*
>
> • *processes which recognise, teach, reward and celebrate positive behaviour;*
>
> • *processes, rules and sanctions to deal with poor conduct.*
>
> *(DfES, 2007, para. 3.1.6)*

Schools must also have an anti-bullying policy, covering physical, verbal and emotional bullying and incorporating active measures against racist or homophobic behaviour.

You must be clear about the sanctions that you may use. Corporal punishment in maintained schools has been illegal since 1986, but in certain circumstances teachers may use physical force to restrain a child. The Education and Inspections Act 2006 makes it clear that you:

> *may use such force as is reasonable in the circumstances for the purpose of preventing a pupil from:*
>
> *(a) committing any offence,*
>
> *(b) causing personal injury to, or damage to the property of, any person (including the pupil himself), or*
>
> *(c) prejudicing the maintenance of good order and discipline at the school.*
>
> *(HM Government, 2006, para. 93)*

Further guidance explains that physical restraint should be a last resort, and that teachers should avoid anything likely to cause injury or be regarded as indecent. Written records must be made of any incidents when force is used, explaining what happened, why it was considered necessary to use force and what the consequences were. You would obviously report this immediately to the headteacher.

Some schools' policies have implied that teachers should never touch a child. At the time of publication, the Secretary of State has expressed an intention to clarify his guidance to confirm that it is appropriate for teachers to touch pupils to restrain them when necessary or to comfort them if they are distressed.

Remember to consult the behaviour policy when planning lessons that present particular hazards, such as some PE and technology sessions, and when designing opportunities for out-of-school learning.

Child protection

Safeguarding Children and Safer Recruitment in Education (DfES, 2006) lists schools' duties in safeguarding children, and provides a framework for protecting them from abuse. Schools are required to work closely with other professions to protect children from harm and report instances where staff members are concerned about individuals. Schools must have a child protection policy and a designated person (usually the headteacher) to liaise with statutory agencies. You should read the policy and its associated procedures, so that you are alert to signs of possible abuse and know what steps to take. To read in more detail about your responsibilities regarding child protection, read Chapter 8.

It is worth remembering that teachers can help children to develop resilience. The work you do in building children's self-esteem and increasing their communication skills can strengthen their confidence to speak out if they are being ill-treated.

Most teachers never fall foul of the law. Awareness of your duties and responsibilities, and a determination to act in good faith, is the key to ensuring that your career runs smoothly.

Activity

When on placement, find in the staff handbook the policies about behaviour, bullying, rewards and sanctions, child protection and health and safety. Check them against the legislation and regulations outlined in this chapter, to enhance your understanding of the way in which headteachers and governors apply the law to the day-to-day running of schools.

Teachers' professional ethics

Jacques (Jacques and Hyland, 2007 p.202) points out that professionalism involves behaving in a principled way towards clients. Your 'clients' include not only children and parents, but also society at large. You also have ethical responsibilities to the teaching profession. Among professional attributes, Jacques identifies three incorporating overt ethical duties (p.202):

- maintain detachment and integrity in exercising personal judgement on behalf of a client;
- establish direct personal relations with clients based on confidence, faith and trust;
- collectively have a particular sense of responsibility for maintaining the competence and integrity of the profession as a whole.

Standard Q3(b) complements the third bulleted attribute: Q3(b) Be aware of the policies and practices of the workplace and share in collective responsibility for their implementation.

These principles may seem abstract. However, when translated into situations that are typical occurrences for teachers, they can clarify some of the ethical dilemmas which you will meet in your work. Consider the questions posed in the following task, and identify their relationship to the bulleted points above:

> ## Activity
>
> 1. You find some children very amiable, and others more difficult to like. How do you ensure that your personal preferences for particular character traits do not lead you to treat certain children more favourably than others?
>
> 2. During a parents' evening, Louise's mother says, 'How is Louise doing compared with her friend Anna?' How can you politely explain to Louise's mother that it would be ethically wrong to disclose to her information about another child?
>
> 3. During a placement you observe a low ability group continuing with a literacy task while the rest of the class enjoys an art lesson. You are told that this is in line with the school's policy, which targets competence in English as a major objective. You think the group is being deprived of a broad and balanced curriculum and that the children may feel negatively towards literacy, sensing that they are being punished for making slow progress. What would you say or do?

The questions encapsulate various ethical issues facing teachers. Question 1 reflects the concept of 'teacher's pet'. Children quickly sense teachers' approval or disapproval and dislike it if teachers act unfairly towards individuals or groups. It is only human to have preferences about people that we like or dislike. It would be understandable if teachers liked children who applied themselves to their work, showed interest and asked intelligent questions. However, it is important to recognise your preferences then take steps to ensure that you communicate positively with **all** your pupils. This is implicit in Standard Q1: Have high expectations of children and young people including a commitment to ensuring that they can achieve their full educational potential and to establishing fair, respectful, trusting, supportive and constructive relationships with them.

As Jacques and Hyland point out (Jacques and Hyland, 2007, p.151ff) equality of opportunity is a statutory right of all pupils. Standard Q1 illuminates the difference between equality of opportunity and equality of outcome. Children's educational potentials differ, so their attainments will differ. Your responsibility is to know enough about each child's prior knowledge, interests and capacities to enable you to set appropriate expectations for the next stage of learning. Consequently you will have varying levels of expectation for different individuals. The ethical imperative is to ensure that your expectations are based on detached, objective judgements, unclouded by personal prejudice or preference.

Question 2 asks you to maintain confidentiality meticulously, while preserving good relations with a client. This example shows that professional ethics often have to be accompanied by personal tact. You must not disclose details of a pupil's performance to another child's parent, but you also have a responsibility to maintain positive relations with that parent.

In some circumstances you would be right not to maintain confidentiality. One is if you believe a child to be at risk of abuse. Another is if you learn of what appears to be a serious breach of professional conduct, or an illegal activity, by someone in the school community. Schools have 'whistleblowing' policies, guaranteeing that those reporting these things will not suffer adverse consequences unless acting maliciously.

Question 3 is about professional judgement in matching the curriculum to the pupils' needs. You are entitled to hold a personal view about professional issues. As a trainee teacher, you are a guest in the school and at most you might discuss the matter privately with your mentor, to develop an understanding of the school's thinking. If you are employed at the school, you could ask for a discussion at a staff meeting, then present a reasoned argument for changing the policy. It would be unprofessional to disregard the school's policy and substitute your own approach. Open discord among the staff of a school jeopardizes the integrity of the profession in the eyes of pupils and parents.

In some aspects of your work you may have reservations about what you are required to do, whether by the headteacher or by legislation. Upholding practices with which you disagree is often unpalatable but, unless the circumstances are so extreme as to threaten children's welfare, the ethical approach is to apply the policy while arguing for a different course of action in the privacy of the head's office or staffroom.

A different aspect of professional ethics concerns a teacher's duty to promote children's moral development (Ewens, 2007, p.138f). You may think this is not your job, especially since there are sincere differences of opinion in society about moral codes. But a moment's thought will convince you that you are imposing moral codes on your class regularly: be quiet, don't interrupt, wait your turn, and so on. Some of this may be conscious implementation of the school's behaviour policy; at other times you are conveying your own values, consciously or sub-consciously. Sometimes you help children to work through their own understanding of right and wrong, perhaps using drama or fiction to promote moral decision-making. It is vital to remain aware of your own moral principles and how these may differ from the beliefs of others. Children will neither benefit from teachers who apply ultra-rigid codes to them, nor from those who allow them to do whatever they wish. Pupils prefer teachers who are authoritative, firm but fair, treating children with respect and regard. Your professional conduct in the classroom will teach children as much about morality as your moral education lessons.

Teachers' knowledge, understanding, skills and attitudes

The standards outline areas of professional competence that you must display before gaining QTS. You can usefully consider them under the headings subject knowledge, knowing how learners learn, pedagogy, and the school and wider contexts.

Subject knowledge

Your need for a command of the subject matter that you want your pupils to learn is underpinned by Q14: Have a secure knowledge and understanding of their subjects/curriculum areas, and Q15: Know and understand the relevant statutory and non-statutory curricula and frameworks. This requirement is more complex than it first appears. At one level, each subject can be viewed as a collection of pieces of information that the teacher conveys to the class, to be memorised and recalled when required. Beneath this superficial, though important, level lie other features of subject knowledge. For example, each subject has its set of skills; examples are estimating in mathematics, hypothesising in science and jumping in PE. At a still deeper level are the key concepts, the big 'ideas' on which the subject is founded. Examples include fair tests in science, timbre in music and worship in religion.

Classroom tasks related to any concept can be simple or advanced. For instance, reception classes can discuss how to make a sampling task a fair test and a medical research team, addressing the same concept at an advanced level, ensures that plans for testing new drugs incorporate blind trialling with control groups. The concept – a fair test – applies at both levels.

The three types of knowledge – information, skills and concepts – are distinct from one another but complementary, and you can add a fourth aspect, attitudes. For example, environmental studies can be a means of encouraging an attitude of responsibility towards our planet.

You need to develop an appreciation of the information, skills, concepts and attitudes associated with each subject. A shallow education, restricted to transmission of factual information, may produce a class of quiz champions; a rich educational diet, incorporating all four elements, equips learners to apply and extend their knowledge and gradually grow into independent, lifelong learners.

Knowing how learners learn

Two standards focus specifically on this topic:

Q18: Understand how children and young people develop and that the progress and well-being of learners are affected by a range of developmental, social, religious, ethnic, cultural and linguistic influences, and

Q19: Know how to make effective personalised provision for those they teach.

Educational psychology has illuminated how children's minds develop in a sequenced way and this has sometimes resulted in an 'ages and stages' approach to curriculum planning. Be careful not to fall into the trap of 'waiting until the children are ready' before introducing more complex ideas that you judge to be theoretically beyond their capacities. Bruner (1960) and Vygotsky (1978) showed that learners can pass more rapidly through stages of learning when teachers provide scaffolding to support their development.

Appreciating psychology's contribution to your understanding of children's development as learners is an important professional attribute. Another is knowledge of how children's home and community backgrounds influence their educational chances and progress. Attitudes towards learning expressed at home, various medical conditions, whether the internet is available at home, whether adults can spend time helping with homework, whether English is spoken at home: these, and many other factors, impact upon a learner's development. In being aware of these issues, you must ensure that you do not create self-fulfilling prophecies, for example by expecting lower achievement from children from a particular background. Remember that the first standard, Q1, requires you to have high expectations of **all** children, so that they can achieve their full educational potential.

Pedagogy

The word 'pedagogy' refers to the science (or is it an art?) of teaching. The key standard here is Q25.

Q25: Teach lessons and sequences of lessons across the age and ability range for which they are trained in which they:

- (a) use a range of teaching strategies and resources;
- (b) build on prior knowledge, develop concepts and processes, enable learners to apply new knowledge, understanding and skills;
- (c) adapt their language to suit the learners they teach...using explanations, questions, discussions and plenaries effectively;
- (d) demonstrate the ability to manage the learning of individuals, groups and whole classes.

Pedagogy links the two previous sections, 'subject knowledge' and 'knowing how learners learn'. Children are not empty vessels which teachers fill with knowledge. They bring ideas, impressions, abilities and information from outside school. Naturally inquisitive, they explore, ask questions and make discoveries for themselves. Your task involves capitalising on these characteristics through your understanding of how learners learn, then exposing your pupils to a well-selected range of knowledge, understanding and skills drawn from across the curriculum. An influential report explained the central thrust of pedagogy in this way:

> *While it is self-evident that every individual, to an extent, constructs his/her meanings, education is an encounter between these personal understandings and the public knowledge embodied in our cultural traditions. The teacher's key responsibility is to mediate such encounters so that the child's understanding is enriched.*

> (Alexander et al., 1992, para. 64)

This point is well illustrated in the following case study:

....

Case Study: Warren's placement progress review meeting

At his mid-placement review, Warren agrees that the major priority should be to ensure a better match between the subject matter in his weekly plans and the learning styles that the children use. He agrees with his mentor that he spends too much time transmitting factual information to the class, and has planned insufficient variety in the tasks that he sets for children. Consequently, many pupils have failed to apply the new knowledge that Warren has introduced, and have not fully understood the work. The class also becomes restless if Warren speaks for too long. Warren identifies the following targets, related to Standard Q25.

- Teach the children some skills that they can use to find something out for themselves.

- Select knowledge that children need to acquire, then design tasks so that they access the desired knowledge, using the skills they learned.

- Prepare questions and exercises to assess how well they have understood the material.

- Study the children's answers to diagnose misconceptions, then prepare explanations and re-teach as necessary.

The mentor is planning to stretch Warren's skills by pressing him to carry out the assessment, diagnosis and re-teaching during plenaries, since prompt feedback is particularly valuable.

....

Notice how Warren's plans involve thinking about pupils' roles in the lessons, rather than his role. Inevitably, early in your training you will focus on what you will do during lessons. With experience, you can move forward rapidly, by planning what the children will do. By planning activities appropriate to the learners' needs, you turn the spotlight away from yourself and concentrate on supporting children's learning. Twiselton (2005) describes how trainee teachers progress from seeing themselves as managers of tasks, to being deliverers of the curriculum and finally to a stage where they enable children to build concepts and skills. Warren's mentor has this progression in mind when advising Warren about his targets.

The school and wider contexts

Part of your professional expertise involves working as a team member, understanding that learning progresses through the combined efforts of the school staff and the children's parents and carers. The following standards are especially relevant:

Q5: Recognise and respect the contribution that colleagues, parents and carers can make to the development and well-being of children.

Q32: Work as a team member and identify opportunities for working with colleagues, sharing the development of effective practice with them.

Superficially, a classroom may appear to be directed by the classteacher, and independent from the rest of the school. You quickly appreciate that the truth is more complex.

First, within the classroom you notice the teacher working regularly with teaching assistants or volunteers, operating as a team leader. Analyse how the teacher shares the lesson plans with other adults. Assistants obviously need clear instructions about the task for which they are responsible, but they must also appreciate why the teacher has set the task, so notice how the teacher explains the intended learning outcomes as well as describing the task.

Next, observe liaison between school and home. Reading books often go home, accompanied by a notebook in which teachers and parents exchange messages about all sorts of things, not just reading. Some parents like to chat with staff when dropping off or collecting children, and more formal arrangements, such as parents' evenings and annual written reports, allow teachers and parents to communicate. Teachers need an ability to get on the right wavelength with each parent, so think carefully about the language you use. Too much educational jargon may mystify a parent; on the other hand, if you 'unpack' the technical vocabulary too much you may appear patronising. In this aspect of your work there is no substitute for experience, so seek opportunities for contact with parents during placements.

Finally, since classrooms do not exist in isolation, you need to be conscious of the range of expertise among the staff of the school.

Initially, you will probably work with your classteacher on curriculum and lesson planning. Other staff may be involved, especially in a large school with more than one class for each age group. Later, you may want further advice about specific areas. Your mentor can point you to appropriate colleagues. The breadth and depth of the primary curriculum places great demands on teachers' subject knowledge. Consequently, most schools appoint subject leaders or curriculum coordinators, teachers with specialist subject knowledge who assist their colleagues, have an overview of the subject throughout the school, and take responsibility for a coherent, sequenced scheme of work. Asking for help from a subject leader is not a sign of weakness, but provides evidence towards standard Q32 since it shows you understand the purpose of teamwork. Similarly, you will probably consult the school's SENCO to discuss the work of pupils with SEN in your class.

The picture of a primary teacher in this section points to the need for a wide range of knowledge and skills. Much of this develops gradually through classroom experience, but it is helpful to use the QTS standards as a checklist, to address both the breadth and depth of your professional obligations.

Teachers' accountability

Jacques and Hyland (2007, p.202) identify 'membership of an organised body involved in testing competence and regulating competence and conduct' as one mark of professionalism. Achieving the standards and passing your training course form the first steps to being recommended for QTS. After that other sets of standards apply to different stages of your career. Judgements made by senior colleagues each year will check that you continue to meet the relevant professional standards. Failure to do so results initially in a programme of support and development, and possibly the withholding by the school's governors of an incremental point on the salary scale. Continued underperformance could lead to disciplinary action including, ultimately, dismissal. These arrangements are how you demonstrate your accountability as fit to work as a teacher.

When appointed to a school you are accountable to the governing body for performing your professional duties. A mentor will support you, and monitor and review your work against the relevant standards. You are expected to be active in undertaking continuing professional development activities, in line with standard Q7 (a): Reflect on and improve their practice, and take responsibility for identifying and meeting their developing professional needs.

Apart from your general accountability as an employee, there are other ways in which you are answerable for the quality of your work. Your contribution to the school is reflected in inspection reports and in results published in performance tables. You have to provide written reports at least annually to parents and carers, and attend parents' evenings to discuss children's work. You are accountable to your fellow-professionals, for example by participating actively in teamwork for planning, assessing and recording.

Importantly, you are answerable to the children for the quality of your planning, teaching, assessment and feedback, for the care and guidance that you provide and for ensuring that they experience equality of opportunity and the chance to fulfil their educational potential.

Finally, you are accountable to yourself. If you believe that teaching is a vocation as well as a profession, you may find that it takes you over, to the detriment of your home life and leisure activities. Finding an appropriate work/life balance is vital. Teachers should be rounded people with a range of interests and life experience who bring something into school from the outside world, and model to children the possibilities that lie ahead for them. While satisfying your conscience that you have done sufficient work to do a good job, make sure that you also have a fulfilling life outside school.

Learning Outcomes Review

Thinking about the school in which you are working or have recently worked, respond to the prompts after each intended learning outcome, to identify your knowledge and understanding of the issues covered in the chapter.

- **An understanding of the concept of a profession and what makes teaching a profession:**
  - Identify from the staff handbook instances of teachers' duties or responsibilities that exemplify Jacques and Hyland's description of professional characteristics.

- **Knowledge of professional and legal frameworks within which teachers operate:**
  - What policies and procedures have been adopted by your placement school to ensure that teachers deal with pupils' behaviour lawfully?
  - What information tells you what to do should you become seriously concerned about a pupil's safety and welfare?
  - Identify two occasions when you collaborated with other staff members (not counting your mentor or classteacher) to make effective provision for the children.

- **An appreciation of ethical principles underpinning teachers' practice:**
  - How have you avoided showing favouritism to particular children or groups in your class?
  - Supposing you had reservations about the actions of a fellow staff member, do you think that remaining silent would be more or less unprofessional than gossiping about it with a colleague?

- **An awareness of the professional knowledge, understanding, skills and attitudes which teachers must display:**
  - Identify one non-core subject that you find hard to teach. Make a list of key concepts associated with this subject, then select examples of skills and information that you could teach to help children understand these concepts.
  - Identify an example of when you changed teaching and learning methods in your planning because of a lesson evaluation.
  - Which member(s) of staff would you turn to for advice about teaching the subject(s) that you find hard to teach? How clear are you about the system of subject leadership operating in your school?

- **Your knowledge of the mechanisms by which teachers' accountability to pupils, parents/carers, employers, fellow-professionals and the public is monitored:**
  - Think of an occasion when your performance as a trainee teacher was reviewed. Identify how the quality of your work was measured, and what part you played in assessing your own achievements.
  - Think about how you might prepare for a parents' evening in your first job. What could you usefully find out during your placement to help you be ready for this?
  - Identify ways of saying 'no', politely but firmly, to requests to do additional tasks that you really do not wish to undertake.

Further Reading

The book by Browne and Haylock provides a comprehensive overview of the professional status of teachers and its practical implications, while the Bristol Guide (which is regularly updated) gives full coverage of the laws, statutes and regulations applicable to the work of all professionals and volunteers in schools.

Browne, A. and Haylock, D. (eds) (2004) *Professional Issues for Primary Teachers*. London: Paul Chapman Publishing. See especially the chapter by Manning entitled *Teaching as a Profession*.

University of Bristol (2008) *The Bristol Guide: professional responsibilities and statutory frameworks for teachers and others in schools*. Bristol: the Graduate School of Education.

References

Bruner, J. (1960) *The Process of Education*. Cambridge, Massachusetts: Harvard University Press.

DfES (2006) *Safeguarding Children and Safer Recruitment in Education*. London: DfES

DfES (2007) *School Discipline and Pupil Behaviour Policies: Guidance for Schools*. London: DfES.

Eraut, M. (1994) *Developing Professional Knowledge and Competence*. London: Routledge Falmer.

Ewens, A. (2007) 'Spiritual, moral, social and cultural values in the classroom' in Jacques, K. and Hyland, R. (3rd edn) *Professional Studies: Primary and Early Years*. Exeter: Learning Matters.

HM Government (2006) *Education and Inspections Act 2006*. London: The Stationery Office.

Jacques, K. and Hyland, R. (3rd edn, 2007) *Professional Studies: Primary and Early Years*. Exeter: Learning Matters.

Schön, D. (1983) *The Reflective Practitioner: How professionals think in action*. London: Temple Smith.

Twiselton, S. (2005) 'Developing your Teaching Skills' in Arthur, A., Grainger, T. and Wray, D. (eds) *Learning to Teach in the Primary School*. London: Routledge.

Vygotsky, L. (1978) *Mind in Society: The Development of Higher Psychological Processes*. Cambridge, Massachusetts: Harvard University Press.

www.publications.parliament.uk/pa/cm201011/cmhansrd/cm100602/debtext/100602-0008.htm accessed 19/10/10.

www.tda.gov.uk accessed 11/10/10.

www.teachernet.gov.uk/wholeschool/behaviour/schooldisciplinepupilbehaviourpolicies accessed 13/10/10.

Pay and conditions of service

The Blue Book: *The School Teachers' Pay and Conditions Document.* London: DfE, updated annually, can be viewed at: www.publications.education.gov.uk/default.aspx

The Burgundy Book: *The Conditions of Service for schoolteachers in England and Wales.* London: Local Government Employers, can be viewed at: www.lge.gov.uk/lge/core/page.do?pageId=119369

Websites of professional unions and associations

ATL Association of Teachers and Lecturers: www.atl.org.uk

NASUWT National Association of Schoolmasters Union of Women Teachers: www.nasuwt.org.uk

NUT National Union of Teachers: www.nut.org.uk

Voice (formerly Professional Association of Teachers): www.voice.org.uk

7. Establishing your own teacher identity
Denis Hayes

Learning Outcomes

By the end of this chapter you will:

- understand how motivation for teaching influences your actions and decisions;
- have a clearer view of the kind of teacher you want to become;
- understand the meaning and significance of teacher identity;
- have learned how to develop as a reflective practitioner;
- understand the significance and impact of different teaching approaches;
- have gained an overview of professional responsibilities and development;
- have learned about appropriate conduct and behaviour on school placement.

Standards

Q1 Have high expectations of children and young people including a commitment to ensuring that they can achieve their full educational potential and to establishing fair, respectful, trusting, supportive and constructive relationships with them.

Q2 Demonstrate the positive values, attitudes and behaviour they expect from children and young people.

Q3(a) Be aware of the professional duties of teachers and the statutory framework within which they work.

Q7(a) Reflect on and improve their practice, and take responsibility for identifying and meeting their developing professional needs.

Q8 Have a creative and constructively critical approach towards innovation, being prepared to adapt their practice where benefits and improvements are identified.

Q9 Act upon advice and feedback and be open to coaching and mentoring.

Q32 Work as a team member and identify opportunities for working with colleagues, sharing the development of effective practice with them.

Motivation for teaching

What kind of teacher do you want to be is a question frequently posed by tutors and lecturers to their trainees. Answers invariably include reference to attributes such as being kind, fair and caring; to skills such as being a good listener; and to general aims such as helping children to learn and reach their potential. These aspirations provide a core set of beliefs for teachers and yet, in practice, some teachers are more successful than others, which raises a number of issues, not least whether everyone has the potential to be a teacher – or only those who have natural talent.

Every study shows that people become primary teachers because they love to work with children; as such, they are almost invariably very fond of the children in their care and, like a responsible parent, want to do everything possible to ensure each child's welfare. Primary teaching has traditionally been a female-orientated profession and teachers historically see themselves as substitute parents with moral responsibility for children. More recently, there has been an increase in the number of men working with primary age children and, to a lesser extent, the early years' sector (children 3 to 5 years of age).

The fact that primary teachers care deeply about children is indicated by the frequent reference they make to 'my' children. Such affection is not confined to the working day but taken home every evening, occupying minds and actions to such an extent that over time the emotional demands, coupled with the physical exertion and long working days, can lead to mental and physical fatigue. Although teaching primary age children is fun and challenging, you must learn to pace yourself and build your expertise and effectiveness gradually, aided by tutors, colleagues, your own studies and constantly thinking about ways to improve.

Teacher self-identity

In addition to the centrality of altruistic (wanting to help others) motives on their desire to teach, primary teachers tend to judge their own worth as persons in terms of their success at work. As a result, failings in school – whether real or imagined – affect every aspect of their lives. While teachers are always interested in finding ways to boost the self-esteem of children, it is also important that they pay attention to enhancing their own confidence and *self-identity*.

A number of factors influence self-identity: competence and skill level; affirmation by others; practical support from more experienced colleagues; and last but not least, moral conviction, including religious faith, driven by a deep-seated conviction that your teaching makes a positive difference to children's lives. It is often stated that 'schools exist for kids'; while that statement is obviously true, it is also the case that schools are places where large numbers of adults work, each of whom deserves to be nurtured and valued.

Mullen (2007) suggests that the construction of teacher identity is largely affective (the power to move the emotions) and that an investigation of the emotional components of the job helps in an understanding of the teacher's self-identity. Your emotions control the extent to which you will resist or embrace advice and change affects your professional growth; as such, the way you handle your feelings strongly influences your development as a teacher.

Activity
Use the following list as a basis for considering what kind of teacher you want to become.
1. Well-informed about the subjects I teach.
2. Kind and compassionate towards children and colleagues.
3. Approachable, pleasant and responsive.

4. Good listener and communicator.
5. Keen sense of humour.
6. Clear in explaining things to children.
7. Patient but decisive.
8. Make fair judgements.
9. Make sensible decisions.
10. Careful time manager.
11. Clear about what I want children to learn.
12. Willing to respond positively children's genuine interests and questions.
13. Team player and cooperative.
14. Offer positive comments and suggestions.
15. Take account of criticism from others and act appropriately.
16. Take every opportunity to encourage my colleagues.

Now make a list of the characteristics you want to avoid.

Values and teaching

It is helpful to think of education as being grounded in five fundamental values: spiritual, cultural, environmental, aesthetic and political. Each of these values is expressed in terms of your *personal* values with regard to self; your *moral* values with regard to others; and your *social* values with regard to the community in which you are placed. For instance, one of your personal values might be to treat others as you wish to be treated; a moral value might be to listen carefully and respond compassionately to colleagues' concerns; a social value might be to volunteer for an after-school club in a desire to contribute expertise for the benefit of others.

Eaude (2006) argues that 'the person' as a teacher cannot be separated from the person you are at all other times. As a result, the values that you bring to the classroom, through your personality, enthusiasm, emotions and priorities, combine to influence children and affect their feelings of self-worth and desire to learn. The relationship (bond) between you and the children is therefore an essential factor in determining your success as a teacher. Children respond well to adults who relate to them naturally and are always approachable. No amount of posturing and forcefulness on your part will compensate for establishing and maintaining caring relations with the children for whom you have responsibility. See also Chapter 4 in this book.

Teacher identity and integrity

Studies about teachers' professional identity indicate that we must pay careful attention to: (a) the relationship between concepts of 'self' and 'identity'; (b) the importance of what counts as 'professional' in professional identity; (c) the impact of the educational setting in shaping identity; and (d) the place of emotions, temperament and personality. In 1997, P.J. Palmer wrote an influential article in which he defines identity and integrity (Palmer, 1997a (online)). Thus, *identity* is described as:

An evolving nexus [set of connections] where all the forces that constitute my life converge in the mystery of self: my genetic makeup, the nature of the man and woman who gave me life, the culture in which I was raised, people who have sustained me and people who have done me harm, the good and ill I have done to others, and to myself, the experience of love and suffering...

In similar vein he explores the related characteristic of *integrity*:

Integrity requires that I discern what is integral to my selfhood, what fits and what does not – and that I choose life-giving ways of relating to the forces that converge within me. Do I welcome them or fear them, embrace them or reject them, move with them or against them?

Palmer goes on to say that by choosing integrity, you become more whole, but that wholeness does not mean that you never make mistakes. He identifies the relationship between the two qualities of identity and integrity such that *identity* lies in the diverse forces that make up a life, whereas *integrity* consists of forces that bring the person wholeness and life rather than fragmentation and deadness. See also Palmer (1997b).

Activity

Think of three teachers you have known well and evaluate their identity and integrity as outlined by Palmer (1997a). List the sorts of key decisions you need to make and priorities you need to establish as you seek to develop your own identity and integrity as a teacher.

Adopting a reflective approach

As the prime satisfaction for most primary teachers is the pleasure of interacting with children and positively affecting their lives – rather than a desire for monetary rewards or status – a teacher's value position is rooted in a need to cherish, serve, empower and benefit the children in their care. As a result, primary teachers constantly need to evaluate their work regarding the fundamental purpose of what they are doing as educators and the daily task of translating those beliefs into practical teaching. A key ambition in your professional life should be to become a 'reflective practitioner', both during lessons (reflecting 'in' teaching) and following teaching sessions (reflecting 'on' teaching).

Activity

If you haven't done so already, begin the reflective process by keeping a record of your classroom experiences (for example, assessing how clearly you communicate ideas and instructions to children) under four main headings.
1. What I did: e.g. *I explained how children should set out their work.*
2. Why I did it: e.g. *I wanted to improve the appearance of their written work.*

> 3. What was good about it: e.g. *I spoke slowly and carefully and answered their queries using child-friendly language. My pedagogical knowledge was good.*
> 4. What could have been improved: e.g. *I need to ensure that every child is paying attention before I speak.*

Your personal values and ideas about priorities in education and life more widely have a strong impact on shaping classroom practice, as you encourage children to respect other viewpoints, speak plainly but courteously, collaborate, weigh up situations, summarise key points, evaluate options and communicate ideas carefully in a supportive (non-judgemental) way.

Research Focus: Teachers as reflective practitioners

Larrivee (2008) reviewed the research on creating a learning climate conducive to facilitating the development of teachers as reflective practitioners and concluded that the process involves a willingness to be an active participant in professional growth. The author argues that the aim of reflective practice is to think critically about one's teaching choices and actions. Consequently, reflective practice involves teachers questioning the goals, values and assumptions that guide their work and entails interrogating the way things are done, the purpose of education and the contexts in which learning takes place. See also Ghaye and Ghaye (1998).

Motivating the children

Your enthusiasm for a subject is important but is not of itself a sufficiently strong factor to ensure that children are motivated to learn. You also need empathy, compassion, commitment, patience, spontaneity and an ability to make sound judgements to produce what is sometimes described as 'loving relations' in the classroom. O'Quinn and Garrison (2004) argue that by nurturing loving recognition and by being brave enough to take risks in learning to allow for children's own shortcomings and vulnerabilities, you can help to develop a tolerant, harmonious and caring learning climate. Children are not only impressed by your knowledge and teaching skills but also by human qualities such as your patience, kindness and encouraging manner.

Values education

A good education is founded on developing the human personality in all its dimensions – intellectual, physical, social, ethical and moral (Sridhar, 2001). Thornberg (2008) argues that *values education* does not depend on following a planned programme of work but is often unplanned and should be embedded in everyday school life. In common with Palmer (see earlier), Thornburg argues that values reflect the personal concerns and preferences that help to frame relationships between children and adults. In other words, your effectiveness as a teacher has as much to do with the heart (emotions) as with the mind (intellect). In practice, teachers use this spontaneity in conjunction with the curriculum to enhance the social and emotional aspects of learning, usually referred to as SEAL.

The values that you bring to the classroom should be the result of careful and informed thinking, as you seek to dovetail your personal morality (inner beliefs) with impartial justice (fair to all). The reason for taking such care is well expressed by Richards (2009) when he refers to the teacher as a 'frighteningly significant person whose teaching helps to shape attitudes to learning at a most sensitive period in children's development' (p.20). While most children grow up to develop competent moral skills, a small number of them fail to do so and cultivate a highly sophisticated form of deviance (Rossano, 2008). In the light of this trend, the author recommends the promotion of deliberate moral practice, suggesting that religious participation provides the basic elements to facilitate it.

You must decide how best to inculcate children into behaving appropriately, while resisting the temptation to give the impression that your way is the *only* way – their parents may have different ideas. For example, you might impress on the children that bullying is wrong, while some parents might be telling them to 'stand up for themselves', even at the expense of others' suffering. Whatever you discuss or declare, it pays to be aware that children often repeat at home things they hear you say in school, so be clear with them about what is right and wrong but be cautious about imposing your own morality on them in a way that might invite criticism.

Developing your teaching approach

Factors influencing your teaching

A teaching approach consists of the methods and strategies that teachers employ to help children learn effectively and reflect the beliefs that practitioners hold about the nature of learning and education in general. Thus, one teacher might believe that children learn best when they are motivated by opportunities to explore ideas as a group, while another teacher may be convinced that they learn best when working individually. Again, one teacher may employ a considerable amount of direct teaching, utilising question-and-answer supported by repetition of facts, while another teacher prefers a problem-solving method in which children are encouraged to raise their own questions and seek their own solutions. One teacher's style may be informal and strongly interactive, using humour and good-natured banter, while another teacher might adopt a more detached and serious manner. Many teachers vary their approach depending on the subject area; thus, an investigative science session might involve a large percentage of group work whereas a phonics lesson will probably be geared towards a more systematic, teacher-led approach.

As a trainee teacher, you will gradually develop your own style of teaching, influenced by five factors: (a) Your evolving beliefs about effective teaching and learning; (b) The approach that works best for you; (c) The influence of more experienced teachers; (d) The approach that children seem to enjoy best; (e) The approach the regular teacher uses with the children. The final point is important – if you are on school placement and attempt to use a significantly different approach from the usual teacher, the children might struggle to understand your intentions and what is expected of them. It is better to observe the regular teacher's methods and closely follow them for a time before gradually introducing small changes of your own.

Whatever teaching approach you adopt, teaching primary-age children relies heavily on the creation and maintenance of a bond of trust and mutual respect between adult and child. You need to have insight into the things that children find significant if you want to create effective communication networks that will enhance learning and maintain good relations. Children appreciate adults who are fair, interested in them as individuals, transparent in their dealings, clear about their intentions, helpful in their explanations, non-judgemental in their attitude yet unflinching in confronting unsatisfactory situations. They benefit from teachers who are prepared to listen carefully to what children say to them, which enhances self-esteem, motivation and academic success. Your positive attitude, enthusiasm and high expectations can make a considerable difference in the way that children view learning, their behaviour and the extent they are willing to persevere.

Research Focus: Views of teaching

An interesting insight into primary teachers' views of teaching was exposed by Taylor (2002) who found that out of a group of 55 experienced teachers, over 80 per cent of them opted for an approach that can be broadly defined as 'child-centred' (Doddington and Hilton, 2007), defined as follows.

- Learning comes naturally to children.
- Children/students learn because they want to learn and not because they are told to do so.
- Play and work are indistinguishable.
- Learning is a communal activity rather than individual.
- The main aim of teaching is to develop the whole person (academic, social, spiritual).
- The curriculum should be related to the child's or student's needs.
- The teacher should encourage children to develop their own mode of learning (see p.34).

Child-centred philosophy

Taylor (2002) – see Research Focus above – notes that the results of his research are almost identical to those carried out among primary teachers some twenty-five years earlier (Ashton et al., 1975). Only about one-fifth of the teachers in Taylor's sample group aligned themselves with a view encapsulated in the ideology promoted in recent years, notably that:

1. real learning cannot possibly be easy;

2. children must be made to work rather than do so out of interest;

3. play is not work unless it is highly structured and controlled by adults;

4. learning is an individual matter;

5. the main aim of teaching is to develop the intellect, not the emotions;

6. the curriculum should relate to the needs of society; and

7. the teacher's job is to motivate and direct learning rather than involve children.

Instead, Taylor's findings that the majority of teachers preferred a *child-centred approach* reflected research carried out among aspiring teachers in England by Hayes (2004) and in Australia (Manuel and Hughes, 2006). Manuel and Hughes concluded that many prospective teachers enter teaching 'with a sense of mission to transform the lives of young people and open opportunities for growth through learning and connecting' (p.21).

> ## Activity
> To what extent do each of the seven principles based on the work of Taylor (2002) reflect your own view of teaching and learning? Take each principle in turn and for each one select from: agree strongly/agree/tend to disagree/disagree strongly. Discuss your conclusions with others.

Continuous professional development

Teachers are required to undergo continuous professional development (CPD) from the moment they enter a course of training until they retire from the job. CPD is defined as the systematic maintenance, improvement and broadening of knowledge and skills, together with the development of personal qualities, all of which are necessary for the execution of professional and practical responsibilities throughout a working life. See Chapter 10 for further discussion on CPD. Qualified teachers commonly refer to CPD as *in-service training* or INSET as they are developing expertise 'on the job'. Over time, you are expected to expand your subject knowledge; improve your organisation and management of teaching; learn new skills (e.g. specific uses of information technology) and increasingly contribute to the school's academic performance and attractiveness – especially to parents. Great teachers are forged from a combination of inspiration and perspiration; you need a substantial amount of *both* qualities.

Newly qualified primary teachers tend to use the teaching approach that they developed during training or modelled on a teacher whom they admire. As they progress, teachers gradually extend the reaches of their experience, focus their energies more efficiently and become more upbeat about school life, though a few older members of staff grow bitter and cynical. As a new teacher, you are advised to avoid being drawn into negative conversations with pessimistic colleagues. Instead, smile, nod and quickly find something else to do.

Reflecting in and on action

As noted earlier, you need to improve your competence through a process of self-evaluation in two ways: (a) At the end of a lesson or series of lessons (reflection *on* action) (b) During the lesson (reflection *in* action). In other words, you must not only take time to 'stand back' at the end of the session but be mentally active throughout the session(s) in evaluating your role and assessing how well the children responded to what you said to them and concentrated on their allocated work.

It is helpful to reflect *on* action by asking two key questions: (1) How well did I undertake and exercise my responsibilities as teacher? (2) How well did the children learn? The second question is more difficult to answer than the first because learning is never smooth and uninterrupted; most children learn a little, forget a little, become confused for a time then understand better, grapple with imponderables and gradually digest knowledge as they think and talk about ideas and reinforce their tentative understanding by asking questions, practising skills and exploring problems.

The model of teaching and learning that advocates a linear progression – *Teach...learn...evaluate learning and modify the next lesson...teach...learn* and so on – fails to take account of the complexity of the learning process and the need for constant reinforcement. Assessing and evaluating a small portion of work, followed by allocating grades or giving marks to represent attainment, is deceptively appealing. You *do* need to evaluate children's progress – and giving a grade or mark can be useful, providing they understand its significance – but you also need to recognise that learning is complex and cannot be reduced to a simple formula. See Chapter 3 in this book for further details.

Reflection *in* action presents its own challenges, not least the fact that it takes place during the lesson at a time when you have so much else to consider. Nevertheless, you will need to discipline yourself to think on your feet, evaluate your teaching spontaneously and make decisions about a range of issues, including:

- the length of time you spend on each part of the lesson (lesson phase);
- the length of time you spend assisting each child or group of children;
- the way that you respond to children's questions;
- the way that you handle instances of indiscipline;
- the standard of work that you accept from children;
- the opportunities you offer for children to explore ideas, investigate and discover new knowledge for themselves.

It is normal for inexperienced teachers to spend more time reflecting *on* action than *in* action. However, over time and with perseverance, you will find it easier to keep a 'mental running commentary', as you rapidly evaluate your actions and the children's responses and make rapid adjustments to what you say and do. It pays to concentrate on one or two aspects of your classroom practice at a time. For example, during one lesson you might make a conscious effort to differentiate the questions you use to ensure that less capable children can respond to simpler ones and more capable children have to think hard about tough ones; in a second lesson, you might pay particular attention to the nature of pupil feedback and your use of praise.

Professional advancement

The need for teachers to provide evidence that children have benefited directly from their teaching has been integral to career advancement, so teachers have to be able to point to measurable and verifiable aspects of pupil learning. Most teachers take advantage of internal promotion opportunities in the school but only a very small number become head teachers. See Neil and Morgan (2003) and Bubb (2004) for an overview of issues attached to professional progression across a career. The establishment of the 'National College' (www.nationalcollege. org.uk) in England – known as 'National College for Leadership of Schools Children's Services – for preparing and training aspiring subject leaders, deputy head teachers and head teachers signals that professional advancement is increasingly dependent on external forms of verification. See Chapter 10 for more about professional advancement.

Professional responsibilities

In recent years, a lot of legislation has been passed specific to the role of teachers that has had an impact on the way that they relate to children in school. A teacher's responsibility for pupil welfare has grown beyond the original standard of *in loco parentis* (standing in the place of the parent). Depending on the age of the children, the person or persons with a primary duty of care must ensure that all reasonable precautions have been taken to protect and safeguard their welfare (Nixon, 2007).

There has been a substantial increase in the amount of litigation in society generally and this trend has influenced the work of adults in school. Consequently, all teachers are obliged to keep abreast of the way in which laws and codes of practice impact upon their behaviour. Teachers must also conform to their professional duties as required by the head teacher, in line with their contracts of employment. A refusal to do so can be interpreted as a breach of contract and invite disciplinary procedures. All new teachers receive a letter of appointment from the school governors/school board specifying matters such as salary, duties and tenure.

Teachers' professional values and practice includes having high expectations of every pupil, respecting a child's social, cultural, linguistic, religious and ethnic backgrounds, and showing wholehearted concern for their academic and social development. The establishment of standards for qualified teacher status and what amounts to a national scheme for teacher training is intended to maintain overall competence.

The need for an acceptable standard of teacher behaviour is discussed in detail in Chapter 6. It is important because primary teachers act as models or examples to their children and local communities. General Teaching Councils (GTCs) in Wales, Scotland and Northern Ireland exist to promote a sense of collegiality and consistency across the teaching profession. However, the GTC (England) was disbanded in 2010. Teachers are bound by formal and implicit codes of ethics that specify how they are to fulfil their duties and obligations with respect to the education they provide. Teachers can be reprimanded for misdemeanours as diverse as repeatedly failing to hand in planning and assessment files to the head teacher for monitoring; demonstrating overt insensitivity to children; or using inappropriate language in front of children and colleagues.

To avoid problems, make every effort to be positive about life in general, avoid complaining and listen respectfully to the things that children and colleagues say. At all cost, avoid any trace of arrogance or giving the impression to staff that you can manage perfectly well on your own and don't need their advice. You can enhance your reputation by arriving in good time for school, staying behind to complete tasks, being courteous and pleasant to colleagues, using your time productively during the day and persevering to improve your teaching skills.

School placement issues

A significant part of a teacher-training course is time spent on school placement. To make the best use of these periods you need to do a lot of thinking and preparation before and during the placement. *Before* you begin, you will be given plenty of advice by tutors and allocated tasks that you must undertake during the time in school. There is nearly always a lot of paperwork to complete, so grit your teeth and get on with it! In the case of extended placements, it is normal to make a preliminary visit to the school or educational setting to meet staff and children and become familiar with the set-up. Don't forget to be friendly, smile a lot and reassure the host teacher by your positive but mature attitude that you will be an asset and not a liability.

During the placement, it takes time to adjust to a new situation, so don't be discouraged if you struggle and feel a bit overwhelmed, especially during the first few days. Hayes (2009) suggests that however hard you work and however sincere is your level of commitment, the time you spend on placement in school is always going to be challenging as well as rewarding. The placement provides opportunities for you to hone your teaching skills and learn about the various teacher roles, supported by a tutor and the school staff. One of the most important things to do is to learn the children's names. Another is to clarify with the teacher/tutor/mentor precisely what is expected of you, when you will be taking responsibility and what you need to prepare. A third is to show a willingness to 'get stuck in'. Don't try to endear yourself to the children by being over-familiar; you can be friendly without compromising your teacher status.

As the placement begins and you do more teaching, you will discover that a variety of practical factors over which you have no control interfere with your carefully laid plans; for example, the school may have a special event that requires time-consuming rehearsals or a special visitor might arrive causing a session to be curtailed at short notice. Occasionally, the regular teacher is ill or absent for other reasons and you have to negotiate with one or more substitute teachers, which tends to delay or accelerate your rise to stardom. Your reaction to unexpected twists and turns reveals a lot about your suitability for teaching, so try to be flexible and view such difficulties as opportunities rather than annoying hindrances. Save your complaining for when you meet your friends in the evening.

Research Focus: Issues facing new teachers

Research carried out by Jacklin et al. (2006) about the issues faced by new primary teachers indicated that one of the greatest challenges was taking full responsibility for the whole class, including establishing and enforcing boundaries of behaviour, pupil safety, registration, liaising with parents, and so on. Trainee teachers are partially protected from this all-encompassing role but still need to recognise that there is more to being a teacher than teaching lessons. The authors go on to say that differentiated teaching, supporting and extending the least and most able children, and above all, setting high expectations and standards for all, irrespective of gender, ethnicity, race, disability or social background, are all part of the day to day role of a primary teacher.

The majority of placements are satisfactory or better; occasionally a placement is disappointing, either because you receive inadequate support, guidance and help from the host teacher/mentor or for some unaccountable reason you don't get on with the children. In such cases it is important to do your best to stay positive, refuse to countenance failure and make constructive use of your tutor and mentor. The reality is that although occasional setbacks are inevitable, they can be used as an incentive to do better and do not spell the end of your teaching career. Use Activity 4 as a guide for evaluating your progress.

Case Study

Two trainee teachers, who had spent time in separate schools as part of their teaching placement, reflected on ways in which their professional development had been affected by widely differing experiences. In the first example, Chris explains how she persevered with an unpromising situation. In the second example, Emma describes her 'dream placement' in a school where pupil behaviour was good and she felt welcomed by the host teachers. The case studies are in the trainees' own words.

Chris (Working with Year 5 children)
'The placement didn't get off to a very good start because in my first meeting with the teacher/tutor, she confessed that she had not really wanted another trainee, so I felt like an intruder. I worked with a group of children whose classroom and learning behaviour was very challenging. They were hard to motivate and showed little interest in the work they were given to do. Many of them seemed to have

→

switched off from school altogether. Several children had serious learning difficulties that were not recognised or being addressed by the teacher or catered for in lessons. A small group of unsettled and uncooperative children dominated much of teacher's attention throughout the school day with the result that other children's needs were not being well met. The classroom environment was poor and uncared for; for instance, there was minimal work on display and children's work was often left unmarked, just lying around gathering dust. Unfortunately, my college tutor was off sick during much of the placement and the school was a long way from the University, so I felt very isolated. There was so much that I wanted to learn, see and do, but owing to the challenging conditions much remains unseen and undone. So, overall this placement was not what I had hoped for at all but in a way I learned more than in my previous school where the children were lovely, the teachers were highly supportive and I was made very welcome. The most important lesson I learned was that I have inner reserves of strength that I didn't know I possessed. I made up my mind to be the very best teacher I could possibly be in the circumstances and refused to become negative or cynical, though there were times of intense frustration. I also became aware of the sort of teacher I definitely did not want to become. Mind you, I still hope my final school placement is easier than the one I've just finished. It would have been easy to imagine that everything was my fault when in fact I think I coped well and made good progress despite the situation. Even so, I envy those some of my friends who didn't have to endure the inner turmoil, strains and stresses that I experienced. Emotions play such a powerful role in teaching, so being unsettled in school has an adverse effect on every other part of your life, too'.

Emma (Working with reception children)
'I was really fortunate with my placement in that I was quickly able to fit in really well with staff at the school and soon became regarded and treated like a fellow teacher and colleague. The class teacher and the two teaching assistants I worked with were highly skilled, supportive and cheerful. They gave me loads of ideas, resources and assistance with my small-scale research I had to do as part of the placement about ways that children learn through play. I felt myself grow in confidence and become a member of the team rather than a trainee teacher sitting in the corner of the room! Having such positive support and encouragement meant that the class felt like my own and as a result the children responded well to me. Support from my class teacher really helped me when I was uncertain or struggling with an issue, as she offered advice in a constructive and pleasant way. I was never afraid to approach her even when I mucked things up, as she always tried to be positive instead of moaning. One unexpected bonus from being accepted as a teacher was the fact that parents increasingly came to me and asked about their children's progress. I was thrilled when some of the parents told me how excited their children were about what I was teaching them in school. My school mentor was very experienced and I felt 100 per cent confident about his guidance (unlike my previous school experiences). He was kind, supportive and caring, which made

→

it my favourite placement of the year. I intend to make sure that I'm as supportive to the trainees that come into my classroom when I'm qualified'.

The above instances show that both trainees developed their expertise and sense of self in different ways. In the first case, the trainee had to draw on her inner strength and belief and learn to be self-reliant in an unpromising situation. In the second case, the trainee had the luxury of a supportive environment and well-behaved children.

Activity

1. What were the different professional challenges facing Chris and Emma?
2. In what ways might Chris have made more progress as a teacher than Emma?
3. What sort of factors combined to create the 'inner turmoil' described by Chris?

All teachers can be persuaded that you are an asset if they see that you respond to their advice, strive to do your best and do not threaten their way of working (Hayes 2003). Despite any reservations you may hold, try to view the teacher as your ally and strive to keep channels of communication open. Stay positive, focus on the children's learning, listen to advice, do your best to implement it and keep paperwork up to date. Thankfully, the large majority of trainee teachers enjoy their placements, though moments of uncertainty and self-doubt are inevitable. Be encouraged that the vast majority of trainees are successful and complete the time in school feeling much more like Emma than like Chris.

Activity

Evaluate your professional progress using the following coding: (1) Progressing well (2) Progressing satisfactorily (3) Requiring attention (4) Requiring urgent attention.

a) I am being positive about my situation and avoid moaning.
b) I am maintaining open communication with colleagues, especially the class teacher.
c) I am listening carefully to advice.
d) I am thoughtfully acting upon advice.
e) I am being friendly, courteous and warm towards others.
f) I am acting in a considerate and caring manner.
g) I am preparing and evaluating lessons thoroughly.
h) I am maintaining necessary paperwork, including assessment of pupil progress.
i) I am reflecting on my teaching during lessons and after the session.
j) I am interacting with parents and keeping them informed.
k) I am becoming familiar with school policies for safeguarding children.
l) I am taking opportunities for leisure and recreation to 'recharge my batteries'.

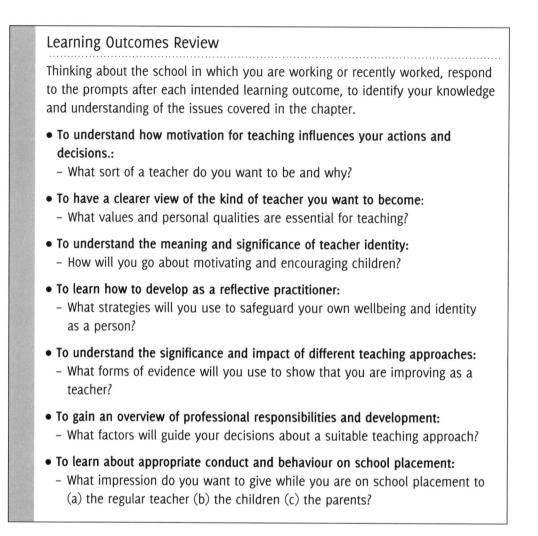

Learning Outcomes Review

Thinking about the school in which you are working or recently worked, respond to the prompts after each intended learning outcome, to identify your knowledge and understanding of the issues covered in the chapter.

- **To understand how motivation for teaching influences your actions and decisions.:**
  - What sort of a teacher do you want to be and why?

- **To have a clearer view of the kind of teacher you want to become:**
  - What values and personal qualities are essential for teaching?

- **To understand the meaning and significance of teacher identity:**
  - How will you go about motivating and encouraging children?

- **To learn how to develop as a reflective practitioner:**
  - What strategies will you use to safeguard your own wellbeing and identity as a person?

- **To understand the significance and impact of different teaching approaches:**
  - What forms of evidence will you use to show that you are improving as a teacher?

- **To gain an overview of professional responsibilities and development:**
  - What factors will guide your decisions about a suitable teaching approach?

- **To learn about appropriate conduct and behaviour on school placement:**
  - What impression do you want to give while you are on school placement to (a) the regular teacher (b) the children (c) the parents?

References

Arthur, J., Davison, J. and Lewis, M. (2005) *Professional Values and Practice: Achieving the standards for QTS.* London: Routledge.

Ashton, P., Kneen, P. and Davies, F. (1975) *Aims into Practice in the Primary School.* London: Hodder and Stoughton.

Bubb, S. (2004) *The Insider's Guide to Early Professional Development.* London: Routledge.

Doddington, C. and Hilton, M. (2007) *Child-Centred Education.* London: Sage.

Eaude, T. (2006) *Children's Spiritual, Moral, Social and Cultural Development.* Exeter: Learning Matters.

Ghaye, A. and Ghaye, K. (1998) *Teaching and Learning through Critical Reflective Practice.* London: David Fulton.

Hayes, D. (2003) *A Student Teacher's Guide to Primary School Placement*. London: Routledge.

Hayes, D. (2004) Recruitment and retention: insights into the motivation of primary trainee teachers in England. *Research in Education*, 71, 37–49.

Hayes, D. (2009) *Primary Teaching Today*. London: Routledge.

Jacklin, A., Griffiths, V. and Robinson, C. (2006) *Beginning Primary Teaching*. Maidenhead: Open University.

Jeffreys, M. (1971) *Education: Its nature and purpose*. London: Allen and Unwin.

Larrivee, B. (2008) Meeting the challenge of preparing reflective practitioners. *The New Educator*, 4 (2), 87–106.

Manuel, J. and Hughes, J. (2006) It has always been my dream: exploring pre-service teachers' motivations for choosing to teach. *Teacher Development*, 10 (1), 5–24.

Mullen, C. (2007) *Curriculum Leadership Development*. London: Routledge.

Neil, P. and Morgan, C. (2003) *Continuing Professional Development for Teachers*. London: Kogan Page.

Nixon, J. (2007) Teachers' legal liabilities and responsibilities, in Cole, M. (ed) *Professional Attributes and Practice*. London: David Fulton.

O'Quinn, E. and Garrison, J. (2004) Creating loving relations in the classroom, in Liston, D. and Garrison, J. (eds) *Teaching, Learning and Loving*. London: Routledge.

Palmer, P.J. (1997a) The heart of a teacher: identity and integrity in teaching, on-line at www.newhorizons.org/strategies/character/palmer.htm

Palmer, P.J. (1997b) *The Courage to Teach: Exploring the inner landscape of a teacher's life*. San Francisco: Jossey-Bass.

Richards, C. (2009) Primary teaching: a personal perspective, in Arthur, J., Grainger, T. and Wray, D. (eds) *Learning to Teach in the Primary School*. London: Routledge.

Rossano, M.J. (2008) The moral faculty: Does religion promote moral expertise? *International Journal for the Psychology of Religion*, 18 (3), 169–194.

Sridhar, Y.N. (2001) Value development, *National Council for Teacher Education (NCTE)*, Value Orientation in Teacher Education conference, New Delhi.

Taylor, P.H. (2002) Primary teachers' views of what helps and hinders teaching. *Education 3–13*, 31 (2), 34–39.

Thornberg, R. (2008) The lack of professional knowledge in values education. *Teaching and Teacher Education*, 24 (7), 1791–1798.

8. Safeguarding children
Pat Macpherson

Learning Outcomes

By the end of this chapter you will have had the opportunity to:

- think about a range of safeguarding and child protection issues, both generally and with specific reference to children in the primary age phase;
- consider implications for your professional practice with regard to safeguarding and child protection in meeting national standards for gaining qualified teacher status and maintaining your licence to teach;
- know about the roles of key school and other agencies' personnel related to safeguarding and child protection. Reference is made to key documents including current statutory and non-statutory guidance;
- become aware of key statutory and non-statutory documents related to safeguarding and child protection.

Standards

Q1 Relationships with children and young people.
Have high expectations of children and young people including a commitment to ensuring that they can achieve their full educational potential and to establishing fair, respectful, trusting, supportive and constructive relationships with them.
Q3 Frameworks.
a) Be aware of the professional duties of teachers and the statutory framework within which they work.
(b) Be aware of the policies and practices of the workplace and share in collective responsibility for their implementation.
Q6 Communicating and working with others.
Have a commitment to collaboration and cooperative working.
Q21 Health and well-being.
(a) Be aware of the current legal requirements, national policies and guidance on the safeguarding and promotion of the well-being of children and young people.
(b) Know how to identify and support children and young people whose progress, development or well-being is affected by changes or difficulties in their personal circumstances, and when to refer them to colleagues for specialist support.
Standards also related to the safeguarding and protection of children are Q2, Q4, Q5, Q15, Q18, Q20, Q30, Q31, Q32, Q33.

Introduction

As a trainee teacher you will 'be' the teacher for much of your time on placement. Even in the early days of your education and training to become a teacher you will be in role as a teacher when you are in school. Through your university-based learning and practical experience on placement you will develop over time your knowledge and understanding of children together with your skills and competences in managing an appropriate learning environment for them. Safeguarding and child protection are essential parts of your work as a trainee teacher and so have to be central to all of your practice and interactions with children and colleagues. You will explore this further within this chapter but please remember that links can be made with other chapters in this book.

> *Every child should be safe. Sadly, not every child is. Shockingly, some children are at risk of harm from the very people they should be able to rely on for love and care. We all have a responsibility to do everything possible to protect those vulnerable children.*
>
> (DfES, 2009)

The quotation above exemplifies the principles and commitments that underpin legislation and policy in safeguarding and child protection. Safeguarding is everybody's responsibility but this is particularly the case for professionals – including teachers – who work with children. The statement also helps us recognise and understand the enormous responsibilities teachers have in ensuring they play their part in helping to keep children safe and protected – at school and, as part of a wider, multi-disciplinary team, at home and in the community. In this chapter the constituent parts of that responsibility will be introduced and explored. No hierarchy is intended in the order in which these are presented; rather they reflect my approach to considering safeguarding and child protection for intending teachers.

There are three elements that help inform your understanding of how a (shared) responsibility for safeguarding and child protection in primary schools and other educational settings can be demonstrated in and through your practice. These elements are the emotional, legal and professional dimensions and each will be explored further as you work your way through the chapter.

The emotional dimension

Thinking about how you respond to a child for whom there is a safeguarding concern can be very upsetting. You may feel anger and resentment towards abusers, frustration that not all children are indeed protected fully from abuse or fear that you will not be able to fulfil your professional obligations and duties.

> ## Activity
> Write down two or three feelings which come to mind when thinking about child abuse and child protection.
> Consider and reflect on the range of feelings that you have identified.

What feelings emerged? You may have listed any or all of the following: anger, frustration, confusion, panic, self-doubt, disgust, despair, feeling overwhelmed, disbelief, fear, protectiveness. You may have mentioned other feelings and emotions and you may have experiences in your past which inform those feelings. Whatever your starting point in thinking through feelings and emotions that emerge when you think about safeguarding and child protection, it is important to recognise that child abuse does raise strong emotions for many people and that it is a subject influenced by our personal value systems and experiences. You also need to remember that you are not alone in dealing with safeguarding cases because there will be other professionals (both in and out of the school setting) who will work with you and support you.

Research Focus

Baginsky and Macpherson (2005) carried out research which led into the development of a training pack for trainee teachers published by the NSPCC. They set out to identify the extent to which trainee teachers:

- learned about child protection on their courses;
- were supported on their placement in developing their understanding of child protection;
- felt confident about responding to child protection issues.

The concerns that trainee teachers reported to the researchers included:

- the sensitivity of the subject matter;
- the belief that the reality would be much harder to cope with than they had been led to believe by the course;
- the importance of the approach taken by the school and the support offered;
- a recognition that time constraints in their ITE course and other factors meant that the coverage had been superficial and was not adequate preparation;
- the failure to deal with the subject in an integrated way throughout the initial teacher training course;
- a fear of dealing inappropriately with a disclosure.

In light of these concerns, review how your own course (including placements) helps assuage similar concerns that you may have.

Another important aspect of understanding our emotional responses to issues of safeguarding and child protection is acknowledging why children need protecting and from what. Children are largely disempowered and that lack of power makes them potentially vulnerable. Teachers, along with other professionals, are a central part of the multi-professional team helping to counter-balance that lack of power and safeguard them. Teaching allows you to establish close and, hopefully, productive relationships with children, and social and emotional interactions that occur each and every day in the classroom lie at the heart of those relationships. If you get the relationships right then children will feel welcomed and valued in your classroom and, if they feel welcomed and valued by you as their 'teacher' then they are more likely to tell you if something is going wrong in their life. Safeguarding and child protection derive from many aspects of your practice – classroom climate, a good grounding in child development (including emotional development and how children develop feelings of security and resilience) and your knowledge and understanding of different patterns of family life and the position of children in families and communities. To summarise, establishing an appropriate emotional climate in your classroom (as well as an appropriate learning environment) requires a genuine commitment from you to children's well-being. Get it right and you will be the sort of teacher that children can trust; someone to whom they can turn to or talk to about problems and issues.

Activity

When you are on placement, obtain a copy of the school's policy on safeguarding and child protection; find out who the designated teacher for safeguarding (sometimes called the safeguarding or child protection officer) is, what you should do if on placement a child discloses to you that they are being abused or you have suspicions from the way a child behaves that they may be being abused. Annotate the policy with aspects that impress you and points you want to find out more about.

The legal dimension

There is a range of legislation and statutory guidance that underpins your work as a trainee teacher. These relate to a wide range of activities undertaken in a primary school: compulsory schooling, the national curriculum, statutory assessment and reporting, accountability and Ofsted inspections, teachers requiring a licence to teach, health and safety in the workplace (school) and of particular relevance in this chapter, safeguarding and child protection. Your school(s) will be expected to comply with all legislation concerned with health and safety at work and you, as a visitor and/or employee in the school, are required to comply with the school's guidance on this. You need, therefore, to check the school's policy and procedures on this matter also. One aspect of health and safety that you may encounter relates to out-of-classroom or out-of-school learning experiences and activities. Your duty of care extends to these situations but ultimate responsibility lies with the head teacher and governing body. For some trips outside of the classroom you will need to gain formal permission from the governors to undertake the visit as well as completing a risk assessment; for others it will be enough to complete a risk assessment only. The class/head teacher or educational visits coordinator will be able to provide information on this. Other sources of support in the area of out-of-school activities are the teaching trade unions and you will find they provide useful guidance and information. Basically, though, it is essential that you you follow all elements of the school's policy and procedures in organising and conducting out-of-school activities and trips. These can vary in detail from school to school but all will require that the following checklist has been completed satisfactorily:

- full, detailed planning of all aspects of the trip – travel, transitions, access to meals and drinks, toilet break, spending money (if this is permitted), educational opportunities from the visit;
- supervision ratios and arrangements;
- a completed risk assessment;
- contact details for children's parents and/or carers.

As you read the case study below, think about the responses would you make, both before and after the trip if you were Simon's friend.

Case Study: A school trip

Simon's class teacher intends to provide an out-of-school activity for the children. He is asked to read the school's policy on out-of-school trips prior to meeting with her to go through the planned activity. Simon tells his friend that he has read the policy but that he does not see the point of it. 'Common sense is all that is needed,' he says.

After the visit, Simon reflects on his experience. He shares with his friend that he now understands how important it is to follow the school's policy and procedure. For example, he explains the reasoning behind one teacher driving her own car to the venue instead of all staff and adults travelling on the coach with the children. He understands that in this case, one teacher drove her own car to provide immediate access to transport should an emergency arise. She had checked that her own personal car insurance covered her for work-based travel.

In relation to safeguarding and child protection you need to be aware especially of the various Children Acts (1989, 2002, 2004 and 2007), statutory guidance on safer recruitment (DfES, 2006), and statutory guidance on multi-professional working in Working Together to Safeguard Children (DCFS, 2006 and 2010).

There is also wider legislation that makes an important contribution to understanding safeguarding and the teacher's role in this, especially human rights legislation that accords children a range of universal rights. Children, then, have a number of legal entitlements or rights. Your role as a trainee teacher brings with it responsibilities to help ensure children's rights are met. Children are protected in law through having rights. Children should be protected by schools, through you (and your colleagues) exercising and carrying out your professional obligations (see Chapter 6 about your professional responsibilities). That is, safeguarding goes with the job of teaching and we owe a professional and legal obligation to all of the children we teach.

What this means in practice is that you as a trainee teacher have a duty of care towards children and that this duty of care in the safeguarding and child protection process requires you to do three things.

- *Notice* – that something might be wrong (from your observations, from what a child says or writes, from what someone else tells you, from what can be best be termed as a listening ear to your professional warning bells).

- *Record* – write down what you have seen, heard, read etc. Date your notes and sign them.

- *Report* on to the class teacher or your school's designated teacher for safeguarding. This person may have a different title such as the child protection officer but the role will be the same.

This sequence of actions is important because teachers make such a crucial contribution to helping identify children who are being harmed or who are in possible danger of being harmed. As a trainee teacher you are required in law and professionally to play your part. At its simplest this means that you have to notice that something may not be right, record it and pass it on to the class or designated teacher (as determined in the school's safeguarding policy). Senior personnel in the school (in particular the designated teacher, the head teacher and the school governor with responsibility for safeguarding) have a higher duty of care and, therefore, greater responsibility. This is support for you also. You will not be working alone to help safeguard children. You need also to be aware that you can never promise to keep secret information you find out (from whatever source) that relates to safeguarding. You must pass the information on.

One of the more worrying aspects of a trainee teacher's role relates to physical contact with children. The law is very clear on some aspects of this.

First, there must be no sexual contact or sexual relationship of any kind with children. This would be considered a very serious abuse of trust as well as being against the law. It might seem obvious that any form of sexual contact with a child is wrong but teaching (and other professions associated with children) involves close, trusting relationships and contact with children, a genuine trust of you by a child. Sometimes such trust is broken. Because of this teaching is a profession that adheres to employment practices which deter the unsuitable. Statutory guidance on safe recruitment to teaching makes it clear that schools (inter alia) must 'help to deter, reject or identify people who might abuse children, or are otherwise unsuited to work with them' (DfES, 2006).

Second, it is illegal for teachers to use physical punishment or chastisement when disciplining children. This includes all forms of corporal punishment – striking, hitting, pushing, using implements etc. Chapter 13 on behaviour management will help you know and understand a range of behaviour management strategies that bring about orderly classrooms and appropriate learning environments.

Other aspects of physical contact with children are not as clear, though. For example, consider whether, as a trainee teacher, you can you touch children at all. There is no law that says you cannot touch children in a non-sexual way. Indeed, statutory guidance makes it clear that this is not the case: 'It is not realistic to suggest that teachers should never touch pupils' (DfES, 2006). In fact, try stopping children touching you! It's actually quite usual for children of primary age to seek some contact of this nature – wanting to hold your hand in the playground, stand very close to you when they get the chance, or seek some physical comfort when they are upset or hurt. There has been much discussion of this recently. Some schools have as part of their school policy a ban on teachers and other adults (including trainee teachers) touching children at all even if they are hurt, have fallen over or are upset. Other schools, though, will consider such practice to be not in a child's interests and even detrimental to a child's emotional well-being or development. You need always to ask for the school's safeguarding policy when you start a new teaching placement or when you begin your work as a qualified teacher. The policy will reflect to a large extent what the school considers to be good practice and appropriate behaviours between teachers (including trainee teachers) and children.

The government has promised to bring in clearer, shorter guidance about physical contact with children, making it clear that some contact is in a child's interest and, hopefully, removing the fears that some schools have that any contact of any kind could be considered inappropriate and the teachers' motives questioned. Clarity and a professional freedom to respond appropriately to children are to be welcomed. However, such professional freedoms require good practice to underpin them, In determining whether or not any physical contact is appropriate, you need to consider who initiates contact, where physical contact takes place (location), where the child is touched (parts of the body); whether other people are there or whether you are alone with a child.

Physical restraint is also something that worries trainee teachers and is a feature of professional behaviour that the government has promised to attend to and simplify. There is recognition already in the statutory guidance that physical restraint may sometimes be required and appropriate: '[teachers], and other staff in schools or FE colleges, have the right to use reasonable force to control or restrain children in certain circumstances' (DfES, 2006). Again, though, you need to take great care and moderation in exercising this professional right and you should always work with colleagues and senior staff if you find yourself teaching a child for whom physical restraint is a necessary strategy. For further advice, see DfES Circular 10/98: *The Use of Restraint of Pupils – Force to Control* available at www.teachernet.gov.uk/childprotection/guidance.htm.

The final strand of the legal dimension is defining child abuse and responding to its occurrence or suspicion. There are a number of types of abuse which fall into the following broad categories – sexual abuse, emotional abuse, physical abuse and neglect. More recently other types of abuse have been recognised. These include financial abuse, bullying, children affected by gang activity, fabricated or induced illness, forced marriage, honour-based violence and female genital mutilation. The foundation of this lies in the Children Act 1989 which introduced the concept of significant harm – actual or suspected – as a justification for compulsory intervention in family life. However, as the document makes clear, there are no absolute criteria on which to rely when judging what constitutes significant harm. Further detail and explanations of abuse and neglect can be found in the statutory guidance *Working Together to Safeguard Children* (DCFS, 2006) and below (taken from DCFS, 2006).

Physical abuse
Physical abuse may involve hitting, shaking, throwing, poisoning, burning or scalding, drowning, suffocating, or otherwise causing physical harm to a child. Physical harm may also be caused when a parent or carer feigns the symptoms of, or deliberately causes, ill heath to a child whom they are looking after. This situation is commonly described using terms such as factitious illness by proxy or Munchausen syndrome by proxy.

Sexual abuse
Sexual abuse involves forcing or enticing a child or young person to take part in sexual activities, whether or not the child is aware of what is happening. The activities may involve physical contact, including penetrative (e.g. rape or buggery) or non-penetrative acts. They may include non-contact activities, such as involving children in looking at, or in the production of, pornographic material or watching sexual activities, or encouraging children to behave in sexually inappropriate ways.

Emotional abuse
Emotional abuse is the persistent emotional ill treatment of a child that may cause severe and persistent adverse effects on the child's emotional development. It may involve conveying to children that they are worthless or unloved, inadequate, or valued only insofar as they meet the needs of another person. It may feature age or developmentally inappropriate expectations being imposed on children. It may involve causing children frequently to feel frightened or in danger, or the exploitation or corruption of children. Some level of emotional abuse is involved in all types of ill treatment of a child, though it may occur alone.

Neglect
Neglect is the persistent failure to meet the child's basic physical and/or psychological needs, likely to result in the serious impairment of the child's health or development. It may involve a parent or carer failing to provide adequate food, shelter and clothing, failing to protect a child from physical harm or danger, or the failure to ensure access to appropriate medical care or treatment. It may also include neglect of, or unresponsiveness to, a child's basic emotional needs.

Policy into practice

There are a number of broader issues associated with safeguarding and child protection that you may wish to explore further. These include cultural understandings and interpretations of safeguarding, the debate on whether parents should be banned in law from smacking their children, domestic abuse and the sexualisation of children in the media.

This research focus concerns the impact of domestic abuse on children's development.

Research Focus

Ward et al. (2010) produced a Government-commissioned report into the impact of domestic violence on young children. They sampled a number of very young children who were identified as suffering, or likely to suffer, significant harm before their first birthdays and were then followed until they were three. Although the report was designed to inform governmental policy, it has significant implications for your practice.

The potential impact on children included delayed speech and language development and aggressive behaviour. There were also high levels of frustration in responding to a range of situations reported. The authors of the study indicated that these behaviours are likely to impact on children's chances of making progress at school.

The research above was welcomed by a number of agencies and associations. The spokesperson for the Women's Aid Federation of England said that it was essential that domestic violence was discussed openly in schools because children 'have a right to know about their own safety' (TES, 2010). Given this, consider the implications for schools and teachers in responding to the issue of domestic violence.

If you teach a child for whom there is any safeguarding or child protection concern – suspected or known – then you may be involved in the investigation of that concern. Investigations are undertaken under Section 47 of The Children Act 1989. The investigation will be led by an experienced social worker. Your input to the investigation may be through direct involvement (you attend and participate) or indirect involvement (your school's designated teacher represents the school) but your contribution will be an essential source of information about the child and her/his needs and how they are being met. Teachers – including trainee teachers also – can and do provide information that arises from a disclosure (directly from a child or from something they have said) or indicators of a potentially abused child (unexplained bruising or injuries, sexually explicit language or actions, or a change in behaviour observed over time). The aim is that all professionals involved in legally safeguarding children do so in a co-ordinated way which focuses on a child's needs. You can further information on this in *What to do if you are worried a child is being abused* (DFES, 2006).

The professional dimension

As a trainee teacher you are required to act professionally at all times. Determining what counts as professional behaviour (as opposed to unprofessional behaviour) is, therefore, critical if you are to be successful and if your practice is not to be called into question. In working towards and achieving qualified teacher status you will be assessed against all of the standards related to your practice as a trainee teacher. This will cover all elements of practice as outlined in the standards: relationships with children, frameworks, communication with others, subject knowledge and children's learning. The QTS standards listed at the beginning of this chapter show just how many standards relate to safeguarding and child protection. For example, the standards concerned with subject knowledge and teaching and learning are obviously directed at discrete subjects but they also relate to personal, social and health education; the being safe strand of Every Child Matters, health and well-being, and the notion of a protective curriculum in the primary school; achievement and diversity; the learning environment; team work and collaboration.

Your work as a trainee teacher (and later, once you are qualified) is underpinned not only by legislative and statutory frameworks but also by professional frameworks for working with children. A key principle of any professional framework will relate to safeguarding and child protection and will be written in a way that makes it clear and explicit that you need to put the wellbeing and development of children first (GTCE, 2010).

Case Study: Professional dialogue

Jessica is on placement in a class that is shared by two teachers, one working in the first half of the week and the other working in the second half of the week. The two teachers meet every Wednesday to review planning and the children's achievements. Jessica notices over the first three weeks of her placement that one particular child in the class exhibits different behaviours on Mondays and Fridays and she mentions it during the following Wednesday meeting. The class teachers are very grateful for Jessica's observations, realising that their focus in meetings has tended to be about children's attainment and progress and less about non-academic matters. As a result they set up a way of being able to monitor the particular child's behaviour over each week.

In order to put the wellbeing and development of children first you need to demonstrate commitment to their learning and development – personal, social, emotional as well as academic. You need also to demonstrate good practice in how you meet that commitment so that your practice is considered appropriate and so that no one questions your motives for working with children in the primary age range. This applies to all aspects of your work as a trainee teacher: when teaching and managing the curriculum for children, in how you establish relationships with children and with which children; what classroom routines and procedures you make use of and how they are applied; in interactions with children and their parents/

carers and with colleagues. You need to ensure that you treat all children as equally as you can, with no obvious favourites among the children. This is not always as easy or straightforward as it might seem. At times you may teach children who you find it very easy or very hard to like and for a variety of reasons. Remember that you must keep the relationship professional. All children in your class deserve to be in an environment where they feel, and where they are, welcomed and valued. You, as the professional, have to create the right sort of climate for this to happen. Children are more likely to tell you when something is wrong in their life or circumstances if you have the right sort of relationship with them. So, you need to make sure that you do not ignore or put down a child who you find it hard to like; you need to make sure that you do not have favourites and that you do not single out favoured children for special treatment.

Protecting yourself from allegations of poor practice or abuse

All of the above paragraph will also help ensure that you protect yourself, too. Schools themselves create risks for children – children are easily accessible, there is a power imbalance between children and the teachers/adults, there are opportunities to touch children (and have children touch you), there are occasions when children are changing clothes or are undressed, for example in PE or when visiting a swimming pool, there are opportunities to see children alone. How you conduct yourself in these situations will form the basis of how others judge your practice and whether you are considered to be professional in the relationships you establish with children.

Case Study: The impact of school context and policy

Jagdeep has undertaken three placements in different schools. He notices that each school has a different policy towards children changing for physical education sessions. For example, he sees that the policy for each school has been influenced by the school context, including:

- the gender of the teacher;
- the age of the children;
- the changing facilities available.

He talks about his observations with his mentor. She explains that each school formulates an understanding of what constitutes good practice and that this varies from school to school. She reminds Jagdeep that all schools have a safeguarding policy and that he should always check how this impacts on other elements of his professional role. She goes on to say that she previously worked in a school that had only one policy covering all elements of relationships in the school. It was called 'The personal and social policy' but it comprised safeguarding, bullying, health education and extra-curricular activities as well as personal and social education.

Remember that the full range of the school's policies may impact on judgements made about your practice and behaviour. For example, the school may have procedures and/or a policy about other aspects of school life which relate to safeguarding and the notion of good practice for trainee teachers as well as qualified teachers. For example, what is the school's policy and procedure for break times/playtimes and children staying in to finish work? Is it considered appropriate to leave a child in a classroom; does the teacher have to remain in the classroom with the child; are teachers expected to take children who are staying in to a central area where supervision and care of them is shared and more public?

The final aspect of professional good practice considered in this chapter is that of vigilance. Vigilance firstly, of the children through what they do, say, write, draw. What will you do about the child who is often hungry, dirty, smelly, loud, anxious, bruised, sleepy, poorly dressed?

Vigilance secondly of the other trainees, teachers and adults in the school – is their practice good; do you see things that worry you or that cause you to question an adult's motives for working with a child or group of children?

Vigilance thirdly, of yourself and your own practices so that you undertake a regular review of your classroom routines and procedures, of your interactions with individual children and the class, of the type of classroom climate you establish and promote. Do you create a climate that encourages children to feel safe and to talk to you if they have any safeguarding or child protection issues? How confident are you that you are the right sort of teacher? Do you treat all children well? How do you respond to children who are dirty, smelly, loud, unhappy, anxious etc? Good practice means operating in an atmosphere of transparency so that no one questions your motives or actions.

Drawing the three principles together

In this chapter three principles have been presented to underpin the trainee teacher's role in safeguarding and protecting children: recognising and understanding that complex emotions are involved; complying fully with all legal and professional duties; demonstrating good professional practice and vigilance.

- Be aware of your own emotional responses and needs as well as those of the children. Remember that you are part of a team – both within the school and in the wider multi-professional network.

- Be absolutely clear that you have a duty to safeguard children and that this is both a legal and a professional obligation.

- Make sure that you demonstrate good practice at all times. Avoid initiating touching children but, if you do touch a child, make sure you do so in an open, public area and in an appropriate way ensuring there is no touching of a child's more intimate areas; use appropriate language when talking to children; dress appropriately; do not swap mobile telephone numbers or personal email addresses with children; do not add children as a 'friend' on social networking sites; maintain a good professional distance – not too distant, though, or else there is a danger that you will not establish a protective relationship with the child; ensure you know and understand what is required when in the role of a teacher so that you know who key personnel for safeguarding and child protection in the school are and what safeguarding/good practice means in each school. This list is not finite and new recommendations will emerge in time. For example, a few years ago the notions of cyber bullying and inappropriate internet use were not well-known. New forms of technology and communication will come on line in the future and so good practice in this area will vary and change depending on those developments.

- Be vigilant – of the children, of all other adults in school, of what you see/hear, of yourself. As a professional you need to be transparent in your practice and your actions need to be open to scrutiny.

Finally, remember and take heart from the fact that it is not laws and/or statutory guidance or a school's policies or professional registration requirements per se that keep children safe and protected from harm; rather, it is teachers themselves – trainees included – who do this through being informed, understanding legal requirements and undertaking their professional role with a view to good, or when possible, best practice in all of their dealings in school and with children.

Learning Outcomes Review

From your reading and from thinking about the school in which you are currently placed, or in which you most recently undertook a placement, respond to the questions which follow each of the intended learning outcomes, as a means of identifying your knowledge and understanding of the issues covered in the chapter.

- **A range of safeguarding and child protection issues, both generally and with specific reference to children in the primary age phase:**
  - Give examples of the range of emotions and feelings raised by the issue of safeguarding children and child protection.
  - What issues are raised in trying to recognise children who may be or are in need of safeguarding and protection?
  - Which of these are relevant to classroom practice and which are relevant to wider family contexts that involve other professionals?

- **Implications for your professional practice with regard to safeguarding and child protection in meeting national standards for gaining qualified teacher status and maintaining your licence to teach:**
  - What is good practice when working with children in the primary school?

- What boundaries should you be aware of at all times when working in a school?
- In what ways do you try to create and sustain an appropriate classroom climate so that children feel able to trust you? How do you do this, and how effective is it?
- List the ways in which your professionalism is judged through your behaviours and actions in both university and the school and classroom.
- Identify examples from your placement(s) when you demonstrated appropriate professional practice and conduct in your relationships with children.
- In what ways can you help ensure that you do not face allegations of poor practice or child abuse when working in the primary school?

- **Know about the roles of key school and other agencies' personnel related to safeguarding and child protection:**
  - What agencies are involved in safeguarding and protecting children?
  - What should you do if you have a concern about a child and this concern relates to a possible safeguarding and child protection issue?
  - What is your role as a trainee teacher in the safeguarding process?

- **Become aware of key statutory and non-statutory documents related to safeguarding and child protection:**
  - Which governmental acts of parliament and statutory and non-statutory documents guidance underpin and influence your work with children?
  - Give examples from your placement school(s) of how you have made provision to address the 'being safe' theme in Every Child Matters.

Further Reading

Daniel, B., Wassall, S. and Gilligan, R. (2005) *Child Development for Child Care and Protection Workers.* London: Jessica Kingsley Publishers.
This book summarises thinking on child development and applies it directly to practice. Through case studies it examines the impact of child abuse and neglect.

Department for Children, Schools and Families (2009) *The Protection of Children in England: action plan – The Government's response to Lord Laming.* London: TSO.

Department for Children, Schools and Families (2010) *Working Together to Safeguard Children: A guide to interagency working to safeguard and promote the welfare of children.* London: TSO.
This document outlines current governmental policy and procedures for all agencies involved in working with and helping to safeguard children and young people who are in need of, or may be in need of, safeguarding and protection. Of particular relevance is chapter 2 which outlines

the roles and responsibilities of agencies including schools and chapter 9 which discusses lessons from research.

Department for Education and Skills (2003) *Every Child Matters.* London: HM Government.
This document was produced following the government's detailed response to Lord Laming's report into the death of Victoria Climbié, and a report produced by the Social Exclusion Unit on raising the educational attainment of children in care. The five outcomes are presented.

Department for Education and Skills (2004a) *Every Child Matters: Change for Children.* London: HM Government.
This further develops the every child matters agenda. It focuses on working together to ensure better outcomes for children and developing integrated services. Attention is given to the five key outcomes and the 25 specific aims for children derived from those.

Department for Education and Skills (2006) *Safeguarding Children and Safe Recruitment in Education.* Nottingham: DFES Publications.
This document focuses on ensuring everyone involved in education shares the objective to help keep children and young people safe.

Department of Health (2000) *Framework for the Assessment of Children in Need and their Families.* London: TSO.
This document explains the rationale behind the development of a common assessment framework and the roles and responsibilities of those contributing to its use to safeguard and protect children. Specific reference is made to education services and the special education needs code of practice.

HM Government (2006) *What To Do If You're Worried a Child is Being Abused.* London: TSO.
This is non-statutory guidance intended for anyone working with children. Its aim is to assist practitioners to work together to safeguard and promote children's welfare.

HMSO (1989) The Children Act. London: TSO.
Section 3(5) provides useful guidance on what is reasonable in safeguarding and promoting children's welfare.

Kay, J. (2003) *Teacher's Guide to Protecting Children.* London: Continuum.
A practical guide and useful reference to the teacher's role in the child protection system.

Lawrence, A. (2004) *Principles of Child Protection: Management and Practice.* Maidenhead: Open University Press.
This book considers theory and practice in child protection. It is based on research in the UK and Australia and it contains sections on the origins of child protection practice and social constructs of childhood.

Walker, S. and Thurston, C. (2006) *Safeguarding Children and Young People.* Lyme Regis: Russell House Publishing Ltd.
The central theme of this book is the need for professionals (including teachers) to develop

more effective, holistic and integrated practice. The chapter on children and young people at risk provides a good overview of the types and causes of abuse; signs, symptoms and effects of abuse; and risk and resilience factors in children and young people.

Wyse, D. and Hawtin, A. (eds) (2000) *Children: A Multi-Professional Perspective.* London: Arnold.
This book covers key ideas in the study of childhood including theories of development and links to education. Multi-professional approaches and taking account of the views of children are included.

References

Baginsky M. and Macpherson P. (2005) 'Training Teachers to Safeguard Children: Developing a Consistent Approach'. *Child Abuse Review,* 14: 317–330.

HM Government (2006) *Working Together to Safeguard Children: A guide to interagency working to safeguard and promote the welfare of children.* London: TSO. pp.191–199.

Department for Education and Skills (2009) *The Protection of Children in England: action plan – The Government's response to Lord Laming.* London: TSO, p.1.

Department for Education and Skills (2006) *Safeguarding Children and Safe Recruitment in Education.* London: HMSO, p.20.

DfES. Circular 10/98. *The Use or Restraint of Pupils – Force to Control.* at: www.teachernet.gov.uk/childprotection/guidance.htm

NSPCC (2003) *Learning to Protect – A Child Protection Resource Pack for Teacher Training.* www.nspcc.org.uk/inform/TrainingLearningToProtect.asp

DFES (2006) *What to do if you are worried a child is being abused.* Nottingham: DFES Publications.

GTCE (2009) *Code of Conduct and Practice for Registered Teacher.* Birmingham: GTCE.

Ward, H., Brown, R., Westlake, D. and Munro, M.R. (2010) *Infants suffering, or likely to suffer, significant harm: A prospective longitudinal study.* DfE Research Brief DFE-RB053.

9. The School Community: being part of a wider professional environment
Tony Ewens

Learning Outcomes

By the end of this chapter you should have developed and clarified:

- an understanding of the concept of community, and its application to the school as a community;
- an appreciation of the notion of 'community cohesion' and the way in which the work of the teacher can support it;
- an awareness of the importance of understanding pupils' social and cultural contexts when planning their learning;
- your knowledge of the ways in which the local and wider community can offer a rich setting within which learning can take place, and how community members can enhance classroom activities;
- an understanding of key factors in planning safe, effective and stimulating opportunities for pupils to learn outside the classroom and at home.

Standards

Q18 Understand how children and young people develop and that the progress and well-being of learners are affected by a range of developmental, social, religious, ethnic, cultural and linguistic influences.

Q19 Know how to make effective personalised provision for those they teach, including those for whom English is an additional language or who have special educational needs or disabilities, and how to take practical account of diversity and promote equality and inclusion in their teaching.

Q23 Design opportunities for learners to develop their literacy, numeracy and ICT skills.

Q24 Plan homework or other out-of-class work to sustain learners' progress and to extend and consolidate their learning.

Q25 Teach lessons and sequences of lessons across the age and ability range for which they are trained in which they:

(a) use a range of teaching strategies and resources, including e-learning, taking practical account of diversity and promoting equality and inclusion;

(b) build on prior knowledge, develop concepts and processes, enable learners to apply new knowledge, understanding and skills and meet learning objectives;

(c) adapt their language to suit the learners they teach, introducing new ideas and concepts clearly, and using explanations, questions, discussions and plenaries effectively;

(d) demonstrate the ability to manage the learning of individuals, groups and whole classes, modifying their teaching to suit the stage of the lesson.

Q30 Establish a purposeful and safe learning environment conducive to learning and identify opportunities for learners to learn in out-of-school contexts.

Q32 Work as a team member and identify opportunities for working with colleagues, sharing the development of effective practice with them.

What counts as a community?

We use the term 'community' in a number of ways.

Research Focus

Kerridge and Sayers (2006) summarise a sociological analysis of the term under three headings:

- physical proximity, as in neighbourhood;

- civic identity, as in populace;

- collective identity, as in unity, co-operation and shared interest. (p.23)

An example of the first of these might be the people who live in a particular village, or a district within a town or city. Simply by living in that place, a person counts as a member of that community. The second category can be exemplified in terms of language or ethnicity, as in the Chinese, traveller or black community. The third category, 'collective identity', refers to groups based on interests, sporting or cultural for instance. Examples would include the biking, painting or athletics community. By definition, members of these communities are active participants in their chosen activity. The three categories are not mutually exclusive but overlap and intersect. A group such as a religious community could be described in each of the three ways. The Christian community could refer to locality (for instance, those who attend the village church), to civic identity (members of the population who accept the label 'Christian') or to collective identity (people anywhere in the world who participate in Christian practices such as worship and social activities).

Most people belong to a number of different types of community.

What makes a school a community?

The threefold analysis outlined above can help us to understand various ways in which the school is a community. Consider a school in which you have undertaken a placement. It may be the only primary school serving a village or suburb. If so, it may be a subset of the community in its geographical location. However, this situation has become increasingly rare, because the policy of parental preference in choice of schools results in many children travelling from one area to another to attend school. Pupils and staff may have little connection with the immediate hinterland of the school so, despite many schools being named 'Community Primary School', the relationship between local community and local school may be tenuous.

Activity

Discuss with staff at your placement school the nature of the pupil and staff community. How many live locally, and how many travel some distance? Do some local children go out of the area to attend more distant schools? What reasons might parents have for their choices of school? You might also like to discuss with staff members the benefits and drawbacks of working at a school close to where you live.

Your placement school might, however, have a close relationship with one or more particular communities within its town or city, as well as being the most convenient choice for parents living close by. Groups who are spread across quite a wide geographical area may try to enrol their children in a school where they will learn alongside others who share their cultural identity or philosophical outlook. The school can seek to build on such a feature, for example by offering additional services for children and families, both during and outside school hours. Read the following case study, and consider the ways in which St Agatha's School serves and contributes to the various communities with which it interacts. What does the information provided tell you about the kind of community that the school seeks to be?

Case Study – St Agatha's RC Primary School

Jane is beginning a placement at a Roman Catholic primary school in a large town. During her pre-placement visits she begins to develop an insight into the characteristics of the school population. A proportion of the children are from practising Roman Catholic families, some travelling across the town, or from neighbouring villages, to attend. The parish priest leads worship once a week and the parish also provides Catholic instruction for children preparing for confirmation. However, the school also has a strikingly open admissions policy, and Jane notices that a substantial number of children of Asian heritage are on the register. She discovers that they are from an Indian community, Hindu in faith, and that some also travel lengthy distances to the school. The school offers adult education classes in English as an Additional Language, and there is a good uptake for these. Additionally, many children attend the school because it is the closest to their homes. Jane observes that some of these arrive at school very early, because of parents' work patterns. She finds out that the school provides a well-used breakfast club, and that an after-school club is also fully subscribed. Some children are at school from 8 am to 6 pm. The school's facilities are also used by a local sports club, some of whose members assist with activities for children attending the after-school club.

You can readily see the complexity involved in describing St Agatha's RC School as a community. To some extent it serves the geographical neighbourhood in which it is situated. More widely, it serves two distinct communities characterised by a shared faith or a cultural and linguistic identity. Finally, it plays a small part in supporting the area's sporting community because it allows its facilities to be used by members of the general public outside school hours. Jane's findings reveal that St Agatha's supports various communities, for example spiritually and culturally as well as practically.

However, none of this is enough to make St Agatha's a community in its own right. Much will depend on the way in which those who run the school ensure that those who attend it gain a positive experience of belonging to a community. The climate of values, codes of conduct and quality of relationships (sometimes summed up in the term *'school ethos'*) can make the vital difference to whether children know themselves to be valued persons enjoying cordial and productive relationships with adults and children, as they experience life in an organisation driven by clear goals and civilised values.

Activity
Read these groups of standards: Q1 and Q2; Q4, Q5 and Q6; Q18, Q19 and Q20; Q30 and Q31. What do these standards suggest about the type of community that any school should aspire to become?

The role of the school's governing body

As a trainee teacher undertaking a placement at a school, your understanding of the school community and the communities which it serves will derive from your conversations with your classteacher, mentor and other staff, from your interactions with pupils and from reading school documentation. Even at this early stage in your career, however, it is valuable to appreciate the role of the school's governing body as a key link between school and community.

The governors are responsible for the overall strategic direction of the school, and the headteacher exercises day-to-day leadership and management within the framework of policies adopted by the governing body. Staff and parent representatives are elected to serve as governors, the local authority appoints some governors and the headteacher is automatically a governor. In community and foundation schools, these governors appoint a number of other members to act as community governors. Typically, these include representatives of significant cultural groups in the school's locality, employers, members of voluntary organisations and people who bring specific experience or skills, such as finance, construction or human resource management. In Voluntary Aided or Controlled schools, the sponsoring body (normally a church or other religious foundation) appoints governors to sit alongside staff, parent and local authority representatives. You can readily see how a carefully selected governing body can create and sustain good links with the complex array of communities to which the school may relate.

St Agatha's School, which features in the case study above, includes among its governors the secretary of the Hindu Community Centre, a tutor from the local FE College and a Councillor who sits on the sports and cultural affairs committee, as well as the parish priest and other church representatives. These individuals have been of great help in forming links with different community groups, and you will notice how several of the school's activities link with the experience that they bring with them. Jane, the trainee teacher placed at St Agatha's, learned a great deal about the backgrounds of her Asian heritage pupils from the governor who worked at the Hindu Community Centre, because he came into her class as a volunteer for two sessions each week. Through talking with him, Jane was able to develop her knowledge of the social, religious, ethnic, cultural and linguistic influences on this group of pupils, thus collecting valuable evidence in relation to standard Q18.

How can schools promote community cohesion?

A cursory overview of education legislation reveals two main trends. The teaching and assessment of an academic curriculum is one; the other is a concern with building a harmonious, healthy society on a basis of shared values. In England and Wales, the Education Act of 1944 required local education authorities 'to promote the spiritual, moral, mental and physical development of the community' (DES, 1944, preamble), and regarded the education service as contributing part of the 'glue' that held society together. Detailed attention was also paid to ensuring access to good nutrition and medical services at a time when these were major concerns because of scarcities during a world war. Current social priorities are different, reflected for example in a concern to ensure harmony in a society comprising people from a wide range of ethnic, religious, cultural and linguistic backgrounds, but the underlying principle – that the education service should contribute significantly towards holding society together – remains a key element of public policy.

Research Focus

Gardner (2007) explores and illustrates the social categories that influence the development of each child's identity. Warning against a simplistic view of this process, he demonstrates by means of a Venn diagram (p.21) ways in which dominant and subordinate cultural groups in society intersect. Gardner describes ways in which children attending a school whose roll is drawn from a mixture of social, ethnic and linguistic groups may be introduced to perspectives other than those with which they have grown up, while other children may attend schools in monocultural communities with little or no exposure to the range of cultures represented in the country as a whole.

It follows from Gardner's analysis that each school needs to consider its unique circumstances when planning its work in relation to social cohesion. As a trainee teacher on placement you therefore need both an understanding of the concept of social cohesion and ways in which you might contribute to it, and also an appreciation of the particular setting of your school and its children.

Activity

Read the following summary of guidance to schools, extracted from www.teachernet.gov.uk/wholeschool/Communitycohesion/Community_Cohesion_Guidance/

> Broadly, a school's contribution to community cohesion can be grouped under the three following headings:
>
> **1. Teaching, learning and curriculum**
>
> Helping pupils to learn to understand others, to value diversity whilst also promoting shared values.
>
> **2. Equity and excellence**
>
> To ensure equal opportunities for all to succeed at the highest level possible, striving to remove barriers to access and participation.
>
> **3. Engagement and extended services**
>
> To provide reasonable means for children, young people, their friends and families to interact with people from different backgrounds and build positive relations.

Now read the following standards, noting their connection to the duty to promote community cohesion: Q1, Q10, Q18, Q19, Q25I, Q26(b). Identify some of the challenges to you as a trainee teacher on placement in designing the curriculum and sharpening your professional practice in response to these demanding objectives.

It is important to guard against thinking that, solely because a school draws its pupils from a range of cultures so that children are being taught together, this will automatically lead to a more cohesive community. After all, the children might simply form monocultural groups in the classroom and playground and remain largely unaware of, uninterested in, and even hostile to the backgrounds of their classmates. School staff members have to take active measures to ensure that the guidance outlined above leads to the desired outcomes.

Equally to be avoided is a view that children educated in a largely monocultural environment are necessarily ignorant about wider society. If schools in such areas make full use of visual media, teach a broad and balanced RE scheme, introduce pupils to diversity through literature and the arts and draw on news stories from around the world, children can develop positive attitudes and sound knowledge regarding social diversity.

It is sometimes claimed that the existence of faith schools impedes the achievement of community cohesion. While it can be the case that school admissions policies based on parental religious practice result in children being divided on faith lines among different schools, there are alternative scenarios. Some faith-based schools, like St Agatha's in the earlier case study, actively seek to recruit pupils from a range of different belief communities. Proponents of faith schools also make the point that the major religions teach about the value and worth of all people, and thus promote social cohesion through the beliefs and practices of their faith communities and schools. You will need to think carefully about your own position with regard to this topical debate.

Whatever the type and location of the school, its policies and practice with regard to curriculum design, targets for achievement and attainment, and extended services are expected to lead to positive, identifiable outcomes in terms of community cohesion.

The following case study outlines a project devised by two trainee teachers, Peter and Sarah, who had been placed in very different schools in the same county. Their work demonstrates the value of partnerships among schools and other agencies in creating sustainable opportunities to develop community cohesion.

Case Study: Peter and Sarah on final placement

For a final placement, Peter was placed in an urban school in a city with a mixed population. The majority British–English community was complemented by a substantial British–Pakistani group. At Peter's school, almost 95% of the children were drawn from the latter. The school had noticed that the population near the school comprised approximately equal numbers of British–English and British–Pakistani households. However, many British–English children travelled away from the area to attend schools elsewhere in the city, and conversely some British–Pakistani children on the register actually lived a considerable distance from the school. The headteacher had concluded that decisive action was needed to broaden the pupils' experience of other cultural groups, and she was hoping that Peter's addition to the staff team for a term could help towards this.

Sarah, meanwhile, had been placed in a Church of England school in a small village twenty miles away. All the pupils were British–English and this reflected the local populace. The school had examined its work in promoting social cohesion. The headteacher was pleased with the impact of changes to the curriculum, which had been made in the interests of encouraging greater awareness of diversity and promoting positive attitudes towards differences in ethnicity, religion and culture. However, he wanted the children to meet people from different groups, as well as learning about them in the classroom. Sarah offered to help with this.

Through the on-line discussion board linked to the university's Virtual Learning Environment Peter and Sarah became aware of their respective schools' plans, and decided to work together. With the support of both heads they arranged an informal 'twinning' between their two classes. Initially, letters were exchanged, and this led to a substantial ICT project enabling children and staff to share

→

information and respond to one another's questions. The project culminated in an exchange of visits, each class experiencing a day in the life of the other school and taking it in turn to host their visitors. Several parents and governors from the two schools accompanied the visits.

Evaluation of the project revealed that, in addition to realising the key intention that the children should meet people from different ethnic, religious and cultural backgrounds, the visits had highlighted differences between urban and rural settings. Indeed, many of the children had been more surprised by the environmental context of the other school than by differences of ethnicity or culture. The schools have resolved to build upon this promising beginning.

A key point arising from the work done by Peter and Sarah is that, while you must be clear about the objectives of collaborative work between schools, you must also be ready to adapt the project in the light of your findings from ongoing monitoring. Initially, Peter and Sarah thought that the opportunity to mix with children from a very different school was the main vehicle for promoting community cohesion. However, they came to appreciate that the children actually gained greater knowledge of each other when they worked in mixed groups on tasks that were only incidentally related to their personal and social education. This judgement shows clearly that you should not see your teaching of the subject-led formal curriculum as being separate from your work in helping children with the formation of their beliefs, values and attitudes. Both aspects of education are most effectively pursued when planned and taught in an integrated manner.

Activity

Read the following extract from Ofsted's Evaluation Schedule for Schools, the document which forms the basis of inspections under the current methodology.

The effectiveness with which the school promotes community cohesion. Inspectors should evaluate:

- the extent to which the school has developed an understanding of the religious, ethnic and socio-economic characteristics of its community in a local, national and global context;
- the extent to which the school has taken an appropriate set of planned actions based on an analysis of its context and is evaluating the impact of its work;
- the extent to which the school's actions have a positive impact on community cohesion within the school and beyond. (Ofsted, 2011, p.52)

Consider the case study (above) of Peter and Sarah's placement. To what extent does the work they did provide evidence of the success of their respective schools in promoting community cohesion when measured against these statements from Ofsted?

Learning about belonging to a community

'The most important single factor influencing learning is what the learner already knows. Ascertain this and teach him accordingly' (Ausubel et al., 1967, p.vi). David Ausubel's advice applies not only to children's learning of traditional subjects but also to how they can most effectively learn about their relationships to and within the communities to which they belong. You will rightly be expected to apply your knowledge of techniques in assessment for learning (AfL) to identify pupils' prior knowledge in each subject, and to use your findings as the basis for planning lessons in which the concepts and activities are appropriately matched to children's developmental needs as learners. The same processes and procedures apply to personal and social learning, by which I mean learning about how individuals relate to groups.

When you start working at a different school or with a new class you should consequently find out as much as you can about the social and cultural settings from which the children are drawn. Teachers need to know about the preconceptions and expectations that children bring with them to school, which reflect the beliefs and values of their parents and carers. Initially, you will probably be able to identify general data about ethnicity, socio-economic circumstances, language, religion and culture. Gradually, you will be able to sharpen this information as you get to know individual children's family circumstances, interests and strengths, and the process is further refined when you meet parents and carers at open evenings and informal school events. You may think that this approach appears to be inappropriately intrusive on your part, but if you take Ausubel's advice seriously you will recognise the importance of gaining a rounded view of each child. Remember, then, the crucial need to maintain strict professional confidentiality regarding sensitive personal information. You must also monitor your own reactions to the contextual information about the class that you acquire. In particular, in the light of standard Q1, it is crucial that you do not allow your high expectations of children to be affected by any personal views and prejudices that you may hold about any sector of society. To give just one example, it is a misconception to assume that pupils for whom English is not the first language are less likely to perform well; studies (e.g. Baker, 2006) have shown bilingualism to be advantageous to learning in the medium to long term.

Having built, and checked the accuracy of, a picture of the groups from which your pupils are drawn, you should then analyse your data and devise ways of extending the children's knowledge of people from other backgrounds, to enhance and enrich their experience of diversity. This will probably involve a mixture of face-to-face contact, as in the earlier case study involving Peter and Sarah, and classroom learning using a variety of media.

Case Study: Children learning about community

The following table offers brief outlines of activities undertaken by a number of teachers. Notice how they are based on reflective analysis by teachers of their

→

observations, and also that many of the ideas are quite simple in conception and implementation. Can you identify ways in which they respond to Ausubel's advice to identify the stage that pupils have reached in their learning?

Staff at a large primary school noticed that pupils rarely interacted with children from other age groups. They experimented with mixed age groupings for drama, and observed that much of the role-play that occurred mirrored typical scenarios involving relationships among siblings. The children developed their abilities to explain how interactions between children of different ages could succeed or fail. It was decided do extend the experiment, despite timetabling difficulties, and to look for other opportunities for mixed-age learning.

At a small village school teachers noticed that most children had little regular contact with elderly people, and that very few had grandparents living nearby. The head spoke to the local pensioners' association, whose members started attending lunch at the school once a week. Mixed tables of children and pensioners were arranged. Initially, topics for conversation were suggested by the teachers, but this soon became unnecessary. The children gained much knowledge about their village from the pensioners, and their oral English, powers of concentration and table manners also benefited.

The head of an all-British–English primary school wanted to extend the children's knowledge and experience of ethnic diversity. He booked a speaker from the Commonwealth Institute to give a presentation about India, its geography, culture and customs to the Key Stage 2 pupils. He invited a school from another district, some of whose pupils were British–Indian, to attend the occasion. The school meals contractor provided a selection of Indian food for lunch. The visit provided a stimulus for a substantial project about India at both schools, and the families of the British – Indian pupils were able to help with information in response to questions from pupils and staff at both schools. The Y6 teacher at the visiting school commented that the event had led to an interesting debate in her class about the extent to which children felt themselves to be British and/or Indian.

At a rural church school the head discussed with the chair of governors (the parish priest) her concern that the children had almost no knowledge of religious diversity. She had been disturbed by negative comments made by one child about Muslims. It was agreed to build visits to places of worship into the school's RE scheme, including a mosque and a synagogue as well as three different Christian denominations. At each place of worship the children explored the building and formulated questions which were answered for them by members of the respective congregations. The teachers evaluated this learning approach very positively. They found that basing the content on children's queries helped to match it to their levels of understanding, whereas presentations by members of the religious communities might have been inappropriately pitched.

→

Staff members at a large urban school with a very mixed catchment were concerned about tensions in relationships among children from different communities. In addition to providing direct guidance about conduct during school assemblies, and arranging tighter monitoring of break times, the head decided to tackle the issue through the curriculum. As part of the school's 'SEAL' (Social and Emotional Aspects of Learning) work, children in one year group took part in structured role play involving encounters between people from different groups. Once children had grown accustomed to this way of working, they began to show insight into the links between the fictional situations explored and their own relationships at school. Encouraged by their initial evaluation of this approach, the staff decided to extend it to other year groups.

The examples presented in this case study share the common characteristic that, in each case, teachers were careful to consider the developmental stage that pupils have reached in their learning. The starting point for each piece of work was thorough analysis by staff members of incidents and situations that they have noticed in their schools. They then used their knowledge of the children, their understanding of teaching methods and their skills in tailoring the curriculum to their pupils' needs in order to help the children to progress. You will frequently have encountered this model of working in connection with English, mathematics and other subjects, and you can feel confident that the same approach is effective in promoting children's learning about what it means to live in a diverse society and to belong to a community.

You will also notice from these instances the importance of teachers and other staff members working together. In each case, identification of the issues needing to be addressed came from staff discussion, and the success of the actions taken resulted to a large extent from collaborative working by teaching and support staff, with the approval of the governing body in specific cases. When you analyse what happened at the different schools, it becomes evident that staff members at each school were in agreement about the values and attitudes that they wished to foster in their pupils. This raises the issue, discussed in Chapter 7, as to whether teachers and others who work in schools are required to subscribe to specific sets of beliefs and values as representing the basis for an ideal society.

The topics under consideration here point to the fact that during your placement you will be part of the adult community at the school, not just an individual teacher working with one class. As a member (albeit temporarily) of the staff room, you can learn a great deal from your colleagues' conversations about the local area and the circumstances of the children who attend the school. You can also extend your knowledge of the children in your class by talking with other staff members who have worked with them and their families previously. The range of perspectives that you will encounter is in itself an eloquent illustration of what it means for a school to operate as a community.

Local and wider communities: their contributions to learning

A school's curriculum can be significantly enhanced if it incorporates ways of using the communities which it serves, or among which it is placed, within the children's regular programme of learning. People, buildings and activities situated close to the school can provide opportunities for learning at first hand about the businesses and services that help society to function as well as about the locality's historical, religious and cultural infrastructure. An emphasis on the types of employment available in a district is a particularly helpful curriculum focus, as it can help children to appreciate how some of what they learn at school relates very closely to knowledge and skills required in different types of work. As you will know, one strand of the Every Child Matters (ECM) strategy referred to helping children towards achieving economic well-being. Since the early 1980s, when it was termed Economic and Industrial Understanding, introducing primary age children to the world of work has been a vital aspect of the curriculum, even if it later tended to be obscured by the subject-driven National Curriculum. ECM revitalises the topic, and the community around the school can be a helpful resource.

The following case studies exemplify some of the potential of working in this way. Can you identify ways in which the teachers concerned have drawn upon their local communities in order to enrich the curriculum?

Case Study: Curriculum and community

- Children at a small rural school regularly walked to the top of a hill overlooking the village. They made sketch maps of the locality then, back at school, produced a large scale map of the village. They identified key buildings and also studied land use. Visits to a farm, the post office, the pub and the church enabled them to interview members of the community about people's work and its value to the community. They also studied how other services were provided for local residents (doctor, vet, police, public transport, mobile library, secondary education). A group of older residents visited the school and were questioned about ways in which the village had changed over the past fifty years.

- A Key Stage 2 teacher from a school in a market town acquired detailed statistics from the school's liaison police officer about road traffic accidents on the busy main road that passed the school. The class analysed the data, producing charts and graphs to show the frequency of different types of accident, and highlighting accident blackspots and the most hazardous times of day, days of the week and months of the year. The local police used the children's work as the basis of a road safety campaign.

$\rightarrow$

- Children from a reception class visited a sub-post office. The class teacher invited the sub-postmistress to visit the school and together they helped the children to set up a post office counter in the classroom. Subsequently the children designed, produced, wrote and sent postcards to other members of the school community, bought and sold 'stamps' at the counter and arranged a delivery system around the school.

These examples raise several points about the link between curriculum and community. First and foremost, a community cannot be divorced from its physical setting. An influential curriculum planning document on environmental education (DES, 1986) emphasised the interaction between people and places. It illustrated how the physical and built environment influences human activity and conversely how human aspirations and values help to shape what is built and how land is used. You need to consider this fundamental factor when planning units of work around the community.

Secondly, there is a balance to be achieved between taking children out of school to visit people and places in the community and inviting community members to come to the school to work with the children. The first of these is obviously easy to accomplish when you are dealing with the community as a particular geographical locality. However, as we saw earlier in this chapter, a community is not necessarily contained within neat physical boundaries. The Chinese community, for example, may be spread across a wide geographical area, and this might mean that visitors to school would be the best approach. Either way there are vital issues to be addressed to ensure the children's safety and welfare, whether you are planning an educational visit or inviting community representatives to school. You need to be fully aware of your placement school's policies and procedures and ensure that you comply with them.

If you plan to take children out of school you should, after discussion with your class teacher and mentor, consult the school's Educational Visits Coordinator. This colleague will advise and support you regarding the permissions to be obtained and the risk assessments to be undertaken prior to the visit. There will also be a need to ensure that an appropriate number of adults will accompany the visit, and that they meet the school's requirements regarding vetting volunteers. It is important not to allow these daunting procedures to deter you from undertaking out of school learning with your class. The first hand experiences gained during a well-planned and organised visit can stimulate interest in a topic that continues back at school long after the event itself.

If visitors are being invited to school, you will equally have to ensure that you have followed the school's procedures. You should follow school policy on asking whether visitors must hold a recent CRB clearance and check that the children are at all times being supervised by a member of the school staff. You must also brief your visitor about what you want them to do while they are with you. Remembering that not all adults are skilled at matching their input to the needs of primary age children, you may find it valuable to base the session on questions that the children have previously devised, rather than on a presentation planned and delivered by the visitor.

The value of linking the curriculum to communities is not limited to those which are close to the school. Once children have formed a set of concepts about what communities are, and what it means to belong to them, through a study of the immediate locality, they are in possession of a powerful model for understanding distant communities as well. You can therefore build on the knowledge gained from studying the school's locality by planning a topic about a distant place, using a 'compare and contrast' approach.

Finally, and with a further reference to Ausubel's thinking about the crucial importance of beginning with what the learner already knows, you may like to think about the links between the school and the community as represented by homework. Each child's closest community is the home and the close circle of family and friends. Homework tasks which are carefully thought out can provide children with an opportunity to learn from and alongside other family members, and this process can result in narrowing the gap between home and school. Ideas presented in this chapter should provide you with effective starting points for activities to be undertaken at home.

Learning Outcomes Review

Thinking about the school in which you are working or have recently worked, respond to the prompts after each intended learning outcome, to identify your knowledge and understanding of the issues covered in the chapter.

- **An understanding of the concept of community, and its application to the school as a community:**
  - What communities are represented among the children in your class?
  - Which of these are local to the school, and which more distant or dispersed?
  - What features of the school's organisation and day-to-day operation provide children with experience of what it means to belong to a community?
  - What sort of community do you try to create and sustain in your classroom? How do you do this, and how effective is it?

- **An appreciation of the notion of 'community cohesion' and the way in which the work of the teacher can support it:**
  - Identify examples of times during your placement when you contributed to the three aspects of community cohesion identified by OFSTED:
  Teaching, learning and curriculum
  Helping pupils to learn to understand others, to value diversity whilst also promoting shared values.
  Equity and excellence
  To ensure equal opportunities for all to succeed at the highest level possible, striving to remove barriers to access and participation.

Engagement and extended services
To provide reasonable means for children, young people, their friends and families to interact with people from different backgrounds and build positive relations.

- **An awareness of the importance of understanding pupils' social and cultural contexts when planning their learning:**
  - Give a couple of examples of how you have adapted your planning and teaching to take account of the experiences that pupils bring with them from their lives outside school. How have you used this approach to affirm and enrich children's understanding of belonging to communities?

- **Your knowledge of the ways in which the local and wider community can offer a rich setting within which learning can take place, and how community members can enhance classroom activities:**
  - Identify one or two instances in which you have drawn upon the local environment of people and places to enhance children's learning.

- **An understanding of key factors in planning safe, effective and stimulating opportunities for pupils to learn outside the classroom and at home:**
  - In what ways did your class experience learning outside the classroom, and how did you ensure that these occasions were both stimulating and safe?
  - Identify ways in which you designed tasks to be done at home which could foster dialogue and cooperation between children and their families?

Further Reading

Whalley's book asserts that those working in schools need to be proactive in engaging parents and carers as partners in helping children to learn. Curtis and Pettigrew explore, from a variety of perspectives, the relationship between learning and the ever-changing nature of culture.

Whalley, M. (ed) (2007) *Involving parents in their children's learning*. London: Paul Chapman Publishing.

Curtis, W. and Pettigrew, A. (2009) *Learning in contemporary culture (Perspectives in Education Studies series)*. Exeter: Learning Matters.

References

Ausubel, D., Novak, J. and Hanesian, H. (1978) *Educational Psychology: A Cognitive View* (2nd edn) New York: Holt, Rinehart & Winston.

Baker, C. (2006) *Foundations of Bilingual Education and Bilingualism* (4th edn). Clevedon: Multilingual Matters.

DES (1944) *The Education Act.* London: HMSO.

DES (1986) *Environmental Education from 5 to 16: Curriculum Matters Series.* London: HMSO.

Gardner, P. (2007) 'Living and learning in different communities: cross-cultural comparisons' in Zwozdiak-Myers, P. (ed) *Childhood and Youth Studies.* Exeter: Learning Matters.

Kerridge, V. and Sayers, R. (2006) 'Community education: innovation and active intervention' in Sharp, J. et al. (2006) *Education Studies: An Issues-based Approach.* Exeter: Learning Matters.

Ofsted (2011) *The Evaluation Schedule for Schools.* London: Ofsted.

www.teachernet.gov.uk/wholeschool/Communitycohesion/Community_Cohesion_Guidance/ accessed 3/10/10

10. Personal professional development
Sandra Eady

Learning Outcomes
....

By the end of this chapter you will have considered:
- the role of Personal Professional Development (PPD) through QTS standards to Core standards;
- what actually counts as PPD;
- how PPD works in the Induction year;
- what is meant by Master's in Teaching and Learning and other Master's routes;
- about the possibilities of working at Master's level as an ITT trainee teacher;
- ways to juggle being a busy teacher/NQT with further study.

Standards
Q7 (a) Reflect on and improve their practice, and take responsibility for identifying and meeting their developing professional needs.
Q7 (b) Identify priorities for their early professional development in the context of induction.
Q8 Have a creative and constructively critical approach towards innovation, being prepared to adapt their practice where benefits and improvements are identified.
Q9 Act upon advice and feedback and be open to coaching and mentoring.
Q29 Evaluate the impact of their teaching on the progress of all learners, and modify their planning and classroom practice where necessary.

The role of personal professional development

One of the most effective ways to support children's learning and development is by actively engaging in Personal Professional Development (PPD) right from the beginning of your teaching career. There is now a great deal of choice and support offered and the professional standards can be a useful way to think about and guide your PPD choices. They can help you review your professional practice, identify further professional development needs and ultimately inform your future career choice.

The framework for professional standards came into operation in September 2007. It aimed to bring coherence to the professional and occupational standards for the whole school workforce.

The professional standards cover the following career stages:

- Q – qualified teacher status;
- C – core standards for main scale teachers who have successfully completed their induction year;
- P – post-threshold teachers on the upper pay scale;
- E – excellent teachers;
- A – advanced skills teachers.

The standards are arranged in three inter-related sections and show clearly what is expected at each career stage in terms of:

- professional attributes;
- professional knowledge and understanding;
- professional skills.

Each set of standards builds on the previous so that a teacher being considered for 'threshold' would need to have satisfied the threshold standards and have met the core standards. A teacher aspiring to become an 'advanced skills teacher' would need to satisfy the standards specific to that status as well as meeting the preceding standards, although they can apply for an AST post before going through the threshold. The full set of standards can be downloaded at www.tda.gov.uk/teachers/professionalstandards/standards.aspx

The professional standards form part of a wider framework of standards for the whole school workforce. This includes the occupational standards for teaching/classroom assistants and professional standards for higher level teaching assistants. Finally, there are also national standards for head teachers. These standards recognise the key role head teachers play in engaging in the development and delivery of government policy and in raising and maintaining levels or attainment in schools in order to meet the needs of every child.

What counts as personal professional development?

Personal professional development (PPD) is about engaging with new or challenging ideas about a specific aspect of your practice. It is about reflecting on this in view of what you currently do and deciding on ways to change your practice in order to adopt and embed the new ideas/ways of working. It may also be helpful to consider PPD as a two way process. Not only does there need to be a stimulus or input from another person, event, book, but most importantly *you* also need to actively engage and be open to listening and ready to reflect on advice, the activity, or the input in question. Thus, if you are to find PPD an effective and worthwhile activity, you need to consider how you might make changes to what you are currently doing in the classroom in order to enhance children's learning. Remember, PPD is not something that is 'done *to* you' but is something that is 'done *by* you' ultimately to support children's learning and development.

Continuing professional development (CPD) has a similar definition and is often seen as meaning the same as PPD. However, whilst PPD focuses purely on your developmental needs in relation to the children learning; CPD tends to include a broader collective view of professional development that locates it more in a national or local policy context where CPD priorities are primarily based on the school's development priorities which may or may not be the same as yours.

The TDA (www.tda.gov.uk/teacher/developing-career/professional-development.aspx) identified three different ways that PPD could take place. These are by using:

- within-school expertise (e.g. induction, coaching, mentoring, lesson observation);
- across-school networks (these could be face-to-face meetings or virtual networks organised through Local Authorities HEIs or school networks);
- other external expertise (e.g. external courses or funded study external speakers, consultants, or further study).

CPD as reflective practice

Thinking about CPD in terms of critical reflection on your classroom practice is a powerful way of evaluating how you are supporting children's learning and whether your approaches to teaching are making a difference. The TDA defines this kind of 'CPD as a reflective activity designed to improve an individuals' attributes, knowledge and understanding and skills'. It supports individual needs and improves professional practice. This definition of CPD would suggest that a whole range of both formal and informal activities engaged in could be defined as CPD as long as they involve reflection on practice. Further discussion of the value of reflection on and in action can be found in Chapter 7.

The case study below illustrates how often informal conversations in the staff room may be just as effective in getting you to reflect and develop a deeper understanding of what you are trying to achieve than actually attending (an often costly) course run by an external provider.

Case Study: Informal conversations as PPD

Over lunch time break Lauren was having an informal chat to a fellow teacher about some children in her Year 2 class who were constantly calling out whenever she asked a question, despite the fact that she had told them on several occasions that they should put their hands up and wait to be asked. Her colleague agreed this was also a problem she had faced until she had been introduced to a questioning strategy whilst studying for a Master's degree. The strategy aimed to get all children involved in answering class questions by putting each child's name on a 'lolly' stick and then randomly selecting one of these when a question was asked. This removed the need for anyone in the class to raise their hands. Based on this informal discussion Lauren decided to use this strategy with her class. Later she also extended the lolly stick idea by using it as a way of randomly selecting 'talk partners' or mixed working groups or deciding seating arrangements.

Lauren's case study is a typical example of how a chance conversation can lead reflection and to changes in classroom practice. However, formalised PPD also has a role in helping you develop your knowledge and expertise in supporting children's learning and this may range from observing a more experienced teacher in your school and discussing this with a mentor, to attending a local conference run by your local authority on a specific topic.

Research Focus

A systematic review of research by Cordingley et al. (EPPI, 2005a and 2005b) recommended that teachers should be involved in identifying their own PPD focus, and whilst PPD can involve the use of external expertise, it should also involve:

- reflection, observation and feedback from peers;
- experimentation in applying new skills in classroom teaching over a sustained period of time;
- an emphasis on peer support.

In fact the PPD that has the greatest impact on classroom practice and is more likely to become embedded and sustained over time is long term and is collaborative in nature. Such PPD can have a positive impact on teachers' attitudes, knowledge and skills and improve children's learning (Cordingley et al., 2005a and 2005b).

PPD related to career stages

Another way to think about your PPD is in relation to what is a priority to you at this point in your career. In this sense the professional standards can be a useful way to gauge your professional needs and prioritise PPD related to your career stage. For example, early on in your career, PPD might be focused on classroom behaviour or matching teaching activities to children's abilities in your class. This type of CPD may then provide a sound basis for your next career stage or role development which may be more related to middle management or leadership.

Research Focus

In a national survey of PPD, Pedder et al. (2009) found that the types of PPD activities in which teachers spent the most time varied but tended to have an emphasis on supporting the needs of different pupil groups, teaching and learning, evaluating learning and approaches to assessment and curriculum. They also found that teachers with one to two years of experience are more likely to participate in CPD with an emphasis on behaviour management and deepening their pedagogical knowledge than their colleagues with more years of experience.

$\rightarrow$

Pedder et al.'s (2009) survey showed that in general PPD tended to involve the following processes:

- a clear focus on pupil learning;
- observation and feedback;
- coaching and mentoring;
- collaborative working;
- opportunities for practice, research and reflective practice;
- involving teachers in needs identification;
- modelling of preferred practice (e.g. active learning), both in classrooms and in adult learning situations.

Note that for Pedder et al. (2009) effective PPD is likely to be rooted in the professional knowledge base of teaching and learning, with a clear focus on children's learning.

Accredited versus non-accredited PPD

It is also important to understand that some forms of professional development you might undertake will be 'non-accredited'; whilst other forms will be seen as 'accredited' PPD.

Much PPD is 'non-accredited'. This means it is useful in itself to help improve children's learning by providing you with updates on current government initiatives, such as literacy, the teaching of reading, or using ICT to enhance children's learning. It is not benchmarked against any specific Quality Assurance criteria and whilst you may have gained a better understanding of a particular aspect of your teaching, does not necessarily provide you with any recognised or greater expertise in the area. Some teachers feel that if they are investing their time and energies in attending professional development they want some credit and recognition for doing so.

Accredited PPD courses are designed to improve your expertise and will provide you with a nationally recognised qualification in the area which might be more worthwhile, not only in the way you support children's learning but also in terms of progressing your career. Master's qualifications are usually longer term PPD options which will involve further study, reading, reflection and often opportunities to meet with other teachers who are on the same course. However, they can be costly in terms of finance and time. Nevertheless, they are usually recognised as good value for money as they provide greater opportunities to deepen your knowledge and develop your practice in a particular aspect of teaching over time.

PPD as developing an expertise – subject centres, longer-term accredited PPD

Becoming a member of a subject association is another good way of engaging in PPD as many subject associations have face to face local meetings, professional magazines and run annual conferences which often host a range of workshops on specific aspects of teaching and learning for a range of age phases. For example, Association of Science Education (ASE), UK Literacy

Association (UKLA), the Historical Association, National Association of Music Educators (NAME) and many more. Subject specific CPD resources and opportunities are also available on the TDA website www.tda.gov.uk/teacher/developing-career/professional-development.aspx which allow flexible learning and develop opportunities. These resources are often linked to subject association pages which provide another source of PPD courses and opportunities specific to a subject area. The case study below illustrates how active involvement with a subject association can enhance not only individual professional learning but also provide support for others in your school.

Case Study: Networking as CPD

Mohammed was keen to become a science coordinator and on the advice of his headteacher, became a member of the ASE and started to attend local events. He soon began to meet other science coordinators and learn how science was organised and supported in their schools. At an annual ASE conference Mohammed attended a workshop session on the use of 'concept cartoons' (Naylor and Keogh, 2000). He became excited by the potential for supporting children's conceptual understanding by getting children to set up their own investigations and test out their existing ideas. He could also see opportunities not only for promoting pupil discussion and assessing understanding but also for providing in-service training for colleagues within his school. His head teacher agreed that the school should purchase the book so that he could try out some of the ideas in his classroom with the aim of running a staff meeting for other colleagues the following term.

Research Focus

Ofsted (HMI, 2006) found CPD to be most effective in the schools where the senior managers fully understood the connections between CPD and its potential for raising standards, and gave it a central role in planning for improvement. However, they also identified a number of concerns. In the surveys of National Curriculum subjects, inspectors found that arrangements for CPD in the subject they were inspecting were inadequate in about one third of the primary schools. This did not mean that the school's arrangements for CPD were unsatisfactory but, usually, that there had been little or no recent professional development in the subject being inspected. The lack of such professional development was due partly to the schools' drive to improve literacy and numeracy and partly to a lack of specialist subject expertise, which meant that managers were failing to pick up important subject-related issues. For example, there was often a tension between policy-driven priorities and school-specific priorities (HMI, 2006).

School focused CPD versus individual or personal focused PPD

Whilst this chapter focuses on individual professional development, it is recognised that there is often an overlap between school and individual CPD needs and sometimes there is a clear relationship between the two. Theoretically both are concerned with supporting and the enhancement of children's development. However, there can also be a tension with individual needs not always fitting with school priorities. Thus, whilst it might seem important for you to develop behaviour management strategies with some of the children in your class, the school may have as its focus improving the standard of written work for boys. When being on placement you may experience working towards an objective on the school development plan which may be different to your own development needs.

Bolam and Weindling (2006) found there was a fairly common perception among teachers that issues for whole-school improvement are often prioritised at the expense of PPD needs. Furthermore, Pedder et al., (2009) found that some of the reasons why schools have difficulty in achieving a balance of school and individual teacher CPD needs may be due to a school being placed in special measures, where the CPD programme is structured exclusively around school-wide targets. Primary school teachers and teachers in schools with low achievement levels had a narrower range of CPD opportunities offered to them. In primary schools these were frequently focused on improving children's numeracy and literacy skills.

Therefore, it is worthwhile thinking about the kinds of CPD you would like access to and for what purpose. Already we have mentioned that it is important to let your professional development be driven primarily by the children's needs. The databases set up by the TDA and subject associations allow teachers to search for a wide range of CPD opportunities offered by a range of providers. You can search or browse the databases to find relevant opportunities that meet your requirements. However, it is important to make the key priority of your professional development focused on supporting your children and their specific needs.

Activity

Bubb and Earley (2007, pp.55–57) provide a useful list of professional development activities under the headings of 'self study', 'observing other practitioners', 'extending professional experience' and 'working with pupils'. You might find pages 55–57 a helpful prompt when completing the Transition Point 1 task in your Career Entry and Development Profile (CEDP). The key questions are reproduced below. Read the section and identify which ones might be appropriate for you as you move into your Induction year. Set out the professional development need and outline the type of CPD that would help you achieve it. Be as specific as possible.

1. At this stage, which aspect(s) of teaching do you find most interesting and rewarding?
2. As you approach the award of QTS, what do you consider to be your main strengths and achievements as a teacher?
3. In which aspects of teaching would you value further experience in the future?

> 4. As you look ahead to your career in teaching, you may be thinking about your longer term professional aspirations and goals. Do you have any thoughts at this stage about how you would like to see your career develop?

As you move towards the end of your ITT programme or if you are about to start your Induction year, think about PPD in terms of the specific ways you can support children's learning within the context of your classroom practice. Remember that the central reason for all CPD is to improve children's learning. The targets identified in your career entry profile are a useful starting point for the short term. Alternatively, you may also consider your PPD in terms of the broader long term picture of how you see your career in teaching developing in terms of supporting other colleagues to develop effective and innovative ways of supporting children's learning or teaching a subject or age phase. Whilst PPD is likely to focus on generic curriculum teaching, learning and assessment, try not to overlook the subject knowledge development and support that can be provided through subject associations.

PPD in your induction year

Induction has been a feature for all NQTs who gain qualified teacher status (QTS) since May 1999 and wish to work in maintained and non-maintained schools in England. Its purpose has been to ensure that all new teachers are prepared for the challenges they might face in the classroom and are able to reach a uniformly high standard in their teaching. As an NQT, the induction programme will enable you to build on strengths and development needs identified at the end of your initial teacher training, in order to set the pace and direction for your professional development (Totterdell et al., 2008).

Your induction year is a three-term period of assessment which helps to ensure that your teaching career is built on a firm foundation. It consists of two main elements:

- an assessment against the core professional standards for teachers;
- a personalised programme of guidance and support providing you with the tools to be a successful teacher.

Towards the end of each term you will meet with your induction tutor or head teacher for a formal assessment. After the first two meetings they will make a report to the local authority or independent schools council teacher induction panel recording your progress to meeting the core professional standards. After the assessment in the third term they will make a recommendation about whether you have met the requirements for successfully completing the induction period. This will then be confirmed to you in writing.

As an NQT in England you can expect the following support in your induction year:

- a 10% reduction in your teaching timetable to give you time to develop your teaching skills away from the classroom. This is in addition to your 10 per cent planning preparation and assessment (PPA) time;

- support from an induction tutor;
- regular reviews of your progress;
- formal discussions at the end of each term with your tutor and or head teacher.

The NQT year is an excellent opportunity for you to:

- work alongside others and becoming involved in planning with your school;
- observe more experienced colleagues;
- visit schools and settings beyond your work place;
- participate in more formal training events and courses;
- meet with your induction tutor to consider your progress and development.

As previously suggested PPD is about you actively engaging and reflecting with the issues arising out of your classroom practice in order to enhance children's learning. Thus, just doing the above will not prove beneficial unless you engage in meaningful reflection and consider the implications for your practice and how your PPD is helping you to progress against the core standards.

Your induction tutor can help support this process by setting aside time for you both to reflect on specific issues relating to your classroom practice. You could also include discussion and reflection on practice you have seen when observing a colleague teach. Similarly, you might discuss a recent course or training session in terms of the implications for children's learning in your classroom.

Your induction tutor is also likely to observe you teach and provide constructive feedback on specific aspects of your lessons at least once every half term. Following each observation your induction tutor will review with you your progress against your objectives and any PPD or wider CPD you have engaged in and revise this with you. It is a good idea for you to set the agenda or suggest the focus of discussion with your induction tutor so that you can guide the discussion.

Research Focus

Research by Totterdell et al. (2004, 2008) report that evaluations of the induction year suggest it is highly effective in developing classroom practice and increasing retention if there is careful consideration and support given to the novice teacher and experienced mentor in terms of time for meeting and collaborative planning. This effectiveness could be further capitalised on if the induction tutor has the appropriate experience of teaching age/phase as the NQT and support is extended over the first three years of teaching.

You can also learn informally from other professional relationships in school. Consider the following points.

- Planning with another teacher who takes the same year/age group as you or from other subject leaders in school such as a Mathematics Specialist Teacher, the SENCo, or experienced teaching assistants.

- Looking at how other classrooms are organised can help you informally learn about how to display children's work or organise workspace.

- Talking to colleagues who have just been on a specific professional development course or who have just been teaching a long time can help you evaluate your current ways of approaching teaching.

- Talking to parents could also be a learning experience and provide alternative perspectives about how a child learns or behaves.

- Using education internet sites, or subject associations and government websites can again provide many ideas for lessons and enable you to see what recent research says about specific aspects of teaching that might be relevant to your practice.

The key thing is that you feel in control of your own PPD and are driving it in the direction you want it to go. However, when searching for and applying for teaching posts you need to consider the school's agenda for CPD.

The Master's in Teaching and Learning (MTL) and other Master's routes

Research Focus

Totterdell et al. (2008) recommend there was a need 'to start thinking about early professional development that includes the first three years of teaching (or the first five years inclusive of initial training), with certification and accreditation for registered and/or chartered status being part of this process' (Totterdell et al., 2008).

The Master's in Teaching and Learning (MTL)

The TDA describe the MTL as a practice-based Master's programme which has been designed to help you develop knowledge and skills to make a real impact in the classroom. The structure of the MTL is designed to focus on early professional development on classroom practice. The case study below outlines how one region in England has taken this forward.

Case Study: The Master's in Teaching and Learning

From September 2009 NQTs in North West (NW) England and new Heads of Department in National Challenge Schools were invited to register for the MTL by January 2010. £30 million was made available by the government between 2008–09 and 2010–11 for the initial roll-out of the qualification, enabling participants to undertake the MTL free of charge. The first cohort in the NW started in April 2010.

The seven NW HEIs worked in collaboration with the TDA to develop a three phase programme which would be identical in each institution. Phase one of the MTL programme aimed to build on the professional experience of the participants and develop Master's level enquiry skills. Phase two aimed to broaden and embed professional practice with particular reference to subjects and age phase they are teaching. This was achieved by engaging with four interrelated areas of content; teaching, learning and assessment; subject knowledge and curriculum develop-ment; how children and young people develop; and leadership, management and working with others. Phase three aimed to further develop practice within a specialist focus and demonstrate it to be at the forefront of the professional field (NW MTL Consortium, 2009). The funding supports a three way partnership between the NQT, the school coach and the HEI tutor.

A key component of the MTL is that participants are provided with a school-based coach who is an experienced teacher with whom they will have regular contact. They are responsible for arranging professional development opportunities, including coaching. They will help identify the participant's professional needs and plan each stage in their learning ensuring that the MTL work is having a positive impact on teaching and children's learning.

MTL participants are also provided with a university tutor to help develop Master's level thinking and practice for example, research skills. They have expertise in identifying and assessing participant needs against the Master's level framework. They help participants to draw upon resources where appropriate to meet specific needs. The university tutor is responsible for monitoring academic progress against the MTL framework, the professional standards for teachers and the QAA Master's level benchmarks. Due to the recent introduction of this programme, there is currently no evaluation of its effectiveness available although it does respond to Totterdell et al.'s (2004, 2008) research findings.

Other Master's courses

The MTL is just one route into doing a Masters degree. It is also possible to register for a Master's degree in Education or in a specific subject or aspect of education such as inclusion, early years or leadership and management. Subject associations also offer Master's in Education degrees as do most universities. Although not free, as with the MTL, most professional Master's in Education are subsidized which makes them very affordable to schools and individuals.

Often these professional Master's programmes have open content modules which provide inputs on research skills and focus on 'teacher as researcher'. Some promote action research models of learning and study whilst others take a broader approach to research. It is also worthwhile considering what forms of assessment are used. Whilst many Master's programmes require written assignments, more are considering other forms of assessment such as portfolios, pod casts and presentations.

Whilst tremendously worthwhile, studying for any Master's programme is complex and relatively long term PPD. Therefore, you also need to consider how it fits in with your specific context, workload and personal life, both long and short term. Some NQTs are keen to engage with Master's study straight after training believing it will enhance the quality of their teaching and at the same time improve their career prospects. They also feel it will be easier to manage before they take on additional responsibilities at school or have additional ties and commitments at home such as a family. Others however, feel they would at least like to focus on their induction year initially and continue with or register for a Masters in their second or third year of teaching (Jackson and Eady, 2008).

Working at Master's level as an ITT trainee teacher

Accredited PPD at Master's level is about developing the skills to critically reflect on practice in the context of what other research has found. This is achieved by skilfully using evidence from a range of sources including books, documents, observations of others' practice to reflect critically on the implications for your practice.

The notion of Action Research was first made famous by Stenhouse (1975). He introduced the notion of 'teacher as researcher', arguing that it should be the teacher or practitioner doing the research in the classroom and not external researchers. Since Stenhouse (1975), the idea of teacher researcher researching into their own practice has gathered momentum and is now viewed as a powerful way of improving classroom practice, in order to enhance children's learning and achievement. Consequently, this approach to PPD underpins many of the professional Master's in Education programmes run by institutions of Higher Education. Teachers and trainee teachers have found the notion of action research a useful and powerful way to improve or develop their practice in the classroom. They use the action research cycle to reflect on their developing practice.

The case study below illustrates how a trainee teacher adopted a 'teacher as researcher' approach in order to conduct a small scale research project whilst on school placement.

Case Study: Using research to develop practice

Angela was undertaking a Primary PGCE. One of the modules 'Improving Learning and Teaching' was at Master's level and involved undertaking a small scale research project whilst on a five week assessed placement. Although Angela had

$\rightarrow$

carried out some research for her undergraduate dissertation this largely involved using statistics and she found the approach to practitioner research quite different to what she was used to.

The research skills input on the module helped her to learn about practitioner research and the use of qualitative methods within an action research methodology. She applied this approach to focus in depth on improving and developing an aspect of her teaching based on the QTS standards Q10 and 22, and specifically on Q25. The module assignment required that the research was written up in a journal format requiring critical reflection on reading as well as on practice.

The module supported Angela's reflective reading of related literature by providing a critical reading record for her to log the key points from related research and implications for Angela's proposed study. By carrying out reading in this way before the placement, Angela formed a sound understanding of what aspect of teaching she would be focusing her small scale study on, she also had an idea of what other research had been done in this area as well as a basic idea of action research and appropriate methods including how she would tackle issues such as ethics and reliability and validity.

She took advantage of the tutorial support and action learning sets at University to shape and modify her research ideas. Initially, her ideas had been too wide ranging and would have been difficult to do as well as plan to teach. However, by the time she was ready to start placement, she had learned to narrow the focus of her research, planning to collect data as part of her lessons. Not only did her analysis of the data involve ongoing assessment of the children but it also provided her critical reflection of her teaching as well as how children were responding to the strategies she used.

At the end of the practice Angela felt she had a much more in-depth understanding about her issue and about how she would change and develop her practice for the final placement. Her research also provided many more questions she wished to pursue in her final placement and in her NQT year.

The key lessons from Angela's experience are:

- use the QTS standards to help you decide on an area for small scale research;
- read about what other research has found out in the area you want to conduct research as this will help you shape a small scale focus;
- take advantage of any tutorials or action learning set seminars to discuss your ideas with others;
- narrow your focus and keep it on your developing practice rather than on others;
- look at ways in which data can be collected from the lessons you plan and deliver.

How to juggle being a busy trainee teacher/NQT with further study

By the time you get to this stage in the chapter you may be thinking that it cannot be possible to continue with further study whilst embarking on your NQT year. The case study below illustrates that with careful planning and motivation there are ways to manage Master's level study alongside teaching. Your interest and motivation are key to this as well as having a clear plan and rationale for what you want from your PPD.

Case Study: Research as a trainee teacher

Alex was in his final year of a four-year Primary QTS Undergraduate programme. He decided to conduct a small scale research project on his use of questions in science lessons on his second school placement. He collected data by asking a teaching assistant with the class to note down how many questions he asked during a science lesson, indicating if these were open or closed questions. When he analysed his data he found he was asking more questions than he initially thought and the majority of these were closed questions which led to the children guessing the answers or using factual recall. He decided from his evaluation he would reduce the number of questions asked and make them more open ended.

This small scale research into his own practice prepared him for undertaking his final placement where he found that he was now more receptive to children's responses to his questions (Q25c). He found that using just a few open questions and allowing children to discuss the answers first was becoming more productive in terms of quality responses and getting the children to think more deeply. He began to return to the open ended questions at the end of the lesson as well. He also realised when discussing with his school-based tutor that allowing children to discuss with each other was also enabling him to provide opportunities for speaking and listening, something he had not considered previously.

When observed by his school-based mentor and link tutor both were impressed with his ability to structure questions so that he moved children on in their thinking. At the end of the placement the school had a post vacant and asked Alex to apply for it. He successfully secured the post. He also took advantage of continuing his Masters study as an NQT. He could see clearly how his initial focus of developing his questioning would enable him to work towards C29 (a–d).

The key lessons arising from Alex's case study above are:

- focusing on key aspects of learning and teaching arising from the Standards;
- choosing something that is a real interest or issue for you;
- focus on an area that is integral to your day to day teaching;
- consider using your findings from your small scale research on your final practice;

- Talk about your experience of small scale research and findings with enthusiasm when on interview for your first job.

Activity

Look at Q25 outlined below.

Plan a small research project around Q25a, b, c, or d using your lessons as a source of data collection. What specific aspects of teaching and learning would you like to develop?

Q25 Teaching.

Teach lessons and sequences of lessons across the age and ability range for which they are trained in which they:

(a) use a range of teaching strategies and resources, including e-learning, taking practical account of diversity and promoting equality and inclusion;

(b) build on prior knowledge, develop concepts and processes, enable learners to apply new knowledge, understanding and skills and meet learning objectives;

(c) adapt their language to suit the learners they teach, introducing new ideas and concepts clearly, and using explanations, questions, discussions and plenaries effectively;

(d) demonstrate the ability to manage the learning of individuals, groups and whole classes, modifying their teaching to suit the stage of the lesson.

The key message running through this chapter is that PPD is not something that is done to you so that by attending a professional development course, somehow you become a better teacher. Instead, we have seen that active engagement in further study is an ideal way in order to structure your future learning and can be managed if it is seen as part of the everyday role of teaching and reflecting and not as an 'add on'.

Some practical tips for your PPD

- Focus your PPD on developing learning and teaching strategies which will ultimately benefit the children you teach.

- Focus on an issue you are interested in and how it is approached in schools.

- Ensure your further study or research is closely linked to your day to day teaching.

- Keep your research very specific, do not let it get too wide.

- Use children's work as part of your data collection.

Finally, an important factor in your development as a teacher is that you believe in your ability to improve your practice, ultimately for the benefit of the children you teach. This is what Dweck (2008) refers to a developing a 'growth mind set' rather than accepting you have a 'fixed mind set'. Good quality PPD which is carefully planned and then embedded in practice is an effective way to develop a growth mindset, enabling you to expand your knowledge and understanding of what it is to be a successful teacher and make a real difference to the children you teach.

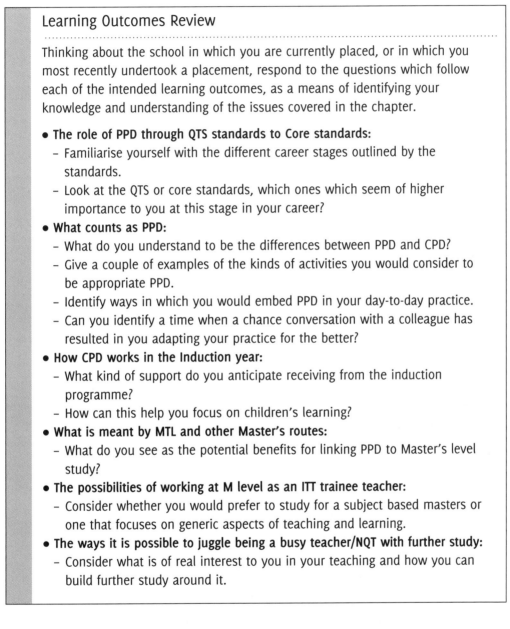

Learning Outcomes Review

Thinking about the school in which you are currently placed, or in which you most recently undertook a placement, respond to the questions which follow each of the intended learning outcomes, as a means of identifying your knowledge and understanding of the issues covered in the chapter.

- **The role of PPD through QTS standards to Core standards:**
  - Familiarise yourself with the different career stages outlined by the standards.
  - Look at the QTS or core standards, which ones which seem of higher importance to you at this stage in your career?
- **What counts as PPD:**
  - What do you understand to be the differences between PPD and CPD?
  - Give a couple of examples of the kinds of activities you would consider to be appropriate PPD.
  - Identify ways in which you would embed PPD in your day-to-day practice.
  - Can you identify a time when a chance conversation with a colleague has resulted in you adapting your practice for the better?
- **How CPD works in the Induction year:**
  - What kind of support do you anticipate receiving from the induction programme?
  - How can this help you focus on children's learning?
- **What is meant by MTL and other Master's routes:**
  - What do you see as the potential benefits for linking PPD to Master's level study?
- **The possibilities of working at M level as an ITT trainee teacher:**
  - Consider whether you would prefer to study for a subject based masters or one that focuses on generic aspects of teaching and learning.
- **The ways it is possible to juggle being a busy teacher/NQT with further study:**
  - Consider what is of real interest to you in your teaching and how you can build further study around it.

Further Reading

The TDA's national continuing professional development (CPD) database can be searched to find opportunities that meet your requirements for CPD. See https://cpdsearch.tda.gov.uk/Register.aspx

The TDA web page (www.tda.gov.uk/teacher/nqt-induction.aspx) provides useful guidance about what to expect in your NQT year and in particular gives a link to the CEDP which is designed to help you think about your professional development.

For further information about MTL, go to www.tda.gov.uk/trainee-teacher/becoming-an-nqt/masters-in-teaching-and-learning.aspx

Chapter 3 'Survival Skills' in Elton-Chalcraft, S., Hansen, A. and Twiselton, S. (2008) *Doing Classroom Research: a step by step guide for student teachers.* Maidenhead: Open University Press. This chapter provides practical advice about getting started with classroom based research either during your initial teacher education or in your first year of teaching.

For further information about the nature of CPD in the induction year and beyond, see chapter 7 (Collaboration and enquiry: sharing practice), chapter 10 (Newly Qualified Teachers and their Induction), and chapter 12 (Early Professional Development) in Bubb, S. and Earley, P. (2007) (2nd edn) *Leading and Managing Continuing Professional Development.* London: Paul Chapman Publishing.

References

Bolam, R. and Weindling, D. (2006) Synthesis of research and evaluation in projects concerned with capacity building through teachers' professional development. Final Report General Teaching Council for England.

Bubb, S. and Earley, P. (2007) (2nd edn) *Leading and Managing Continuing Professional Development.* London: Paul Chapman Publishing.

Cordingley, P., Bell, M., Thomason, S. and Firth, A. (2005a) The impact of collaborative Continuing Professional Development (CPD) on classroom teaching and learning. Review: how do collaborative and sustained CPD and sustained but not collaborative CPD affect teaching and learning? In: *Research Evidence Library.* London: EPPI-Centre, Social Science Research Unit, Institute of Education, University of London.

Cordingley, P., Bell, M., Evans, D. and Firth, A. (2005b) The impact of collaborative CPD on classroom teaching and learning. Review: what do teacher impact data tell us about collaborative CPD? In: *Research Evidence Library.* London: EPPI-Centre, Social Science Research Unit, Institute of Education, University of London.

Dweck, C. (2008) *Mind Set: The Psychology of Success.* New York: Ballantine Books.

Her Majesty's Inspectors (HMI) (2006) *Logical Chain.* London: HMI.

Jackson, A. and Eady, S. (2008) Perceptions of Master's level PGCE, Paper presented at BERA Conference, Heriot-Watt University, 3–6 September.

Naylor, S. and Keogh, B. (2000) *Concept Cartoons.* Sandbach: Millgate House Publishers.

Pedder, D., Storey, A. and Opfer, D. (2009) *State of the Nation.* TDA.

Stenhouse, L. (1975) *An Introduction to Curriculum, Research and Development.* London: Heinemann.

Totterdell, M., Woodroffe, L., Bubb, S., Daly, C., Smart, T. and Arrowsmith, J. (2008) What are the effects of the roles of mentors or inductors using induction programmes for Newly Qualified Teachers (NQT) on their professional practice, with special reference to teacher performance, professional learning and retention rates? In: *Research Evidence Library.* London: EPPI-Centre, Social Science Research Unit, Institute of Education.

Totterdell, M., Woodroffe, L., Bubb, S., Hanrahan, K. (2004) The impact of NQT induction programmes on the enhancement of teacher expertise, professional development, job satisfaction or retention rates: a systematic review of research on induction. In: *Research Evidence Library.* London: EPPI-Centre, Social Science Research Unit, Institute of Education.

11. Assessment
Mary Briggs

Learning Outcomes

By the end of this chapter you will have considered:

- what assessment is and its relationship with learning and teaching;
- your role in monitoring and assessing children's progress in learning across the curriculum;
- how to share assessments with children;
- how to feed back to children on their work and/or responses;
- the role of recording assessments;
- the statutory assessments;
- reporting to parents/carers and consultations.

Standards

Q11 Know the assessment requirements and arrangements for the subjects/ curriculum areas they are trained to teach, including those relating to public examinations and qualifications.

Q13 Know a range of approaches to assessment, including the importance of formative assessment.

Q14 Know how to use local and national statistical information to evaluate the effectiveness of their teaching, to monitor the progress of those they teach and to raise levels of attainment.

Q26
(a) Make effective use of a range of assessment, monitoring and recording strategies.
(b) Assess the learning needs of those they teach in order to set challenging learning objectives.

Q27 Provide timely, accurate and constructive feedback on learners' attainment, progress and areas for development.

Q28 Support and guide learners to reflect on their learning, identify the progress they have made and identify their emerging learning needs.

Introduction

Assessment serves a number of purposes:

- identifying next steps and planning future learning;

- ensuring consistency of standards;
- demonstrating progress;
- accountability.

Assessment is the aspect of teaching that is used for accountability as teachers are judged by the results of the assessment levels their children achieve. As a learner you may still remember the importance given to external assessments made of your work whilst at school. There are two linked aspects of assessment that of attainment and achievement.

Attainment is:

- a 'snapshot' of how a child is doing at a specific point in time;
- linked to National Curriculum Key Stages;
- shown in marks or grades in relevant national tests or examinations or school-based assessment.

Achievement is:

- an assessment of children's knowledge, understanding and skills in relation to their capability;
- reflects the progress they make in relation to children of similar capability;
- a judgement about whether children are doing as well as they can.

There are three main concepts associated with assessment are:

Assessment FOR Learning
This is the assessment that is completed to inform the planning of future learning and teaching. This involved the teacher and child in a process of continual review about progress

Assessment AS Learning
This aspect of assessment has developed from the personalised learning agenda (see Chapter 4), the increased awareness of the learner's role in their own assessment and application of different learning styles to the teaching process. This aspect focuses on reflecting on evidence of learning. This is part of the cycle of assessment where learners and teachers set learning goals, share learning intentions and success criteria, and evaluate their learning through dialogue including self and peer assessment. Learners are able to build knowledge of themselves as learners, and become *meta-cognitive*. In other words, they become aware of how they learn. It also helps learners to take more responsibility for their learning and participate more in the process of learning.

Assessment OF Learning
This assessment provides a summary of the assessment to date. It involves working with the range of available evidence that enables teachers, schools, Local Authorities and government to check on learners' progress and using this information in a number of ways.

Assessment and personalised learning

Associated with assessment is the move to develop a personalising learning agenda. Several of the elements of this agenda are helpful in relation to developing your understanding of current assessment practices. This shifts the focus of assessment from an activity which is 'done to' children to one which is done with children.

Component	Features
Learning how to learn	Giving learners skills, strategies and procedures to enable them to become meta-cognitive and self-managing learners.
Assessment for learning	Developing a wide range of assessment strategies, which place the emphasis on formative rather than summative approaches by engaging the learner in the assessment process
Teaching and learning strategies	Providing learners with a wide range of appropriate options to enable them to learn in the most effective way for them to experience the full portfolio of teaching and learning strategies
Curriculum choice	This involves changing the curriculum experience from the 'set meal' to the 'a la carte' menu. Students are given increasing choice as to what they study and when they study it
Mentoring and coaching	The one-to-one relationship is central to any model of personalising learning – it is the most powerful expression of a commitment to the learning of the individual. Mentoring may be used to monitor academic progress, support meta-cognition and provide focused support for aspects of the curriculum.

Table 11.1 Elements of personalising learning

Research Focus

The Assessment Reform Group (2002) developed the following principles for assessment for learning to guide classroom practice. This will involve all adults working with pupils in schools and early years settings.

Assessment For learning guide to classroom practice: 10 principles

Assessment for learning should:

i)   be part of effective planning of teaching and learning;

ii)   focus on how students learn;

iii)   be recognised as central to classroom practice;

iv)   be regarded as a key professional skill for teachers;

v)   be sensitive and constructive because any assessment has an emotional impact;

→

vi) take account of the importance of learner motivation;

vii) promote commitment to learning goals and a shared understanding of the criteria by which they are assessed;

viii) give learners constructive guidance about how to improve;

ix) develop the learners' capacity for self-assessment so that they can become reflective and self-managing;

x) recognise the full range of achievements of all learners.

(Black et al., 2002)

Planning for assessment

Use of observations, tasks, tests and other activities

Observation is a key skill to develop as part of your teaching skills. You may be asked by your tutors and school based staff to be aware of what is going on all around the classroom at all times, so that you notice if a child goes out of the class without asking or interactions between children become heated. (See Chapter 13 for more on managing behaviour for learning.) This is quite a different observational skill from that needed to make assessments of children. You will not be able to keep track of everything in detail but you will be able to note significant events that will assist all of those working with children to make judgements about progress and achievement in their learning.

By observing young children in play situations you may see them use their knowledge and therefore acquire the evidence upon which to make judgements about their learning. All the adults working with children in the EYFS will contribute to these observations that will be used to compile the profile at the end of the EYFS. There are two kinds of observations of young children. The first will be planned observations which you may plan with the team of adults working in the class and include activities outside as well as indoors and the second will be the spontaneous noticing of significant learning that you will wish to record.

Focused observation can be used with older learners. Although it will give you a wealth of information about their learning, it is time consuming, However you may find this a helpful method of assessment if looking at the use of mathematical skills, knowledge and application when teaching using a cross curricular approach. You may find a sheet like the one that follows as an initial guide to your observations.

Date	Observer		Child/group	
Context Related objective and learning outcomes				
Unaided task	Aided task		Practical task	
Notes 				
Reference to any recording by child/group				
Objective achieved	Objective partially achieved		Objective not achieved	
Notes	Notes		Notes	
Targets set as a result of observation		Review date		

Figure 11.1 Selecting children for intervention strategies/additional input

> *Working with a group can provide assessment information that is more difficult to capture in the whole-class context; it provides an opportunity to discuss the mathematics in more detail with individuals in the group. The focused attention given to a group helps to inform future planning and teaching. It also gives children who are not active contributors in the whole class the opportunity to participate more directly, share their ideas and extend their learning within a small group of peers.*

> *(Williams, 2008, p.67)*

Although the focus in this quotation comes from a review of primary and early years mathematics the same issues apply across the primary subjects.

The main focus is identifying groups of children for guided group work. You can identify children for a guided group through the following strategies.

- Through day-to-day assessment of children's progression in the lesson.

- Following feedback from a teaching assistant.

- As a result of a **planned assessment** activity with a focus on an identified target group.

- Following periodic assessment to track progress in a specific curriculum area.

- In response to school priorities about the attainment of particular groups of children, where there is evidence of underperformance (target group).

Case Study: Using effective guided group work

Going into her final block placement, Samir had a target to focus on effective guided group work in her teaching. Over the first half of the placement, she began to feel more comfortable using it as a teaching strategy. During her mid-placement review, Samir talked with her mentor about what she had learnt about guided group work.

'In terms of assessment, I see how guided group work helps me to build upon the assessment I undertook previously. It really helps me to target my teaching to the appropriate level for each of the children in the group and I can probe and assess children's understanding far better than when I'm working with the whole class. More generally, I now get that it is pretty fluid and it must respond to the children's learning needs. So, I can't plan for it too far in advance. I'm going to work more on using practical and ICT-based resources, as well as thinking about more appropriate subject specific models to develop children's understanding.'

Marking and written feedback

Marking and giving children written feedback on their work across the curriculum is an important part of the role of a classroom teacher. By marking work you gain a sense of outcomes across the whole class and the range of ability including pupils you may not have worked with directly during a specific lesson. This enables you to feed forward into your planning for the next lesson.

Research Focus

Val Brooks (2009) has specifically researched 'marking as judgment' because she believes that this area of assessment has not received the amount of attention it should, deserve despite its pivotal role. This work raises important issues for primary teachers who work predominantly with criterion referenced assessment, that is, you are matching the work against criteria which are pre-established. These criteria come from level descriptors in the National Curriculum, key objectives from the Primary National Strategy or success criteria linked to the learning objectives for a specific task within a lesson. Brook cites the following research when exploring the use of criteria... 'there is no common understanding of what criteria-based means or what it implies for practice... Additionally, the concepts of "criteria" and "standards" are often confused' (Sadler, 2005, p.175). Brooks goes on to argue that teachers need to be familiar with the criteria before they can use these to mark effectively but she also explores the disadvantages of this as once teachers think they have internalised the criteria they still tend to make judgements on the basis of their memories of how children performed tasks and

$\rightarrow$

sought to use the criteria to confirm judgements they have already made. The marker can also suffer from bias as they are likely to be swayed by the neatness of the work and legibility of handwriting. In addition there is the issue of looking at the role of affect – which includes looking for opportunities to give credit. Brook's paper asks us to take another look at the process of marking and the judgements teachers make when completing the task.

Activity

Choose a piece of work from a curriculum area and familiarise yourself with the description of the criteria for the appropriate levels before you mark this work. Jot down what you are paying attention to as you mark and then re-read the passage about Brook's research and try to identify what you were focusing on. Share your thoughts about this process with other trainees on your course.

Oral feedback

There are two different kinds of oral feedback; the planned and the responsive. With planned feedback you will have time to consider how you phrase the feedback for an individual, group or whole class so it is likely to be based upon marking a class set of books or your reflection on a previous lesson in conjunction with your school-based tutor/mentor/class teacher's feedback. This may include general feedback on strengths and areas for development against the objectives that you might give to the class at the start of the next lesson. This can help model feedback for children to use in peer or self assessment situations.

Responsive feedback is usually in the form of comments that you will make during the lesson to individuals, groups and to the class depending, upon the specific activity that is being undertaken. You may find this very daunting as it is part of thinking on your feet whilst teaching. If you are not sure it is worth saying directly to the individual, group or class, then you may want to take away the information and to think about it before you give feedback rather than feeling uncomfortable about the position in which you find yourself. This strategy shows that you have listened and/or observed what is going on and that you are responding. You can then plan a more considered response but you must make sure you follow through with the response and give feedback. Don't forget. It may be an issue that you wish to discuss with your school-based tutor/mentor/class teacher before talking again to the children involved especially if you are new to the class and need guidance on how a child might respond to the feedback given. Don't forget to ensure that all children get some oral feedback, including children with additional needs. For this group you may want to plan your feedback very carefully if it is to be a public feedback. For any pupil negative feedback in a public arena could damage their self-esteem and their attitude to learning. Read Chapter 4 for more on supporting children with additional needs.

Peer and self assessment

Young children are more than capable of making judgements about their own and others' work as part of the process of assessment in schools. Many schools have introduced an approach called 'two/three stars and a wish' and some even produce sheets/templates to put onto children's work.

The idea behind this approach is to get the learners to look carefully at their work and reflect on two or three 'stars' that form the positive feedback and one 'wish' indicating where development could be made. This can be completed as self assessment or can be used to guide peer assessment. The teacher can then talk to the child about how they might work on the area they have identified in the wish category. This approach can be flexible and children can be allowed to give only one star or no wish, or there may be situations where wishes are not appropriate as its overuse could have a negative effect. Children can find it difficult to begin with and focus on holistic areas of their work including the presentation rather than the learning objectives or success criteria agreed for the lesson and the teacher may need to remind them about focus of their feedback for themselves or others. A key element here is that the success criteria are clear and accessible for all learners. Be aware that children can also focus on trying to please the teacher rather than making judgements against the criteria for themselves.

Another approach to self-assessment uses a star diagram where the child is asked to rate themselves against the items indicated. In this case it is some general items in relation to a geography topic on the study of a local area. 1 is a low score and 5 is high. The star can have more arms so more items can be included. You can use the results from individuals to evaluate teaching approaches and plan for future approaches to learning.

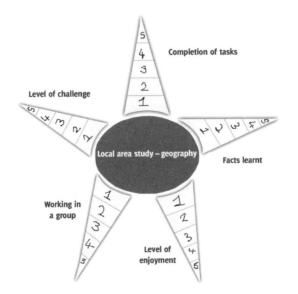

Figure 11.2: Star diagram

Role of peer coaching

Linked to self and peer assessment is the role of mentoring and coaching in the classroom. Mentoring and coaching are terms which are often used interchangeably for two people working together to change outcomes for one of the pair. Sometimes that can be a directive relationship relying on the coach or mentor being a more knowledgeable person than the other where the coach/mentor.

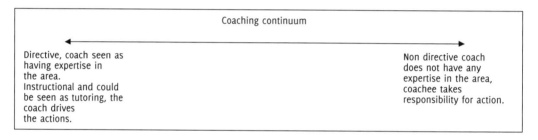

Figure 11.3 Coaching continuum

Children can develop the skills of a coach as Briggs and Van Nieuwerburgh (2010) have shown in their work with Year 5 and 6 children focusing on giving and receiving feedback. Below is an example of feedback given on the drawing of a giraffe and how the child has responded to the feedback in another drawing.

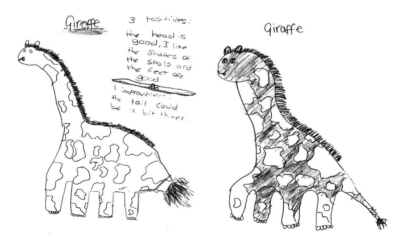

Figure 11.4: Children's drawing of a giraffe pre- and post-coaching

Although the research was carried out with the oldest children in Key Stage 2, in one school a Year 1 teacher had already been working in this way encouraging her class to give and receive feedback.

Record keeping

All teachers keep records of children in their class and these can take a variety of forms from notes scribbled on sticky notes whilst teaching, to in class test results and level assessments against key objectives or attainment targets. What is important about record keeping is that it is useful. You may like to ask yourself the following questions in relation to your own records.

- Can you identify groups of children for whom it would be helpful to work as a group with you on a specific topic they find difficult from your records?
- Does your record keeping help you to compile summary information about children's progress and attainment? If not what other information would you need to collect?
- Would your records allow someone else to be able to pick up and plan for your class rather than trying to assess them all again?

You may have been asked to record information as below to indicate whether or not targeted learning objectives have been achieved in a specific lesson.

Name	Attendance register		Targets achieved		
	Present ✓	Absent ✗			

Figure 11.5 Class record sheet

What kind of information does this give you and is it helpful in identifying specific groups of children for guided group work or for future planning or for summative assessment purposes? What kinds of records would give you more comprehensive information in order to address these questions?

Activity

With a small group of trainees on your course pool any examples of record keeping that you may have collected or been given and see if you can evaluate their effectiveness. See if you can construct a list of the most useful information that you need to keep as a record in the class and why.

Assessing pupil progress

Assessing Pupil Progress (APP) is a voluntary approach to tracking children's attainment. APP is the tracking of children's attainment in English, mathematics and speaking and listening using diagnostic information about individual's strengths and weaknesses. In order to make a judgement about pupil's work you will need to follow a series of steps.

This process begins by needing to plan for the collection of evidence as a teacher in the class. It then becomes a three step process of:

1. Considering the evidence → 2. Reviewing the evidence → and 3. Making a judgement

(National Strategies, 2009)

You can read more about APP in Chapter 3.

Summative assessment points across early years and primary age range

Early Years Foundation Stage (EYFS) profile

The *Assessment and reporting arrangements* (ARA) contains guidance on the early years foundation stage (EYFS) profile curriculum assessment and reporting arrangements. These are updated regularly, so ensure you have the most up-to-date copy.

The EYFS profile is a way of summarising each child's development and learning attainment at the end of the EYFS. For most children, this is at the end of the reception year (Year R) in school. Others may be assessed in settings such as nursery schools, private, voluntary and independent (PVI) settings and by Ofsted-registered childminders. It identifies children's learning needs for the next stage of school, helping Year 1 teachers to plan an effective and appropriate curriculum for each child.

A revised EYFS will take effect from September 2012. This may have an impact on the EYFS profile and its content.

Reporting children's attainment to parents or carers

All EYFS providers must provide parents or carers with a written summary of a child's progress against the early learning goals and attainment within the assessment scales. A copy of the EYFS profile summary scores reported to the local authority must also be provided to parents or carers if requested.

For children in Year R the following must be reported to parents/carers:

- brief particulars of achievements in all subjects and other activities. Comments should be included for each of the six areas of learning, where appropriate;
- comments on general progress;
- arrangements for discussing the report.

For children at the end of Year R there should be a written summary reporting progress against the early learning goals and the assessment scales given to all parents/carers.

Schools must offer parents/carers a reasonable opportunity to discuss the outcomes of the EYFS profile with their child's teacher.

Key Stage 1

Ensure you have the most recent copy of the 'Assessment and Reporting Arrangements (ARA)' as this will give you the most up-to-date information for this age group. The *Assessment and reporting arrangements* (ARA) provides statutory information and guidance on the Key Stage 1 national curriculum assessment and reporting arrangements.

At the end of Key Stage 1, teachers summarise their judgements in relation to the national curriculum level descriptions taking into account the child's progress and performance throughout the key stage, determining:

- a level for reading, writing, and speaking and listening;
- an overall subject level for mathematics;
- a level for each attainment target in science.

The statutory national curriculum assessments must be administered to all children who are working at level 1 or above in reading, writing and mathematics. Their role is to help inform the final teacher assessment judgement reported for each child at the end of Key Stage 1. There is no requirement to report separately the levels obtained from the tasks and tests.

Reporting to parents/carers

Children's overall teacher assessment levels sent to the Local Authority must be reported to their parents or carers. However, for science, only the overall level, not the levels for each attainment target, is reported. For children with special educational needs who are working towards level 1, schools should report progress in the P scales in English, mathematics and science (see below).

Results held by schools as part of an individual child's educational record must be disclosed to that child's parents or carers on request.

For children in Year 1 and above information given to parents/carers includes:

- an attendance record;
- brief particulars of achievements in all subjects and other activities, highlighting strengths and development needs;
- comments on general progress;
- arrangements for discussing the report.

For children at the end of Key Stage 1 this information includes the above plus:

- teacher assessment levels;
- comparative information about the national curriculum levels of attainment of children of the same age in the school and at a national level.

Optional tests in Years 3, 4 and 5

A suite of standardised optional tests provide additional evidence that can contribute to teachers' periodic assessment of their children in Years 3, 4 and 5. They provide schools with an instrument for gathering assessment evidence to support teacher judgements. Schools can use optional tests selectively as part of a range of assessment tools, including the assessing pupils' progress (APP) materials developed by QCDA and published via the National Strategies. The tests therefore present a tool to help schools map their children's progress which schools can decide how to use. They can be used summatively to produce a national curriculum level or used in whole or in part at any point during Key Stage 2 to provide valuable diagnostic information about children's strengths and weaknesses. Teachers may choose to administer the tests alongside written work, class discussions and group activities in a rich variety of contexts. Tests are marked internally and results are not collected or published.

End of Key Stage 2

Ensure you have the most recent copy of the 'Assessment and Reporting Arrangements (ARA)' as this will give you the most up to date information for this age group.

At the end of Key Stage 2, teacher assessment judgements for English, mathematics and science are reported with the national curriculum test results. The tests take place on specific days in May and include the following tests for each subject.

There are three English tests:

- a reading test;
- a writing test (made up of a longer task and a shorter task);
- a spelling test.

There are three mathematics tests:

- *Test A* (a non-calculator paper);
- *Test B* (a calculator paper);
- mental mathematics test.

In science, only selected schools participate in sampling tests.

At the end of Key Stage 2, teachers summarise their judgements for each eligible child, taking into account the child's progress and performance throughout the key stage. They need to determine:

- a level for each attainment target in English, mathematics and science;
- an overall subject level in each of these subjects.

Teachers base their judgements on the level descriptions in the national curriculum and use their knowledge of a child's work over time to judge which level description is the best match or 'best fit' to the child's performance, taking into account written, practical and oral work as well as classroom work, homework and the results of school examinations or tests.

Teacher assessment provides a rounded judgement that:

- is based on knowledge of how the child has performed over time and in a variety of contexts;
- takes into account strengths and weaknesses of the child's performance.

Teachers look at the level descriptions of the attainment targets immediately above and below the level awarded to confirm this level is the closest match to the child's performance.

Reporting results of tests to parents/carers

The following information must be reported to parents or persons with parental responsibility each year during Key Stage 2.

- Brief details of achievements in all subjects and other activities forming part of the school curriculum.
- Comments on general progress.
- Results of any national curriculum tests taken during the year.
- Attendance record
- Arrangements for discussing the report.

In addition to the above, the following information must be reported to parents or carers at some point during the final year of Key Stage 2.

- Teacher assessment levels for reading, writing, speaking and listening, English overall, mathematics and science.
- Comparative information about the national curriculum levels of attainment for children of the same age in the school.
- Comparative information about the national curriculum levels of attainment for children of the same age nationally. Comparative information will comprise a national average from the previous academic year for each core subject, at each level.
- A statement confirming the national curriculum levels of attainment have been awarded in accordance with the statutory arrangements.
- Detail of any National Curriculum attainment targets or subject from which the child is exempt.
- A brief account of what the teacher assessment and national curriculum test results show about the children's progress individually and in relation to other children in the same year, drawing attention to any particular strengths and weaknesses.

Parents or carers must be given an opportunity to discuss the report and the report should include details of how to arrange this.

Inclusion issues in relation to tests

A small number of children within this age group may need to be considered for a slightly different arrangement for their tests. Access arrangements are allowed for children who have a long-term illness or have an injury, such as a broken arm, and for children who have limited fluency in English and children with special educational needs. The support given must not result in a change in the test questions, and the answers must be the child's own. When considering these arrangements schools may look at the following groups of children:

- those with a statement of special educational needs as described in the *Special educational needs* (SEN) or a local equivalent such as Individual Pupil Resourcing Agreement (IPRA);
- those for whom provision is being made in school at *School Action* or *School Action Plus* of the SEN *code of practice*, and whose learning difficulty or disability significantly affects their ability to access the tests;
- those who require alternative access arrangements because of a disability;
- those who are unable to sit and work for a sustained period because of a disability or because of behavioural, emotional or social difficulties;
- those with English as a second language and who have limited fluency in English.

Children working below the levels covered by the tests

QCDA has produced a suite of optional tasks covering levels above and below the test levels. The optional tasks provide additional evidence that can contribute to teachers' assessment of their pupils.

P scales

The use of P scales is statutory for children with special educational needs who are working below level 1 of the national curriculum. In this context, special educational needs are defined in the Education Act 1996 as all those on the school's Special Needs Register. Schools will need to use P scales to record and report the achievements of those children in English, mathematics and science. The P scales must not be used to assess children with English as an additional language (EAL) at any age, unless they have additional special educational needs.

For further discussion about including all children, read Chapter 4.

Reporting religious education

Religious education is a statutory subject for all children registered at a maintained school, except for those in nursery classes and those withdrawn by their parents or persons with parental responsibility under section 71 of the School Standards and Framework Act 1998. It is not a subject within the national curriculum and there is no national programme of study. It is a general requirement that schools report children's progress in religious education to their parents or persons with parental responsibility, but there is no required format for national reporting. *Religious education: The non-statutory national framework* provides guidance for schools and local authorities on assessing progress in religious education using two attainment targets and a non-statutory eight-level scale, which may be used for reporting progress.

Information that is exempt from disclosure

Schools must report a child's national curriculum test level to their parents or persons with parental responsibility. A head teacher can disclose the marks awarded to a child in the national curriculum tests or allow their parents or persons with parental responsibility to see, or have copies of, marked test scripts, but there is no requirement in education law to do so.

The single level test model

The primary purpose of a single level test (SLT) is to confirm a teacher judgement that a child is working at a particular national curriculum level. Within pilot schools, a teacher judgement comprises a teacher assessment of a child's level of attainment using the assessing pupils' progress materials, and a subsequent professional judgement about a child's readiness to sit the test. An SLT confirms a teacher judgement by giving an independent estimate of a child's level of attainment.

SLTs are intended to be age-independent in terms of entry decisions. That means that any child in Years 3–6 is eligible to be entered for any SLT. It does not mean that the items/tests should not be biased with respect to age, as long as that bias is relevant to the part of the programme of study being assessed. For example, if younger children tend to do less well on items that are necessary for the appropriate assessment of a subject, then that is acceptable. It is not acceptable for items to be biased with respect to age in ways that are not relevant to the construct being assessed.

Activity
Read the report of the evaluation of singles level tests QCDA (2010) *Single level test: Report on development and outcomes* available at www.qcda.gov.uk/assessment/84.aspx. Ask another trainee to also read the report and then discuss what you thing the key issues are for the testing process in primary schools. Why do you think these were being considered? Are there different issues for different subjects involved? You might consider the impact that single level testing might have on teaching and the structure of the curriculum.

Tracking children's attainment

Schools make appropriate use of pupil-tracking approaches which include year, class and group curricular targets are set, linked to analysis of assessments.

Teachers:

- use a range of summative assessments to: judge attainment; identify children's progress; inform groupings of children;
- use optional and statutory tests to monitor and assess progress;
- use assessment to establish challenging targets for pupils.

Schools make use of data from the Foundation Stage Profile, end of key stage tests, optional tasks and tests and systems for tracking progress. Other sources of information include tests, tasks, assessing pupil progress (APP) levels and age standardised scores, say, for reading ages.

Tracking can take place across a variety of time periods from across key stages, annually, termly or half yearly, half termly and day to day. With shorter term periods curricular targets, key objectives, progress books and any half termly or termly tests are used as data for judgements made about progress. For day-to-day tracking, teachers use marking, observations, annotations of work and plans, feedback both oral and written and any notes taken as part of lesson evaluations.

Attainment needs to be measured against age-related expectations and progress is measured against the child's starting point. By analysing data teachers can begin to address the following questions.

- How well are we doing? – *Analyse current performance of children.*
- How well should we be doing? – *Compare with national standards and similar schools.*
- What more can we achieve? – *Set clear and measurable targets.*
- What must we do to make it happen? – *Identify and implement improvement plans.*
- What went well?
- What can we do better? – *Take action – review success – start again.*

With the changes to end of key stage assessments, assessment no longer has an end of key stage focus alone. Now there is more emphasis on ongoing assessments and there is a greater need for consistency of judgements

Case Study

As a placement task, Sheila had to find out about the system used in school to track children's attainment and discuss how often teachers add data to this system and the frequency with which they review all the data and what they do as a result. The head teacher showed her a line graph of three children in her class and how they had all increased in levels of attainment over their time at the school.

In addition to this, Sheila was also required to track the attainment of three individuals in her class during the placement. She chose the same three children, but was staggered to find their progress was less than smooth and that the topic being studied had a significant impact on their attainment.

→

Sheila's mentor explained how, over time, learning may appear smooth, but at any one time, learning is a challenging process and is far from linear. They discussed why assessment was such a crucial part of teaching, reflecting on Sheila's revelation.

You can read more about the process of learning in Chapter 3.

School self-evaluation and target setting

Reporting and Analysis for Improvement through School Self-Evaluation, RAISEonline provides interactive analysis of school and children's performance data. This has replaced the Ofsted Performance and Assessment (PANDA) reports and Department for Children, Schools and Families' (DCSF) Pupil Achievement Tracker (PAT) or any use of Assessment Manager to track the data. This system aims to enable schools to analyse performance data in greater depth as part of the self-evaluation process whilst providing a common set of analyses for schools, local authorities, inspectors and school improvement partners.

The system allows the generation of reports and analysis covering the attainment and progress of children in Key Stages 1 and 2 for primary as well as for secondary and these include the facility to explore hypotheses in relation to children's performance. Optional test results can be added to RAISEonline, the joint Ofsted/Department for Education tool for school self-evaluation and target setting. Contextual information about the school is part of the key information and this in turn then allows comparison with schools nationally and locally. The program allows for question level analysis to investigate children's performance in specific subjects. In addition there is a facility to set targets which supports schools in the process of monitoring, challenging and supporting children's performance. The final part of the system provides the ability to import and edit child-level data and create school-defined fields and teaching groups. This information is then used by schools to set targets as part of their learning improvement plan (LIP) which replaces the school improvement plan (SIP). Further information about RAISEonline can be found at www.raiseonline.org

Consultations with parents

As a teacher you will be in a position to discuss their child's learning, behaviour, attitudes and any other aspects of their education with their parents/carers. This can be quite a daunting prospect for a new teacher so it is an activity you should try to observe and then undertake as a mentored task whilst you are in school.

Learning Outcomes Review

Thinking about the school in which you are currently placed, or in which you most recently undertook a placement, respond to the questions which follow each of the intended learning outcomes, as a means of identifying your knowledge and understanding of the issues covered in the chapter.

- **Consider what assessment is and its relationship with learning and teaching**:
  - Look at your lesson plans to identify how you have used assessment to plan and teach specific curricular subjects. Have you used assessment in different ways for different subject areas? What might you improve for your next teaching placement?

- **Consider your role in monitoring and assessing children's progress in learning across the curriculum**:
  - Look at your lesson evaluations to identify how you have monitored children's progress over a sequence of lessons in specific curricular subjects. What strategies have you used for monitoring and recording progress? What have you done as a result of your monitoring – for example selecting children for guided group work? What might you improve for your next teaching placement?

- **Explore how to share assessments with children**:
  - Look at your plans and specifically the success criteria. How have you shared these with the children?

- **Consider how to feedback to children on their work and/or responses**:
  - Consider examples of the written feedback you have given to children and review any notes you made in preparation for oral feedback sessions. What responses did you get from the children? Could you see any impact on their progress and/or attainment as a result of the feedback?

- **Consider the role of recording assessments**:
  - Look at the records you have kept. Can you evaluate its usefulness? What might you improve/change for future teaching placements?

- **Consider the statutory assessments**:
  - Consider the experience you have of any statutory assessment procedures and target any gaps for your next teaching placement. Have you read the current arrangements for primary schools?

- **Consider reporting to parents/carers and consultations**:
  - Review the experience you may have had of reporting to parents/carers. What else might be helpful experience? Have you attended parents' evenings?

Further Reading

Further issues associated with continuity and progression will be addressed in Chapters 5 and 12 of this book.

RAISEonline. Read about using RAISEonline in Hansen, A. and Vaukins, D. (2011) *Primary Mathematics Across the Curriculum.* Exeter: Learning Matters.

Personalised Learning:
www.standards.dcsf.gov.uk/nationalstrategies/sup4/personalisedlearning

Primary assessment area:
www.standards.dcsf.gov.uk/nationalstrategies/sup4/primary/assessment

Transfer and transition:
www.standards.dcsf.gov.uk/nationalstrategies/sup4/transferandtransition

The Assessment for Learning (AfL) strategy:
www.standards.dcsf.gov.uk/nationalstrategies/sup4/aflstrategy

AfL with APP: Developing collaborative school-based approaches:
www.standards.dcsf.gov.uk/nationalstrategies/sup4/aflandapp

References

Black, P., Harrison, C., Lee, C., Marshall, B. and Wiliam, D. (2002) *Working inside the Black Box.* London: King's College.

Briggs, M. and Van Nieuwerburgh, C. (2010) 'The development of peer coaching skills in primary school children in years 5 and 6'. Paper presented at The World Conference for Learning, Teaching and Administration. American University Cairo, Egypt (in press).

Brooks, V. (2009) Marking as Judgment, *Research Papers In Education,* 1–18.

National Strategies (2009) *Getting to grips with Assessing Pupils' Progress.* Nottingham: DCSF.

National Primary Strategy (2010) *Unlocking Progress: helping children achieve their potential.* London: HMSO.

QCDA (2010) *June 2010 Single level tests: Report on development and outcomes.* September 2010, Coventry: QCDA /10/5250/p.

Sadler, D.R. (2005) Interpretations of criteria-based assessment and grading in higher education. *Assessment and Evaluation in Higher Education* 30: 175–94.

Williams, P. (2008) *Independent Review of Mathematics Teaching in Early Years Settings and Primary Schools.* Nottingham: DCSF.

12. Planning
Mary Briggs

Learning Outcomes

By the end of the chapter you will have:

- become aware of the essential components of planning that are undertaken in schools including children's previous experiences, teacher's subject knowledge, vocabulary and resources;
- become aware of the levels of planning that are undertaken in schools;
- looked at the necessary elements of lesson planning in detail including evaluation;
- considered the planning requirements for additional adults;
- considered opportunistic planning and the issues surrounding different locations.

Standards

Q15 Know and understand the relevant statutory and non-statutory curricula and frameworks, including those provided through the National Strategies, for their subjects/curriculum areas, and other relevant initiatives applicable to the age and ability range for which they are trained.

Q20 Know and understand the roles of colleagues with specific responsibilities, including those with responsibility for learners with special educational needs and disabilities and other individual learning needs.

Q22 Plan for progression across the age and ability range for which they are trained, designing effective learning sequences within lessons and across series of lessons and demonstrating secure subject/curriculum knowledge.

Q29 Evaluate the impact of their teaching on the progress of all learners, and modify their planning and classroom practice where necessary.

Introduction

In order to plan effective lessons and sequences of lessons for any subject in the curriculum there are a number of areas that need to be explored. When a trainee teacher observes experienced teachers teaching, it can appear that they can perform without any apparent planning and very little written down. This can be misleading as it can make you think that this is how you need to operate. The experienced teacher is only able to operate effectively in this way through building up their expertise by initially planning lessons in more detail as this helps with the thought processes needed to plan good lessons. It is tempting to want to shortcut this process as it is very time consuming and it may feel like an unnecessary workload during your training course. However, it is worth seeing this as part of the training process like any other and, although it appears that it is the written plans that take precedence, you will be going through a process which involves a number of other elements. Your teaching of a specific topic within the curriculum could be the only time children are introduced to that area during the year, so it should be well planned, organised and taught. In time you will be able to plan good lessons without the weight of apparent paperwork but you will have still undertaken the cognitive activity of thinking through each lesson or session in detail and it will be no less rigorous as a result. This will include the necessary consideration of elements of contingency planning which may well initially look intuitive to the observer but are skills developed over time.

Essential components of planning

The following areas are the general starting points for all planning regardless of the amount of detail that is actually recorded. Your course will have guidance about the requirements and expectations for planning at each stage of your progress, which will also guide your thinking and your actions.

The National Curriculum and National Strategy documentation

The National Curriculum is the statutory document you are legally obliged to teach. Once you know the curriculum areas and topics you are going to be planning to teach it is worth looking at the National Curriculum and the detail of the expectations for the age group you will be teaching. Also look at the National Strategy Frameworks where appropriate. The reason why you should use this material as set out in the guidance of the National Curriculum as follows:

Teachers' planning for schemes of work should start from the programmes of study and the needs and abilities of their children. Level descriptions can help to determine the degree of challenge and progression for work across each year of a key stage (QCA, 1999, p.18).

Children's previous experiences

Securing pupils' progress that builds on their prior learning is a central curricular objective. Because progress is goal-related, the goals of learning must be explicit in order to guide planning and teaching, whether cross curricular or focused on discrete subject content (Rose, 2009, para. 35, p.11).

Previous experience of the topic by the age group you will be teaching

This has two elements, the detail of the activities and tasks given to the children i.e. the teaching that has been undertaken and more importantly the assessments of the pupil's learning and any indication of any errors, misconceptions or areas that need to be recapped that occurred during the previous lessons. It is also useful to know how long ago this area of the curriculum area was last undertaken by the group or class and what the lesson was immediately prior to the lesson that you will be planning. With this information you can think about making connections within the subject and across the curriculum for the children. This can be content knowledge as well as skills developed in other lessons. Even when children appear to have had no previous experience of the topic to be taught they will bring their own ideas about the area to the lesson. This can include any preconceptions they may have established when making sense of their world. For example, they may think clouds cry when it rains. Part of the planning process is to allow space in your lesson to explore ideas children may bring to school with them and only then can you begin to use these in your teaching and address misconceptions and errors. If you don't address these they become harder to shift and can create barriers for future learning in any subject.

Teachers' subject knowledge

In order to plan and teach effectively you will need to look at the progression within a specific topic and the links between the topic to be planned and other areas within the subject being taught or between curriculum areas. Once you know what you will be teaching and you have asked your class teacher and/or mentor about the pupil's previous experiences, attainments and misconceptions, you are ready to explore you own subject knowledge. Your course will include sessions on subject and pedagogic knowledge. Look at your notes for the specific topic you are planning to explore the details of the progression. Use these to understand where the lessons you will be planning and teaching fit into this progression. Try to identify any aspects that you may want to revisit in relation to your own understanding. Explain the key aspects to a colleague to try out your approaches and check your understanding. Be honest with yourself at this point as it is possible to make assumptions about your knowledge.

Vocabulary

Your understanding of the vocabulary needed during any unit/session/lesson is a crucial part of planning effective teaching. Think about how you will explain what each of the words means in the context that it is used within the curricula focus particularly if they are everyday words that have a subject specific meaning. Part of your planning will be to have the words available to introduce to the children on an interactive whiteboard, poster, display and/or cards.

Activity
Choose a subject you are less confident teaching. Look at the appropriate National Curriculum expectations including levels of attainment, schemes of work and any long term planning you have access to, and identify the progression of subject knowledge required for the learner and the teacher. Check your understanding of terms, processes, procedures and all other aspects of content.

Resources

What kind of resources will be needed to help you teach the topic? Ensure you are familiar with the resources available in the school you will be working in. Do they use an interactive whiteboard (IWB) to present and manipulate ideas? How can you vary the resources that you plan to use to support different learning styles or different age groups of children?

Levels of planning in settings and schools

There are three levels of planning in settings and schools – long term, medium term and short term. As a trainee teacher, long and medium term planning is the level you are likely to be given by your placement setting/school, and you are not as likely to have access to the staff discussion about this level whilst you are on placement, particularly if it is of short duration. If you do have the opportunity it is good experience to join in the discussions even if you will mainly be listening to the other teachers. It would also be worthwhile talking to teachers about how the plan was developed so that you can gain a sense of the process. Schools evaluate this level of planning through work trawl scrutiny and a review of children's progress in learning across the curriculum in preparation for the next years' teaching.

Long term planning

This planning is usually the focus for the whole setting or school and is designed to ensure continuity and progression for children in a subject. In terms of coverage this level of planning should ensure that the requirements of the Early Years Foundation Stage and the National Curriculum are met for all children.

Medium term planning

Medium term planning is in greater detail than long term planning and usually comprises half term to termly plans. As a trainee you may find yourself being given the existing medium term plan or scheme of work. It can be difficult to work from someone else's plans as you may not have been part of the discussion about the order of topics or the amount of time to be given for teaching those topics. It is worth making these plans your own by looking at the medium term plan for the placement's duration and adding appropriate detail to support your work and to address the specific standards related to planning across the curriculum.

Mixed year group classes

It can be particularly important to gain an overview of what is to be taught when dealing with a mixed year group class. You will need to ensure the subjects of the whole curriculum to be covered by the year groups coincide so that the same areas are being taught at the same time. This will make it easier to plan in the short term and for you to offer a coherent approach to all children. This level of planning is evaluated either by the whole school or by a member of staff who has responsibility for a subject area or teaching and learning and is usually the agenda for a whole staff meeting, year group or key stage, depending upon the size of the school and its organisational structure. On a longer placement, you may be asked to evaluate the planning for a sequence of lessons either within a subject area or thematic approach and here you will draw on individual lesson evaluations in order to make judgements about the effectiveness of learning and teaching across the sequence. You can also draw upon any feedback you have had from observations of your teaching of appropriate lessons as part of your evidence base.

Block plans/unit plans

If your placement school is using the revised National Strategies framework they will focus on blocks of work. When mapping out blocks and units over the term or year the inter-relatedness of the content and pitch of the units needs to be taken into account. There are various ways that the units can be pieced together to provide children with a coherent learning experience and the example provided can be adapted to suit the specific school context and the pupils' needs. This will be based upon previous teaching and assessment of pupil's learning. Some schools produce their own block plans for subjects like science which they allocate blocks of time on the timetable for teaching these areas.

Other starting points

It is possible to think about planning and the starting points for lessons in different ways. For example you could use a book as the stimulus for planning across the curriculum or a topic approach neither of which may cover all areas of the curriculum. The reasons for this are explained in Chapter 2. These cannot detail all the possible activities, but they offer you a starting point to think about your planning from differing perspectives.

Commercial schemes

Some areas of the curriculum may be taught using a commercial scheme which structures the teaching and learning and supports the teacher's planning. This can include pupil books, teacher books, large text books, posters, IWB resources and others. Be sure that you use these only as a guide or loose framework so that you continue to focus on the children's needs and prior experiences foremost as textbooks cannot be written for a specific class and the potential range of needs.

Research Focus

Despite the importance of planning as part of the teaching process there is little research specific to this area. Much of the research looks at the effectiveness of implementing a teaching strategy and how this is planned by the teacher. Beyer and Davis's (2009) research looked at preservice teachers' use of 'educative curriculum materials' for science teaching in Canada. They argue that teachers need to cultivate the capacity to critique and adapt curriculum materials in productive ways and that for new teachers this is challenging task. They found

→

that the lesson-specific nature of the supports made it difficult for the preservice teachers to recognise the principle underlying the ideas in the supports. Thus, most of them did not use the principle within the educative supports to analyse the lesson plan more broadly or analyse other lesson plans, resulting in missed opportunities to further improve the materials beyond the suggestions given in the support' (p.699). This raises questions for how trainee teachers work with curricular materials and the support you may be given to enable you to work with materials more effectively. It also points to trainee teachers being aware that they need to unpack the principles within materials before use with a class.

Activity

When you are on placement, find out which subjects are taught using a commercial scheme. How does this impact on planning? Does this mean that the planning, teaching and learning for this subject is a separate area and that there is no integrated planning with this area of the curriculum? Look at the commercial scheme material available to you on placement for a specific subject.

- Read through the lesson plan and any guidance.
- Adapt the plans to take account of the least and most able children.
- Annotate a copy of the plans to meet your pupil's needs.
- What ideas could you take for activities from the material?
- How could you change the worksheet offered into a practically based activity?
- If you intend to use a prepared plan as part of your planning consider how you will intervene to monitor progress during the lesson and inform and redirect learning when necessary?
- Discuss any use of scheme materials with your school based tutor/class teacher/ mentor.
- How does this compare with the issues raised in the research focus?

Short term planning

Short term planning is the level that you will have most autonomy over as a trainee teacher. The other chapters in this book encourage you to consider many issues related to planning for children, such as meeting individual needs, planning a motivating lesson, the need to plan for assessment opportunities and so on. This section considers the 'nuts and bolts' of lesson planning.

Daily or lesson planning and lesson formats

Most teachers use their weekly or block plans as the main short term planning rather than working on individual lessons, although you may find schools where teachers plan daily lessons.

However as a trainee you are likely to be required to plan individual lessons, especially when you are being observed. This will also allow you to gain evidence against a number of standards for QTS.

Below is a list of the typical content you will find required in a trainee teacher's lesson planning proforma. While each course will vary as to its format and precise content, what is important is that your plans include all the key elements that are required to ensure a clear effective plan that will support your teaching and progress in learning in the classroom.

The following list is clearly intended for planning lessons according to the features of a three-part lesson. You will find that some teachers use this lesson format to structure their lessons but others will vary the format according to what is being taught. You will need to consider an introduction at the beginning of the lesson where you make the links to previous learning and connections between aspects in mathematics. Plus a review/plenary at the end of the lesson to assist with assessment and give children time to reflect upon their learning. The lesson can be stopped at any point for a mini review which would allow you to monitor progress, pick up on any misconceptions and extend or redirect learning where needed.

In addition to noting the *subject/theme, date, class*, and *number of children*, you will need to consider:

Children's previous experience: Work to be built on from previous lessons, units, years.

The previous previous lesson: Make notes from evaluations and assessment, including children's errors and misconceptions that need to be addressed in this lesson.

National Curriculum references: Include key statements and where appropriate level descriptors. Also consider the relationship with QCDA schemes of work and/or NS frameworks.

Learning objectives: Should be specific to this lesson and measurable and may vary for different groups of children and say how you will share these with the class.

Possible errors and misconceptions or sources of difficulties: This should show you your awareness of potential difficulties children might encounter.

Assessment: **What** precisely do you want the children to achieve in this lesson? **Who** is to be assessed: individuals, group, class? **How** will the assessment be made e.g. observation during intro, group work questioning; marking work?

Cross-curricula focus: Links with other subjects, themes.

QTS Standards: Trainee teacher's personal targets to be addressed during this lesson. Two or three maximum.

Resources: Materials, equipment, ICT, texts.

Safety issues: This could include what you say to the class about the use of potentially dangerous equipment e.g. scissors, compasses or the need for children to wear appropriate clothing if working outside or awareness of allergies if cooking.

Subject specific language: Including introducing and using key vocabulary both by the children as well as the teacher.

Specific expectations for behaviour: (Make clear to children, this could be a general focus on a show of hands or specific targets for individuals or groups.)

Speaking and listening objectives: As appropriate to this subject/lesson.

Introductory activity: Focus on the teacher and the children. Include assessment. May be an oral/mental starter if a mathematics lesson. Include timings.

Introduction to the main activity: Focus on teacher input to start the lesson, what are the key concepts that you want the children to learn. What stimulus will you provide to focus the children's learning.

Main activity: Will include differentiated tasks, including IEPs where appropriate. Include differentiate assessment. Consider mini plenaries where appropriate. What will your role be? The role of other in-class supporting adults? Timings?

Plenary: Key questions to ask/objectives to revisit/areas to discuss; consolidation activity; introduce homework where appropriate; note any errors/misconceptions to address.

Evaluating lessons

In addition to the above aspects to consider, your lesson plan should also provide space for an evaluation of the lesson. Annotate the plan, using a different colour. Add other working notes or changes directly to the plan. After the session consider both the quality of the teaching and whether each of the children really progressed in their learning. Make any relevant notes that will help you plan the following sessions. This may include: comments on timing; the appropriateness of the resources; additional ideas to reinforce the learning; suggestions for alternative organisational strategies.

Did each child really learn what was intended? Remember you can't judge learning just by completion of the work or activities set. Also remember to think about the children's understanding of vocabulary used in the lesson. Make reference to specific children (which may or may not need to go on their records). Make notes on how you might help the children progress in their learning, this can include areas for recap as well as what, where and when with next steps.

In the case study below you will be able to see these headings in practice, in a plan for a Key Stage 2 history lesson planned by a trainee teacher. As you read the plan, think about the extent to which the trainee is responding to each of the areas in her planning.

Case Study: Planning for a history lesson

Subject/ Theme	History – Life in Tudor Times. The Tudor Monarchs
Date:	20th October
Class/year group	Class: 5B **Number of Children:** 28
Children's previous experience:	In Year 3: Explored past photos from 1900s as a source of evidence about changes in the local area. Throughout KS2 children have been encouraged to use to exploring different sources of evidence in order to find out about a specific period of history as part of historical enquiry skills
Notes from previous lesson	Last couple of lessons on Who were the Tudors? and Early Tudors Explored pupil's existing knowledge about the Tudors Arranged dates of Tudor Monarchs in chronological order Placed pictures of Tudor Kings and Queens on a large family tree S.N and M.J had difficulty sequencing large numbers in dates (pick up on this in numeracy as well)
NC references	**NC** SU 2 Life in Tudor Times 4a find out about the past from different sources (e.g. contemporary pictures, portraits, costume)
Learning objectives	**By the end of the lesson most children will:** • Know the Tudor family were a family of kings and queens who reigned in fifteenth and sixteenth centuries • Specifically know who Elizabeth I was and key facts about her reign • Have discussed the evidence and bias about the character and images of the Tudor Monarchs as presented in contemporary portraits e.g. *Holbein's portrait of Elizabeth I* • Have made at least one inference based on the evidence contained in the Tudor portraits.
Possible errors and misconceptions or sources of difficulties	Children may have difficulty relating the centuries to the dates e.g. sixteenth century and 1500s
Assessment	**What?** Can the children identify some aspect of the portrait as evidence to make inferences about the life, status or character of the king or queen e.g. *the padded clothes make the queen look big, strong, powerful.* Symbolism used in Elizabeth's portrait **Who?** Orange group (T), T.A to assess J, M, E, S, D and K **How?** Observation/questioning during intro, focus group activities and plenary
Cross-curricula	Art. Artists and portraits. Hans Holbein, Nicholas Hilliard

→

Focus	Ma. Ordering larger numbers – dates. Group collaboration
QTS Standards	Q25 Use a range of teaching resources Q26 use group activity as an opportunity for making a focused assessment
Resources	National Gallery posters, postcard – Tudor portraits, http://www.marileecody.com/eliz1-images.html
Safety issues	Manage transitions group by group. Discourage dashing from carpet. Bring back if necessary
Subject specific language	Primary source, evidence, inference, portrait, artist, costume, facial expression symbol, chronological order, family tree
Specific expectations for behaviour	Work as a team. Allocate a person to record your ideas about the portraits. Share your ideas. Listen to others, Encourage everyone in group to contribute
Speaking and listening objectives	En 1. Speaking and listening – expressing ides to an audience Paired and group discussion

(Time: 10 mins)	Introductory activity/Mental Oral:
Teacher: *Manage groups to carpet.* *Review* previous lesson on Tudors **IWB.** Display large portrait of Richard III *Discuss portraits* Valuable, important source of evidence/ information about people and life in the past *Why no photographers to take their pictures?* ● *Q.A/Partner talk* ● *Who do you think these people are?* ● *What clues are there?* ● *Give one or two examples, e.g. jewellery, background, facial expression* ● *Why might they be made to look stern, wealthy etc.*	**Children:** Gather on carpet **Partner talk.** Review. What do you remember about the Tudors? Two things you learned about the Tudors Children discuss other clues and what they might tell us about the Tudor Kings and Queens as they are presented in the portraits
● **Assessment: Can the children** identify at least one aspect of the portrait as evidence to make an inferences about the life, status or character of the king or queen e.g. *the padded clothes make the king look big, strong, powerful. The map in the background suggests they ruled over other lands*	

→

(Time: 5 mins)	Introduction to the main activity

Teacher:	Children:
Display portraits of Henry's children in early life and as monarchs so that children can see how children were dressed and any changes once they become monarchs, Edward and Mary and Elizabeth	In groups at tables Each group of 'Time Detectives' discuss Henry's children as presented in the portraits Examine carefully. Describe what they can see
Explain Task Use famous portraits of Tudor Kings and Queens Become Time Detectives. What can we discover about each monarch from the portraits?	Identify what might it tell us? Elect a recorder Use large sheets to record the clues and what it might tell us about the character or life of a each monarch
Model example on flip sheet. e.g. Edward V **Arrange groups (6x5)** • Orange to Teacher • Support group with T.A	

(Time: e.g. 30 mins)	Main activity:	
Group (TA)	Groups	Group (with Teacher)
Pomegranate, With J, M, E, S, D and K To work on carpet **Use IWB** Coronation portrait of Elizabeth Supervise recording or scribe for the children. Record clues and pupil's ideas **Assess each child** as below	**Swan,** Edward **Hawk,** start with portrait of Mary Queen of Scots **Red Rose,** Mary Each group to discuss and record clues/evidence and inferences about monarch	(White Rose) To examine Rainbow portrait of Elizabeth Discuss some examples of symbolism, e.g. serpent, wisdom, dog loyalty etc.
Assessment: Can these children: identify at least one aspect of the portrait as evidence to make inferences about the life, status or character of the king or queen *e.g. the padded clothes make the king look big, strong, powerful? The map in the background suggests they ruled over other lands*	Can these children: identify at least two aspects of the portrait as evidence to make inferences about the life, status or character of the king or queen *e.g. the padded clothes make the king look big, strong and powerful? The map in the background suggests they ruled over other lands*	Can these children: identify at least three aspects of the portrait as evidence to make inferences about the life, status or character of the king or queen? *In addition can they identify some of the symbols and what they might mean? E.g. Crown, orb, serpent?* *Visit website for information.* http://www.marileecody.com/eliz1-images.html

→

Differentiation/target setting including IEPs where appropriate:
A.K – IEP (EAL support) encourage use of vocabulary for everyday items – king, queen, clothes, picture, portrait, costume
Encourage T, W, KM to use of mother tongue where helpful.

Teacher's role during the main activity:
Develop Rose groups' appreciation of symbolism and use internet search if available

Use of in class support, including guidance to supporting adult(s):
See above

(Time e.g. 15 mins) **Plenary:**
Gather children on carpet
Key questions to ask/objectives to revisit/areas to discuss:
What has each group of Time Detectives learned about their child of Henry from their portrait?
What did they notice about the representation of them as children and then as monarch?
What makes Mary Queen of Scots the odd one out?
Each group to display chart and briefly report
Explore the idea of 'bias' in the pictures
Do you think the portraits are accurate?
Why might an artist's portrait be biased?
What would you do if you were an artist in the time of the Tudors?
Reinforce and praise original or independent inferences drawn from portraits
Consolidation activity
Hot seat an artist
Choose a volunteer to be Holbein or Hilliard
Ask them to describe the monarch they painted
Children ask questions about what they were really like!
Introduce homework where appropriate:
Find other pictures of the Tudor Family which might tell us something of their lives or characters

Activity

Use the following lesson plan discussion sheet to evaluate the history lesson above. If possible, talk to other trainees/tutors/your mentor about your findings. What would you alter from the plans?

Lesson Plan Discussion Sheet   Title: _____

        Date: _____

Focus	Yes/no/ partly	Notes and suggestions
Are there clear and appropriate references to the EYFS, NC, relevant frameworks, QCA, School Schemes? Do they match age related expectations? If not why not?		
Are the learning objectives and intended outcomes specific and clearly defined? Is it clear what knowledge, skills, understanding or attitudes the children will gain from the lesson? Are there sufficient opportunities for challenging children? Remember children who find activities either too easy or too hard can become bored, frustrated and disruptive in the lesson. Does the plan indicate how children will know what the objectives for this lesson area?		
Does the plan identify potential errors, misconceptions and difficulties that the pupil's might have with the content or processes?		
Does the plan show that the trainee's knowledge and understanding are accurate?		
Will this be an interesting lesson, set in an appropriate context, relevant to the children's experiences? Remember children who are bored can be more disruptive in lessons.		
Does the lesson plan demonstrate that the trainee teacher is building on an evaluation, assessment and knowledge of the pupil's ability, achievements and needs?		
Does the lesson cater for children with a range of different abilities, SEN, G&T or those with EAL?		
Is there an opportunity to find out what the children already know at the start of the lesson?		

Are there planned opportunities for the children to contribute, talk, interact, communicate and engage in activity?		
Is it clear where and how the class will be organised for the activities, e.g. whole class, group, paired and individual work?		
Are health and safety issues considered?		
Are the activities explained in sufficient detail for another teacher to be able to lead the lesson if necessary?		
Is it clear what both the teacher and children will be doing at each stage of the lesson?		
Have any additional adults in the classroom been planned for?		
Does the lesson have an obvious structure e.g. beginning, middle and plenary? Has the timing of each stage of the lesson been considered?		
Can the outcomes be realistically achieved in the allocated time?		
Have appropriate questions and the introduction of new vocabulary been planned for? Does the plan show how the new vocabulary will be shared with the children?		
Is it clear what resources, including ICT, will be used and how they are to be organised?		
Is it clear who and what is to be assessed and how this lings to the learning objectives?		
Are the activities to be used as opportunities for formative or summative assessment?		
Is it clear what the purpose of the is plenary for this lesson?		
Are there appropriately planned mini plenaries to allow reinforcement of specific issues/address misconceptions/monitor progress with activities/share feedback with the class group from pairs or small group work?		

One issue you may have considered is the standard ability groups within the plans for the main activity. What other ways are there for organising the learning during this phase of the lesson? You may consider individual work, pairs, small groups but not necessarily by ability, splitting the class into two and whole class working depending upon on the content and focus of the lesson to be taught. You may also notice that one of the aims of the lesson was key facts about Elizabeth yet the main focus was Henry VIII's children. What would you do about this?

Planning for other adults in the classroom

Many classes have other adults in who support the learning and teaching of individuals and groups. They can be supporting children with additional learning needs, English as an additional language, behavioural issues or as a learning mentor. They will need to know what is expected of them during the lesson and you may not have much time to discuss your plans ahead of time. A written plan to support them is helpful for both you and them as everyone is clear about expectations.

Subject/theme	
Date	
Group or set including number of children or individual you will be working with	
Children's previous experience Work to be built on from previous lessons, units, years	
Notes from previous lesson Based on evaluations and assessment: (Include children's errors and misconceptions that need to addressed in this lesson)	
Learning objectives	
Activities here detail the activities to be undertaken with the group/individuals	
Assessment by additional adult **What** the children to achieve are to achieve **What will you be looking for?**	Notes from assessments made by additional adult
Resources **Materials, equipment, ICT, texts**	
Safety issues It is your responsibility as the teacher to indicate if there are any safety issues that other adults working in the class should be aware of in relation to the specific tasks you are asking them to undertake with groups/individuals	
Subject specific language Including key vocabulary	
Any specific expectations for behaviour for group/individuals	
Speaking and listening objectives	

Activity

Plan for another adult in your placement class and then gain some feedback about the details of your instructions for future planning for other adults with whom you will work.

Alternatively, plan for the additional adult for the previous history lesson.

Research Focus

Panasuk and Todd (2005) describe a method of evaluating lessons a 'Lesson Plan Evaluation Rubric' (LPER) which is an instrument derived from the Four Stages of Lesson Planning (FSLP) strategy and the empirical results that provide the insight into the elements of lesson planning with a specific focus on mathematics lessons. They begin by exploring other previous writers discussing planning e.g. Clark and Dunn (1991) who said that planning is a psychological process of envisioning the future, and considering goals and ways of achieving them. The teacher makes decisions that affect their behaviour and their students. Schön (1983) described lesson planning as pre-active decision-making that takes place before instruction.

OBJECTIVES formulated in terms of students' observable behaviour HOMEWORK matches the objectives DEVELOPMENTAL ACTIVITES reflect the objectives advance development and learning MENTAL MATHEMATICS activates prior knowledge, prepares students for the acquisition of new concepts	ELEMENTS OF INSTRUCTION *Instructional Environment* ● Inquiry-Based Instruction ● Expository/Direct Teaching ● Labs and Projects *Instructional Approaches based on* ● Problem Solving ● Multiple Representations ● Critical Thinking ● Communication ● Connections *Class Arrangements* ● Individual ● Group Work ● Pair Work

Figure 12.1 Four stages of lesson planning (Panasuk and Todd, 2005, p.216)

Each element of the plan was scored for each teacher's plan and the results identified four factors that influenced the effectiveness of the lesson plans for mathematics.

1. *Worked out problems* – this is about working out the answers to questions that the teachers would ask the children and by examining the questions that the children would complete during the lesson the teachers had a better picture of scope of the concepts that were going to be taught.

→

2. *By-products of the Four Stage Lesson Plan (FSLP)* – this was related to the organisational structure of the lesson, not always the same but planned carefully
3. *Lesson Coherence* – this is related to the links between the different elements of the lesson to maximise the learning for the pupils
4. *Representations* – these were the mathematical representations used by the teachers to support the pupils learning

Activity

Look at one of your lessons using this framework and discuss with other trainee teachers on your course and or teachers in school. What can you learn from this research about planning and its importance?

Opportunistic planning

The following extract is taken from the Rose Review of the Primary curriculum and it sums up the use of opportunities that arise in the classroom which teachers can take advantage of in their teaching.

> **3.58** *As well as planning work, primary teachers are invariably skilful opportunists, always ready to capitalise on the unexpected to build from children's interests. For example, when a 5-year-old announced, 'My new baby brother was born last night', what followed was a lively class discussion covering several aspects of personal development: thinking about the care of babies, how to hold them, why they are weighed frequently, and why milk is better than water for feeding them. This was followed by an invitation to mum and baby brother to visit the class to celebrate the baby's birth and learn more about how to care for him.*

(Rose, 2009, p.75)

Activity

Think about a time when you:
a) allowed an unplanned event to impact on your teaching. How did this affect the children's learning? Or,
b) chose not to follow up an unplanned event and therefore kept following your planned lesson. How did this impact on the children's learning?

Location and planning

So far we have considered planning within a classroom but there are other locations for which you will need to plan. Planning resources for outdoor work is important as you need to consider weather conditions and how you protect recording that children may complete as part of their activities. Outside you can also plan larger scale tasks or use the children themselves as a main resource.

Activity

Walk around the school in which you are on placement. Note outdoor areas including playgrounds, fields, and nature environments. Find out how they are currently used as a location for learning and teaching. Plan in consultation with your school-based tutor/mentor/class teacher to use one of these locations as part of your plans and evaluate the lesson(s).

Learning Outcomes Review

Thinking about the school in which you are currently placed, or in which you most recently undertook a placement, respond to the questions which follow each of the intended learning outcomes, as a means of identifying your knowledge and understanding of the issues covered in the chapter.

- **Become aware of the different levels of planning that are undertaken in schools:**
  - What were the long term plans for the class you were teaching?
  - How were the plans organised? Were they organised in subjects or were they cross-curricula?

- **Consider the required elements of planning, children's previous experiences, subject knowledge, vocabulary, resources:**
  - Identify examples of planning during your placement which shows how you have taken account of:
  pupil's previous experiences;
  your own subject knowledge required before teaching;
  the necessary vocabulary for lessons;
  appropriate resources including the use of ICT to support learning.

- **Become aware of the documentation you need to be familiar with before planning any area of the curriculum (Q22):**
  - Show examples of how you have linked your planning to the appropriate statutory and guidance materials for the curriculum and how this has

influenced the decision you have taken in planning learning and teaching activities. This is more than quoting the references in your planning.

- **Look at the elements of lesson planning in detail (Q22):**
  - Identify an example of lesson planning during your placement where the lesson was successful in promoting learning and one where the lesson was less successful. Try to identify what the differences were in your planning that supported the more successful lesson and why? What changes will you make to the process of planning as a result in the future?

- **Consider the planning required for additional adults (Q20):**
  - Identify an example of planning for another adult during your placement where the activity was successful in promoting learning and one where the activity was less successful. Try to identify what the differences were in your planning that supported the more successful activity for both the children and the other adult and why? What changes will you make to the process of planning for additional adults as a result in the future?

- **Consider how to evaluate planning, teaching and learning and how to use this information to feed into future planning (Q29):**
  - Identify examples of lesson evaluations during your placement which show how you have altered elements in the next lesson as a result of your review. Discuss these with another trainee teacher on the course and compare methods of review. Between you can you draw up a list of questions to assist you both in reviewing future lessons?

Further issues associated with continuity and progression will be addressed in Chapter 11, the assessment chapter of this book.

Further Reading

Medwell, J. (2006) Approaching long term and medium term planning. In Arthur, J., Grainger, T. and Wray, D. (2006) *Learning to Teach in the Primary School*. London: Routledge, pp.81–89.

Medwell, J. (2006) Approaching short term planning. In Arthur, J., Grainger, T. and Wray, D. (2006) *Learning to Teach in the Primary School*. London: Routledge, pp.90–101.

Superfine, A.C. (2008) Planning for mathematics instruction: A model of experienced teachers' planning processes in the context of a reform mathematics curriculum. *The Mathematics Educator*, Vol. 18, No. 2, 11–22.

Threlfall, J. (2005) The formative use of assessment information in planning – the notion of contingency planning. *British Journal of Educational Studies*, Vol. 53, No. 1, March, pp.54–65.

References

Ausubel. D.P. (1968) *Educational psychology: A cognitive view.* New York: Holt, Rinehart and Winston.

Beyer, C.J. and Davis, E.A. (2009) 'Using Educative curriculum materials to support preservice elementary teachers' curricular planning: A comparison between two different forms of support' *The Ontario Institute for Studies in Education of the University of Toronto Curriculum Inquiry,* 39:5 pp.679–703.

Clark, C.M. and Dunn, S. (1991) Second-generation research on teachers' planning, intentions, and routines. In H.C. Wanen and H.J. Walberg (eds), *Effective teaching: Current research* (pp.183–200), Berkeley, CA: McCatehum Publishing.

Panasuk, R.M., and Jeffrey, T. (2005) Effectiveness of Lesson Planning: Factor Analysis. *Journal of Instructional Psychology.* Vol. 32(3), Sep, pp. 215–232.

Qualifications and Curriculum Authority (QCA) (1999) *The National Curriculum for England at key stages 1 and 2.*

Rose, J. (2008) Independent Review of the Primary Curriculum: Interim Report. Nottingham: DCSF Publications.

Schön, D. (1983) *The Reflective Practitioner.* New York, NY: Basic Books.

13. Managing behaviour for learning
Kate Adams

Learning Outcomes

By the end of this chapter you should be able to:
- reflect on your own behaviour as a learner;
- understand the importance of identifying why some children behave inappropriately;
- understand that teaching, learning and behaviour are linked;
- know some strategies for achieving effective behaviour in the classroom;
- recognise links between theory and practice in managing behaviour for learning.

Standards

Q1 Have high expectations of children and young people including a commitment to ensuring that they can achieve their full educational potential and to establishing fair, respectful, trusting, supportive and constructive relationships with them.

Q2 Demonstrate the positive values, attitudes and behaviour they expect from children and young people.

Q7 (a) Reflect on and improve their practice, and take responsibility for identifying and meeting their developing professional needs.

Q10 Have a knowledge and understanding of a range of teaching, learning and behaviour management strategies and know how to use and adapt them, including how to personalise learning and provide opportunities for all learners to achieve their potential.

Q31 Establish a clear framework for classroom discipline to manage learners' behaviour constructively and promote their self-control and independence.

Defining 'good' and 'bad' behaviour

Imagine a school in which every child in every class was on task, put their pencil down as soon as the teacher asked, walked down the corridors without being tempted to run, lined up in silence, always spoke politely to staff and fellow children and hung on every word of the teacher... even on a Friday afternoon when the rain had been pouring since 9 a.m. confining children to the dreaded indoor playtimes. Perhaps you have been fortunate enough to have experienced such a school, in which case you will be the envy of your fellow students, but for many of you this is probably a scenario which you could only dream of.

The behaviour of children is a key concern for all trainees and many experienced teachers alike (ATL, 2006). After all, it only takes one child in a class who displays inappropriate behaviour to unsettle the calm ambience of the classroom and disrupt the learning of other children. For you, as the adult responsible for the lesson, it is essential that children's 'good' behaviour is maximised and their 'bad' behaviour is minimised, either through prevention or by a quick response which ends it quietly wherever possible without a drama.

Life in school is, however, rarely as simple as one would like, particularly because the classroom is a complex setting involving group interactions with social actors who bring with them a wide range of experiences and assumptions which may or may not concur with those of their peers. There are, as the final report of Sir Alan Steer's government-commissioned review of behaviour in schools made clear, no simple answers to the issue of poor behaviour. However, there is the potential for all schools to 'raise standards if they are consistent in implementing good practice in learning, teaching and behaviour management' (DCSF, 2009, p.3). This chapter takes you through some of the key issues inherent in managing behaviour for learning. It encourages you to engage in reflective thinking to clarify your own ideas about what constitutes appropriate classroom behaviour and to explore the reasons why some children do not engage in the type of behaviour you anticipate. Practical advice is offered to help you nurture children's behaviour for learning, whilst recognising the complexities of the task and understanding the links between theory and practice.

At the centre of this chapter is you, the aspiring teacher, so before we explore children's behaviour in more detail, it is necessary to engage in self reflection. Self-reflective practice is a key element in the role of a teacher and a requirement of qualified teacher status. It can bring many advantages, not only in improving your own practice but also in developing yourself – bringing insights into your ideas, motivations and behaviour. But to achieve this also demands an honesty which can be difficult for some people. It is particularly challenging when addressing the issue of children's behaviour because we need to reflect on our own actions within learning settings; we need to be honest about our own behaviour when we are students.

Activity

Thinking of yourself as a learner in a classroom setting (a university seminar/an evening class/as a school child/college student), answer the following questions with as much honesty as you can. Have you ever:

- Engaged in a whispered conversation while the tutor was talking?
- Written notes to a friend while the tutor was talking?
- Gone off task during an exercise or activity, discussing something completely different?
- Failed to have done the prerequisite reading?
- Sent a text message to a friend during the session?
- While working on an online task, checked your personal email?

You may well be the model student and have answered 'no' to all of these, in which case you are to be commended. If you have, you are unlikely to be a serial offender, perhaps only occasionally having indulged in such behaviour, as indeed I confess I have. Whatever your response, you will no doubt recognise these traits in some of your peers. Some students argue that sending a text message during a session is inconsequential because it does not disrupt anyone else's learning; that discussing last night's party is not a problem because the other group members wanted to know what happened, and besides, the task prescribed by the tutor was not that engaging anyway. Fellow students and tutors may well take a different stance, expecting all to take responsibility for their own learning and engage at all levels and demonstrate respect and politeness in the learning environment.

The perceived 'rights' and 'wrongs' of adult students' behaviour could be debated endlessly but at the heart of the issue is this: how do you feel when the children in your classroom behave in similar ways? When you are the teacher, the relatively harmless act of children passing notes to friends or whispering to each other while you are talking has the potential to make a strong impact on you, especially if several children are engaging in such behaviour rather than just one or two. One minor incident is not an issue, as you can end it swiftly and silently, with an appropriate stare to convey your disapproval, but if several pockets of mildly disruptive behaviour erupt the impact on you can be quite disconcerting. You can feel powerless and frustrated, demotivated by the fact that you have spent so long preparing the lesson only to find that few children are interested and few are learning. If you are being formally or informally observed the stress and pressure can be quite overwhelming. In order to avoid being in such a situation there are simple steps you can take to prevent and minimise disruptive behaviour and resolve many issues quietly before they create problems. This chapter will outline some of those steps but it is equally important to consider them alongside the complexities of behaviour in classroom settings, whether it be the behaviour of adult students or young children. One of the most fundamental issues to consider is what is meant by the terms 'good and bad' behaviour, or appropriate and inappropriate behaviour.

Activity

Alongside a friend, independently make lists of what you consider to be 'good' and 'bad' behaviour for primary school children during a lesson. Also include a middle column for behaviour which you do not desire, but would not find offensive, such as a child writing a message to a friend. Now compare them with your friend's list. Are there areas of difference?

While you and your friend will have undoubtedly placed some incidents in the same column, such as a child hitting another in the unwanted behaviour section and working quietly and conscientiously in the 'good' column, you may find that there are areas of disagreement, particularly in the middle column, as this case study illustrates.

Case Study: What do you mean, that was *bad* behaviour?

Carrie, a student teacher, had completed a practical science lesson on magnetism and was receiving feedback from Mr Laughlin, her school mentor.

'So, Carrie, how do you think that went?' he asked.

'I know what you're going to say,' she responded. 'It was awful, especially the noise. The children were so excitable as soon as they got hold of the magnets. At one point I couldn't hear myself think but I did use the hand signals to get their attention, though they were too involved with the materials to notice that I was trying a non-verbal technique.'

'So you think that the noise levels were too high?'

'Oh, yes! It was deafening.' But Mr Laughlin disagreed. Their ongoing conversation highlighted the fact that on a personal level they both had differing tolerance of noise levels. Certainly, he explained, too high a level can be dangerous if you need to attract the class' attention immediately for safety issues. Noise can also make it difficult for some members of the class to concentrate. However, what Carrie needed to focus on is what the children were talking about. If they were excitedly discussing the lesson then that was a positive sign; if they were discussing last night's television viewing then that would be another matter.

In addition to the issue of noise levels, other aspects of behaviour are particularly prone to being classified as grey areas, being acceptable to one teacher but not to another. These types are the most commonly found in schools and are referred to as 'low level' disruptive behaviours.

Research Focus

Government reports such as The Elton Report (1989) and more recently those from Ofsted (2005a; 2005b) consistently note that low level disruptive behaviours are the most commonly reported type of misbehaviour in schools. These are inoffensive behaviours, which Rogers (1998) notes include talking while the teacher is talking, leaving one's seat, calling out or not having equipment. Hayes (2003) adds tapping an object on a table, leaning back on a chair, giggling instead of concentrating and making silly comments at inappropriate times. The most effective means of reducing low level disruptive behaviours is through good quality teaching and learning (Ofsted, 2005a; DCSF, 2009). Serious incidents, including violent acts, remain rare according to the most recent government reports (see DCSF, 2009). Whilst newspaper reports often portray the opposite, presenting a picture of schools in a crisis situation with regards to unruly behaviour, Haydn (2007) argues that these are unhelpful given that research shows that serious incidents remain in a small minority.

Why children behave in the ways they do

Given that there are various ways of labelling classroom behaviours, it is important for you to be clear in your mind what you deem appropriate. However this understanding also needs to be viewed within the context of your school's behaviour policy and ethos. You also need to be flexible in your definitions. A practical lesson is, for example, likely to result in much higher noise levels than a creative writing lesson, so you cannot use a blanket approach to defining an acceptable level of the volume of children's talk.

Alongside your flexibility with regards to definitions, you will also need to consider why children behave inappropriately as these reasons can also vary from one child to another. Every child is different. They come from different backgrounds and have different life experiences and they will not necessarily respond to you, or any other member of staff, in the same way. The more you are able to understand the reasons for a child's inappropriate behaviour, the more easily you will be able to minimise or manage it.

Activity

When next on placement, at the end of your first day, write down the names of the children you have learnt. Clearly, you will not be able to recall all 30 immediately, so it is useful to reflect on why you have remembered the names that you have. It is quite common to have remembered those who had been eager to welcome you and offer help (showing positive behaviour) and those who misbehaved, but very few of the remaining group.

You will have walked away from any classroom with some warning bells in your head, to be mindful of certain children who have the potential to show disruptive behaviour. This is what sociologists call labelling; it is a natural human response but it is potentially damaging for the child who, if labelled as a troublemaker, may well fulfil this prophecy by acting according to adults and other children's expectations of them. Instead it is important to explore the 'why' of the child's behaviour in order to identify the root of their actions.

Case Study: Identifying reasons for behaviour

Shannon was nearing the end of her final block placement and was particularly worried about losing control of her class, taking a relatively strict approach to behaviour management to compensate. She followed the principles of consistently enforcing the school's behaviour policy with little flexibility. One day Robbie, a normally quiet, conscientious and compliant six-year-old began to show disruptive behaviour, throwing rubbers and pencils across the room and refusing to stop. Shannon was taken aback by his unusual behaviour and continued to implement her zero tolerance approach which only caused Robbie to be more defiant. Feeling overwhelmed by her loss of control of the situation, Shannon spoke to her mentor who then went to see Robbie's mother at the end of the day only to be told that his father had left home the previous night. Clearly, Robbie's behaviour was a reaction to this devastating event in his personal life. Shannon then realised that she should not have been so inflexible with Robbie and vowed to take time to explore the reasons why children misbehaved in the future.

The reasons for children's appropriate and inappropriate behaviour are extremely wide. The following tables note some of the most common reasons underlying children's behaviour but are by no means exhaustive lists.

Appropriate behaviour in class	Possible causes
On task behaviours	Engaging lesson High levels of motivation Good self esteem Strong school and class ethos Children have clear expectations

Table 13.1. Possible causes for appropriate behaviour

Inappropriate behaviour in class	Possible causes
Off task behaviours	Uninspiring lesson Low levels of motivation Low self esteem Weak school and class ethos Children have no clear expectations Special educational needs (not necessarily diagnosed) Health issues Emotional problems Disruptive home life Being bullied

Table 13.2. Possible causes for inappropriate behaviour

You will see that the first five causes listed in Table 2 – uninspiring lesson, low levels of motivation, low self esteem, a weak school and class ethos and no clear expectations – are effectively the opposite of the first five potential causes of appropriate behaviour. This is good news because they are elements which you can have a significant influence on, as we will see in the next section. The other possible causes of inappropriate behaviour are not necessarily as daunting as they might first seem because you can still take a role in supporting the child, whether directly or by contacting the relevant people including parents or other agencies. The most important element to recognise is the need to understand why a child behaves as they do. Many children with disruptive behaviours cannot or will not articulate why they display them, so it is important to work in partnership with parents/carers, other staff and other agencies as appropriate in order to begin to explain their behaviour.

Finally, in reflecting on the 'whys' of behaviour it is valuable to consider your own actions in learning settings. At the outset of this chapter you identified situations when you or your peers went off task whilst you were a student/child. Revisit that list and now consider why you did so. It may be that you/they discussed last night's film during a practical task because you believed that the task was boring or irrelevant. Or perhaps you had finished the task early? Did you send text messages to your friend during the lecture because you were bored with the lecture content or were you worried about a situation at home and could not concentrate? Whatever the reasons, they will have implications for your role as the teacher when your children go off task, so always be mindful of them.

Your role in supporting children's behaviour for learning

Thus far, the chapter has shown how important it is for you to acknowledge your definitions of appropriate and inappropriate behaviour, the need for flexibility in applying those definitions and the importance of understanding why children in your class behave as they do. These are underlying fundamental concepts which are essential to your role, but there is also a wide range of practical actions you can take to maximise positive behaviour for learning. This section outlines some of those actions that will soon become second nature to you, but are fundamental to your role as a teacher.

It is essential to note that behaviour management is not an 'add-on' to your teaching role; it is not something which is done on top of your lesson planning. Rather, there is no separation between good behaviour and good teaching and learning/planning (DES, 1989, Cohen et al., 2006, Adams, 2009). Ofsted (2005a, p.15) further endorses the link between teaching, learning and behaviour, commenting that in their own inspections, 'effective teaching and learning is a key to encouraging good behaviour and engaging with those children who have the most difficult behaviour'.

Lesson planning

The previous chapter was dedicated to discussing planning. However, it is worth revisiting because it is a complex notion and one that is crucial to consider in relation to behaviour for learning. From day one of your training, you will be taught to plan lessons in significant detail, a topic which is covered in depth in the following chapter. Your plans are unlikely to make any explicit reference to behaviour yet their content will be inextricably linked to the children's behaviour. How?

One of the key features of a lesson in which children are engaged and on task is one in which children are sure of what they need to do. Clear aims and objectives are therefore important, because if children are unsure of what is expected of them they are more likely to engage in off task behaviours. Naturally, those clear aims and objectives need to be conveyed to the children effectively, which needs to be combined with a stimulating and clear delivery of the lesson itself. It needs to incorporate a range of teaching strategies to cater for different learning styles and keep children purposefully occupied. Further, it needs to be delivered at an appropriate pace (Pollard et al., 2008); too fast and the children will not be able to consolidate learning, and too slow and many will lose interest, again creating unnecessary opportunities for off task behaviour. Overall, Moyles (2001) observes that much unacceptable behaviour can occur when children are unsure of what to do, or are bored with work which is unvaried, so your planning has a crucial role to play.

Personalised learning is also important to your practice. This involves the tailoring of teaching and learning to individuals' needs, providing clear progression routes for children based on assessment for learning and, where relevant, incorporating interventions such as one to one support (see Chapter 4 for a detailed discussion).

The physical classroom environment

In addition to your planning, you can also take other practical steps to prevent much inappropriate behaviour, via the preparation of the physical classroom environment. An experienced teacher will have given considerable thought to the layout of the room – something which is not necessarily discernable to the untrained eye, yet is also relatively obvious once you understand the thinking behind it.

The physical layout of the room has a major positive influence on children's behaviour if set out carefully. Seating plans are crucial for ensuring that appropriate combinations of children are grouped together (DfES, 2006) and it is common for these to be altered over the course of a term as children's relationships with each other change. You have a variety of issues to consider here, such as:

- Will seating friends together enhance their work ethic or allow them to engage in excessive idle conversation?
- Should children with disruptive behaviour be seated with children who are conscientious learners so that the latter can set good examples, or will the disruptive behaviour distract them from their own learning?
- What should you do if the relationship between two children on a table turns sour?
- Does seating children in ability or mixed ability groups enhance their behaviour for learning more effectively?

There are no clear cut answers to such questions and the answers can change according to the different personalities involved – what works for one group of children may not work for another.

Research Focus

Haydn (2007) collected the views of over 100 teachers, 300 trainees and 700 pupils to identify factors which aid teachers to manage learning effectively. A prominent issue in discussions related to whether or not moving children to different places within the classroom was effective, but he found no clear consensus of opinion, even within the same school. Likewise, the use of seating plans gave rise to different views, although some respondents noted that it was difficult for trainees to change established seating plans as this often gave rise to resentment amongst children. Wannarka and Ruhl (2008) reviewed the literature on the effects of seating arrangements on behaviour found no consensus in the literature on seating arrangements and their effects on behaviour and academic attainment. However, some contradictory findings may have arisen due to different methodologies and Wannarka and Ruhl argue that the nature of the task should influence the seating plans, a view also supported by Muijs and Reynolds (2001). For example, seating children in groups may be ideal for discussion based tasks whilst seating in rows may benefit independent work. That said, children were given a voice in Haydn's (2007) research, in which 45.5 per cent stated that teachers who allowed them to choose where they sat in class were having a positive influence on their learning by doing so.

In addition to seating, making resources accessible for children not only minimises opportunities for time wasting but also encourages independence and responsibility. Consider where you keep pencil sharpeners, spare pencils and rubbers; children will need these regularly throughout the day and if they are placed in a tub on the other side of the room, you are providing children with the opportunity to 'waste' considerable learning time by wandering around 'looking for the pencil sharpener'. You can appoint different children to hand out resources such as books or practical equipment. This approach gives children responsibility but also ensures that you avoid groups hovering around one area of the room at the same time, potentially giving rise to unwanted low level disruptive behaviour.

In all aspects of the physical layout of the room, routines are of critical importance. Routines, such as clear procedures for entering and leaving the classroom or what to do when a child cannot find a pencil sharpener, are essential. When children are unsure of what to do, you have unwittingly provided an opportunity for losing learning time at best, or engaging in disruptive behaviour at worst. Clear expectations are vital with regards to all aspects of behaviour management.

The social environment

A second feature of the classroom environment is the social. It has long been recognised that some schools have a strong positive ethos – a warm, caring atmosphere which is dominated by respect and strong values. In such schools, children's behaviour tends to be very positive. Whilst you will be able to develop your own classroom atmosphere this will need to fit into the wider school ethos. Ravet (2007) emphasises the importance of a whole school approach to developing and sustaining it; it is not about presenting words in a policy that have little influence on practice, but it relates to a school where rights, responsibilities, open communication and collaboration are embedded in all areas of the school. It is the responsibility of all staff, not just teachers, to ensure that such values are lived.

Creating a positive ethos permeates all activities and all areas of the curriculum. Key drivers are the spiritual, moral, social and cultural development (SMSC); personal, social, health and citizenship education (PSHCE); the social and emotional aspects of learning (SEAL) and the Every Child Matters agenda (ECM). Aspects of these various elements combine to enable children to develop a strong sense of identity, self-efficacy, self-esteem and self-confidence; they learn to understand their role as being part of a wider community within the classroom, school, neighbourhood community and as a global citizen; they encounter moral issues and learn to manage their feelings and recognise and respond appropriately to others' feelings. For a more detailed discussion of the impact of issues such as identity and self-confidence on behaviour, see Adams (2009). Read also Chapter 4 in this book.

Strategies for managing children's behaviour

Combined with these practical steps undertaken in planning and preparing the classroom environment, you will also employ a range of strategies for managing children's behaviour. Make the most of your opportunities to see other teachers in action whilst you are training as it is easy to become locked into your own relatively small repertoire of techniques which will not necessarily have long staying power with a class, and may not be effective at all with another group of children. All strategies need to be clearly explained to the children so that they are aware of your expectations of them. For example, you can employ some of the following for gaining a class' attention as noise levels rise but be advised that they may well become ineffective after a certain length of time, and in some cases may never make an impact at all, thereby highlighting the need for a wider range to draw upon.

- Count down from five to one, by which time all children should be silent and listening.
- Ring a bell to indicate that noise levels are becoming too high.
- Raise your hands in the air, indicating that all children should do the same and refrain from talking as they do so.
- Hand out stickers to children who are working quietly.
- Place marbles in a jar as noise levels become higher, using a marker to show that when the marbles reach that point, then noise levels are too high.

Activity

Wider issues, some of which are noted in the table below, are also helpful to ensure that you are fully prepared. Before your next teaching session, use this checklist to evaluate your preparation.

Preparation	Check this box if prepared
Ensure that I have a 'teacher presence'	
I am aware of the school's behaviour management policy	
I am aware of my role in managing behaviour whilst the teacher is teaching	
I am aware of individual children's special educational and emotional needs which may impact on their behaviour	
Resources for my lesson are easily accessible	
My lesson plan has clear learning objectives and a range of teaching strategies and I am confident that I know how to communication them effectively to the children	
I have considered the seating plan for my lesson	
I have planned for any transitions such as moving children to their tables, back to the carpet, or into another part of the school	
I have a range of non-verbal strategies to complement the use of my voice	

Behavioural theories

Whilst it is tempting to simply collect a list of tips and practical strategies, theory is important in fully understanding the reasons for poor behaviour and how to manage/prevent it. Theory does not stand alone. It has strong links with practice and in fact underpins many of the routine actions which teachers undertake in the classroom. Take, for example, the use of rewards and sanctions in the school. Each institution will have its own policy and practice, with good reason. As the Steer Report (2005, p.22) states: 'Consistent experience of good teaching promotes good behaviour. But schools also need to have positive strategies for managing behaviour that help children understand their school's expectations. These strategies must be underpinned by a clear range of rewards and sanctions.' You will have seen a range of these on placements. Rewards commonly include stickers, verbal praise, certificates, team points, whilst sanctions may include withdrawal of privileges, a system of warnings, being sent to the head teacher and parents being informed. Behind such apparently simple strategies are, however, theoretical frameworks, a selection of which is discussed here.

Behavioural approaches have a long history in education, offering principles for describing behaviour and theorising that learned behaviours can be altered using conditioning. Psychologist B.F. Skinner developed the theory of operant conditioning which involves voluntary responses to situations whereby a person acts on their environment to achieve a desired outcome. For example, a child who wishes to receive praise from the teacher will work conscientiously in order to receive praise. They will make an association between the situation of working hard and the teacher's response of praise, which is called a positive reinforcer or a reward. Receiving praise may then encourage students to work conscientiously in the future. Conversely a punisher, or negative reinforcer, weakens the association. Long (2005) gives the example of making children collect litter from the school grounds and then allowing them to stop when their behaviour improves. One of the limitations of behaviourism is that it does not consider children's thoughts and feelings.

Assertive Discipline is an approach developed by Canter and Canter (1992) which involves presenting clear boundaries to behaviour and the use of non-verbal methods. A key feature is to consciously seek and recognise children's good behaviour. For example, if a child is sitting quietly, the teacher should consistently praise the child for doing so, explaining what they are being praised for. Rules are often displayed and are regularly reinforced, with a child facing a sanction if they break one, such as their name being written on the board. As Long (2005) notes, Assertive Discipline is a commercial venture, but you will regularly see elements of it in classrooms which are common practice. For example, class rules are often created with children and displayed. Indeed, Steer's final report (DCSF, 2009, p.62) states that 'all parties need to be aware of the expectations of the schools and the rules that apply. Good behaviour management requires excellent communication and intelligent, sensitive and consistent application of the rules'. Similarly, praise is undoubtedly important and Steer's report (DCSF 2009) states that all schools have the responsibility to praise children where appropriate. However, as Muijs and Reynolds (2001) advise, it needs to be sincere and realistic otherwise it becomes tokenistic.

A student-centred approach has long been advocated in education, which is particularly relevant to children's behaviour and focuses on the emotional life of the child. Psychologist Carl Rogers (1983) argued that it is vital for teachers to empathise with children to maximise their learning and personal growth. According to this theory, children who feel that their teacher does not judge them are more likely to share their thoughts and feelings, in turn contributing to a strong class ethos, and positively influencing their behaviour. The concept of empathy has been central to the notion of emotionally literate schools. Weare (2004) argues that strategies establishing clear expectations and administering sanctions are not sufficient for addressing behaviour alone, and that the theory of emotional literacy is essential to understanding children's behaviour. She suggests that teachers need to understand the emotional origins and outcomes of inappropriate behaviour. The notion of emotional literacy has become increasingly mainstream in UK schools in recent years, with an emphasis on encouraging children to explore and share their feelings through activities in PSHCE and SEAL for example. Yet the concept has been strongly critiqued by Ecclestone and Hayes (2009) who argue that a rise in what they term 'therapeutic education' is actually damaging the aspirations and resilience of learners, instead turning them into self-preoccupied individuals.

More recently, the 'behaviour4learning' approach has emerged following a study for the Evidence for Policy and Practice Information and Co-ordinating Centre (EPPI-Centre) at the Institute of Education, London (Powell and Tod, 2004). This was a systematic review of studies which explored the theoretical links to learning behaviour in school contexts. Ellis and Tod (2009) expand upon the framework which has relationships at the heart of children's behaviour: their relationships with themselves, with others and with the curriculum. Each of the three types of relationships has a bearing on children's learning and behaviour but given that relationships are fluid by nature, quick fix strategies are not readily available. Rather, teachers are encouraged to prepare for positive relationships, and encourage children to also work positively towards them. It is not a theory that is intended to replace behaviour management techniques, but rather is intended to complement them and aims to reduce the common misunderstanding that behaviour management is separate to teaching and learning (Adams, 2009; Ellis and Tod, 2009).

Activity

All theories can be critiqued, so consider the strengths and limitations of these theories. Some notes have been made for you – can you add to them?

Theoretical argument	Strengths	Limitations
Breach of a class rule can lead to a sanction whilst obeying rules brings rewards	Children are given clear expectations	It does not teach children to obey rules because it is the right thing to do
Praise should be offered regularly		
Empathy is central to the teacher–child relationship		
It is important to understand the emotional origin of a child's inappropriate behaviour		
Quality relationships with self, others and curriculum can enhance positive behaviour for learning		

Where do I go from here?

Managing children's behaviour is a never ending learning curve because every class and every group of children is different, and some children's behaviour can be different from day to day. Even the most experienced of teachers face disruptive behaviour, albeit from a very small minority of children. Yet that is not a reason to be disheartened. Instead, you should embrace the variety of human nature and recognise that all children are different and will therefore react differently to the same classroom environment. You have many tools at your disposal to prevent inappropriate behaviour from the outset via effective planning and practical organisation, and by your ability to understand why some children display disruptive behaviour. Through self-reflection and the understanding and application of theory, you have the ability to build a repertoire of techniques, and learn from your own experience and that of others. That ideal, 'dream' class will never behave perfectly every day of every school year, so do not impose unattainable targets on yourself but make it your goal to ensure that the learning environment maximises positive behaviour to the best of your ability.

Learning Outcomes Review

Thinking about your own behaviours as a student teacher, respond to the questions which follow each of the intended learning outcomes, as a means of identifying your knowledge and understanding of the issues covered in the chapter.

- **Reflect on your own behaviour as a learner:**
  - When I am a learner, do I behave in the ways that I expect from children?
  - What causes you to behave in particular ways when you are learning?

- **Understanding the importance of identifying why some children behave inappropriately:**
  - What types of behaviour do I not expect from children? Are there times when I can make an exception?

- **Understand that teaching, learning and behaviour are linked:**
  - How effective are my lesson plans for preventing inappropriate behaviours?
  - What do I need to do to improve my behaviour management to maximise children's opportunities for learning?

- **Know some strategies for achieving effective behaviour in the classroom:**
  - How effective are my lesson plans for preventing inappropriate behaviours?
  - How can I create a positive ethos in my classroom?
  - How willing am I to learn new strategies and keep in mind the theories behind some of them?

- **Recognise links between theory and practice in managing behaviour for learning:**
  - How well do I understand the links between theory and practice?
  - What do I need to do to improve my behaviour management to maximise children's opportunities for learning?

Further Reading

Behaviour4Learning website, available from www.Behaviour4Learning.co.uk. In addition to covering the theoretical components of the B4L approach, the website will also keep you up to date with current developments in research, policy and practice. Revisit it regularly.

Cohen, L., Manion, L. and Morrison, K. (2006) *A Guide to Teaching Practice.* Abingdon: Routledge. Chapter 15 provides a relatively concise but thorough overview of approaches to behaviour management, which is grounded in theory.

Rogers, B. (2006) *Classroom Behaviour: A practical guide to effective teaching, behaviour management and colleague support.* London: Paul Chapman Publishing. An accessible text which provides a wide range of practical strategies which are also supported with theory.

References

Adams, K. (2009) *Behaviour for Learning in the Primary School.* Exeter: Learning Matters.

ATL (Association of Teachers and Lecturers) (2006) *Poor Behaviour is an Ongoing Problem, ATL Survey Finds,* available from www.atl.org.uk

Canter, L. and Canter, M. (1992) *Assertive Discipline.* Santa Monica: Lee Canter Associates.

Cohen, L., Manion, L. and Morrison, K. (2006) *A Guide to Teaching Practice.* Abingdon: Routledge.

DCSF (2009) *Learning Behaviour, Lessons Learned. A review of behaviour standards and practices in our schools.* Nottingham: DCSF.

DES (1989) *The Elton Report: Discipline in Schools.* London: HMSO.

DfES (2006) *Learning Behaviour, Principles and Practice – What Works in Schools.* Nottingham: DfES.

Ecclestone, K. and Hayes, D. (2009) *The Dangerous Rise in Therapeutic Education.* Abingdon: Routledge.

Ellis, S. and Tod, J. (2009) *Behaviour for Learning: Positive approaches to behaviour management.* Abingdon: Routledge.

Garner, P. (2005) Behaviour for learning: a positive approach to managing classroom behaviour, in Capel, S., Leask, M. and Turner, T. (eds) *Learning to Teach in the Secondary School: A companion to school experience.* Abingdon: Routledge.

Haydn, T. (2007) *Managing Pupil Behaviour. Key issues in teaching and learning.* Abingdon: Routledge.

Hayes, D. (2003) *A Student Teacher's Guide to Primary School Placement: Learning to survive and prosper.* London: Routledge.

Ofsted (2005a) *Managing Challenging Behaviour*. London: Ofsted. Available from: www.ofsted.gov.uk/Ofsted-home/Publications-and-research/Care/Childcare/Managing-challenging-behaviour/(language)/eng-GB accessed 4/8/10.

Ofsted (2005b) *The Annual Report of Her Majesty's Chief Inspector of Schools 2003/2004*. London: Ofsted.

Long, M. (2005) *The Psychology of Education*. London: RoutledgeFalmer.

Moyles, J. (2001) *Organising for Learning in the Primary Classroom: a balanced approach to classroom management*. Buckingham: Open University Press.

Muijs, D. and Reynolds, D. (2001) *Effective Teaching – evidence and practice*. London: Paul Chapman Publishing.

Pollard, A., Collins, J., Simco, N., Swaffield, S., Warin, J., Warwick, P. and Maddock, M. (2008) *Reflective Teaching: Evidence-informed professional practice*. London: Continuum.

Powell, S. and Tod, J. (2004) *A Systematic Review of how Theories Explain Learning Behaviour in School Contexts*. London: EPPI-Centre, Social Science Research Unit.

Ravet, J. (2007) *Are we Listening? Making sense of classroom behaviour with children and parents*. Stoke on Trent: Trentham.

Rogers, B. (1998) *You Know the Fair Rule*. Harlow: Pearson Education Ltd.

Rogers, C. (1983) *Freedom to Learn for the 80's*. Columbus: Charles E. Merrill.

Wannarka, R. and Ruhl, K. (2008) Seating arrangements that promote positive academic and behavioural outcomes: a review of empirical research. *Support for Learning* 23: 2, 89–93.

Weare, K. (2004) *Developing the Emotionally Literate School*. London: Paul Chapman Publishing.

Index